Homicide in Pre-Famine
and Famine Ireland

Praise for Homicide in Pre-Famine and Famine Ireland

'Based on extensive and thorough research, well organised and lucidly written, this book makes a major contribution to our understanding.'

Professor S.J. Connolly, Queen's University Belfast

'...an invaluable resource for historians interested in violence in historical societies, as well as a useful corrective to a flawed characterization of pre-Famine Ireland.'

Journal of Interdisciplinary History

'*Homicide in Pre-Famine and Famine Ireland* is a solid work of historical analysis with a great number of strengths that make it a pleasure to read. Mc Mahon's analysis is exemplary ... [The book] reveals his exceptional skill for the logical dissection and evaluation of claims other scholars have made ... In doing so, he challenges the fundamental assumptions of some major perspectives on social change, especially social change in Western society over the past several centuries.'

American Historical Review

'...this original, provocative and timely study demands we interrogate further our understanding of the nature of Irish society not only in the early nineteenth century, but also of the manner in which historians, political theorists and commentators arrive at their conclusions as to the nature of pre-modern, and by implication, modern Irish society.'

Studia Hibernica

'Based on thorough research, its central argument is set out lucidly and confidently and should exercise appeal beyond the realm of criminal justice history.'

Continuity and Change

'In straddling the family, the personal, the agrarian *and* the sectarian, [Mc Mahon] has successfully activated a much-needed and more inclusive discussion in a clear and confident manner ... [T]he author suggests further possible avenues of investigation. This book provides those who may wish to explore those avenues with an excellent starting point.'

Reviews in History

Homicide in Pre-Famine and Famine Ireland

RICHARD MC MAHON

LIVERPOOL UNIVERSITY PRESS

First published 2013 by
Liverpool University Press
4 Cambridge Street
Liverpool
L69 7ZU

This paperback version first published 2017

British Library Cataloguing-in-Publication data

A British Library CIP record is available

ISBN 978-1-84631-947-1 cased

ISBN 978-1-78694-092-6 limp

Typeset in Ehrhardt by Carnegie Book Production, Lancaster
Printed and bound in Poland by BooksFactory.co.uk

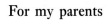

For my parents

Quiet Country Still

This is still quiet country.
The things that happen
leave it quieter still.

A short walk will take you
to the brim of the horizon
from where you can see

houses this side and the far side
of the lough, each with a story
known to all, yet never told.

Tom Duddy

Contents

List of tables and figures

Tables

Figures

Preface

Was pre-Famine and Famine Ireland a violent society? The dominant view among a range of commentators at the time, and in the work of many historians since, is that violence was both prevalent and pervasive in the social and cultural life of the country. This book explores the validity of this perspective through the study of homicide and what it reveals about wider experiences of violence in the country at that time. The book provides a quantitative and contextual analysis of homicide in pre-Famine and Famine Ireland. It explores the relationship between particular and prominent causes of conflict – personal, familial, economic and sectarian – and the use of lethal violence to deal with such conflicts. Throughout the book, the Irish experience is placed within a comparative framework and there is also an exploration of what the history of violence in Ireland might reveal about the wider history of interpersonal violence in Europe and beyond. The aim throughout is to challenge the view of nineteenth-century Ireland as a violent society and to offer a more complex and nuanced assessment of the part played by violence in Irish life.

My debts are many. I would like to thank An Roinn Dlí agus Cirt agus Comhionannais/ the Department of Justice and Equality and the Irish Legal History Society for funding the original thesis on which this book is based. The thesis was supervised by Professor W.N. Osborough of the School of Law at University College Dublin and Professor Desmond Greer of the School of Law at Queen's University Belfast. I owe a great debt to both for sharing their knowledge of and enthusiasm for Irish history with me. I am also grateful for the additional funding and conducive working environment provided by the Moore Institute for Research in the Humanities and Social Studies at the National University of Ireland, Galway, which enabled me to continue my research there. In particular, I would like to take the opportunity to thank the then Director of the Institute, Nicholas Canny, and the project leader, William O'Reilly. I would also like to thank Gearóid Ó Tuathaigh for his support at that time.

W.E. Vaughan read and commented on the original thesis – I am grateful for his advice, support and encouragement. Cormac Ó Gráda and Seán Lucey agreed to read chapter four of the book and I am thankful for their valuable comments. Robert Sapolsky provided some very useful references for and feedback on chapter three, for which I am also most grateful. John Cronin also read and made helpful comments on chapters four and five as well as the conclusion. I am grateful too to Lesa Ní Mhunghaile for reading the original thesis and saving me from many errors. Thanks must also go to John Moulden for sharing his work on Dolly's Brae with me. The book has also been strengthened by the comments and suggestions provided by the readers for Liverpool University Press. I alone am responsible for all errors of fact and interpretation.

Thanks are due also to the staff of the National Archives of Ireland, particularly Gregory O'Connor and Mary Mackey for their advice over the years on the sources available in the archive. I am also grateful to the staff of the National Library of Ireland for all their assistance. The support and assistance provided at the Public Record Office of Northern Ireland is also gratefully acknowledged. I have also benefited greatly from the assistance of the staff of the special collections department in the James Hardiman Library at NUI, Galway. Thanks must also go to Alison Welsby and all at Liverpool University Press for their help with the book. I would also like to thank Pádraic Reaney for kind permission to use his Famine Cottage print as a cover image. I am particularly grateful also to Sheila Duddy for allowing me to use Tom Duddy's poem 'Quiet Country Still' at the beginning of this book.

A number of people were good enough to provide me with a couch, an inflatable mattress or even, at times, a bed to sleep on during my various research trips for this book; in particular, I would like to thank John Cronin, Evelyn Flanagan, David Ryan, Mahipal Ganeshmal, Philip 'Schmills' Graham, John 'Walshie' Walsh and Alexandero de Llado.

Over the last number of years, I have been very fortunate to spend time at a range of history departments and research institutes in Dundee, New York, Stanford, Maynooth, Liverpool and Edinburgh. This has led to the nagging feeling that if I could live my life over I would apply for frequent flyer miles, but has also given me an opportunity to meet welcoming and inspiring people both inside and outside of academia who have made the last few years both stimulating and enjoyable. I am hoping that another book will emerge from these travels and that I can take the opportunity then to thank those who have helped me over the years. For now, however, I would like to thank both Randy Roth and Joe Lee in particular for taking an interest in the work and offering support when it was needed. I wish also to thank Tom Devine and Enda Delaney and, indeed, all at the Scottish Centre for Diaspora Studies in the School of History, Classics and Archaeology of the

University of Edinburgh for providing a stimulating environment in which to carry out my current research project and to finish this book.

I am very grateful too for the support provided by a variety of funding bodies which has helped enormously in sustaining my research. I would like to thank the Harry Frank Guggenheim Foundation, the Fulbright Commission (Ireland), the Royal Irish Academy, the Irish Research Council for the Humanities and Social Sciences, The Pennsylvania Historical and Museum Commission and the Ireland Canada University Foundation for their support.

This book would also have been a far more arduous and challenging task without Catriona who, by joining in early morning swims in the Pollock Holes of Kilkee, guiding me up (and thankfully down) the Munros of western Scotland, and in sharing a life with me in Edinburgh, has always reminded me of an altogether better world beyond the book.

Finally, I would like to thank my family and, particularly, my parents, without whose unstinting love, support and encouragement this study simply could not have been completed. The book is for them.

'A violent society'?

Sir Richard Hussey Vivian, commander of the armed forces in Ireland, addressing a select committee on the state of the country in 1832, remarked on the 'extraordinary carelessness of human life' amongst the mass of the people – declaring that, although generally hospitable, they 'would have no sort of hesitation in taking up a stone and committing a murder'.[1] Before the 1839 select committee on crime in Ireland, Joseph Tabeteau agreed that there was 'a very great disregard' for human life 'manifested in the feelings and practice of the peasantry' and noted that 'even after death it is astonishing how soon the thing passes away, without leaving any remembrance, even at the very inquest there is very little feeling shown.'[2] Maxwell Hamilton, the crown solicitor for the north-east circuit, stated before the 1852 select committee on outrages that there was 'a great recklessness of human life' which arose from the 'great demoralizing effect on the minds of the people' of witnessing murders.[3] For others, Ireland stood out from much of the rest of Europe as a violent place. Writing in the mid-1830s, George Cornewall Lewis claimed that 'in a large part of Ireland there is still less security of person and property than in any other part of Europe, except perhaps the wildest districts of Calabria or Greece.'[4]

---

[1] *Report from the select committee appointed to examine into the state of the disturbed counties in Ireland; into the immediate causes which have produced the same, and into the efficiency of the laws for the suppression of outrage against the public peace, with the minutes of evidence, appendix and index*, p. 93, H.C. 1831–32 (677), xvi, 1 (hereafter cited as Select committee on the state of Ireland, *Minutes of evidence 1831–32*).

[2] *Minutes of evidence taken before the select committee of the House of Lords appointed to enquire into the state of Ireland since the year 1835 in respect of crime and outrage, which have rendered life and property insecure in that part of the empire*, p. 747, H.C. 1839 (486) xi, xii, 1 (hereafter cited as Crime and outrage committee, *Minutes of evidence, 1839*).

[3] *Report from the select committee on outrages (Ireland) together with the proceedings of the committee, minutes of evidence, appendix and index*, p. 160, H.C. 1852 (438), xiv, 1 (hereafter cited as Select committee on outrages, *Minutes of evidence 1852*).

[4] George Cornewall Lewis, *On Local Disturbances in Ireland; and on the Irish Church Question* [1836], (new edition, Cork: Tower Books, 1977), ix.

Travel writers too noted a tendency towards violence and often dwelt on its prevalence in Irish life. Henry Inglis, while recounting a faction fight in the west of Ireland in 1834, reflected on the general 'abundance of fighting', he had encountered on his journey through the country.[5] For John Barrow, travelling along the south coast in the autumn of 1835, fighting was a 'pastime' among the 'lower class of Hibernians' who, particularly when under the influence of whiskey, had an 'extraordinary propensity' to fight. Such fights were, moreover, as often with their 'nearest relations [and] friends' as with 'foes'.[6] Caesar Otway, reflecting on the negligence of the Irish lower classes in curbing the 'tempers of their children', found little surprise in the fact that in Ireland 'the savage hand [was] so often lifted up to strike and commit a homicide.'[7] For Gustave de Beaumont, writing in the late 1830s, Irishmen were both 'violent and vindictive', displaying 'the most ferocious cruelty' in their 'acts of vengeance'.[8]

The view that pre-Famine and Famine Ireland was a particularly violent society is also the dominant perspective within the numerous studies of rural unrest in the first half of the nineteenth century, which have demonstrated how violence and the threat of violence was utilised, often by agrarian secret societies, in order to regulate socio-economic conditions.[9] The extent of such unrest has, indeed, led one commentator, to conclude that Ireland at this time was a 'remarkably violent country'.[10] Similarly, although perhaps less stridently, Sean Connolly has argued that Ireland was 'a violent society in which public order was often precarious and sometimes non-existent'.[11] J.S. Donnelly has claimed that ordinary people in pre-Famine Ireland inhabited an 'extremely violent world'.[12] For Galen Broeker, in the years

---

[5]   Henry D. Inglis, *A Journey throughout Ireland, during the Spring, Summer, and Autumn of 1834* (5th edition, London: Whittaker and Co., 1838), p. 227.

[6]   John Barrow, *A Tour round Ireland, through the Sea-Coast Counties, in the Autumn of 1835* (London: John Murray, 1836), pp. 348–51.

[7]   Caesar Otway, *A Tour of Connaught, Comprising Sketches of Clonmacnoise, Joyce Country and Achill* (Dublin: William Curry, Jun. & Company, 1839), p. 122.

[8]   Gustave de Beaumont, *Ireland: Social, Political and Religious* with an introduction by Tom Garvin and Andreas Hess [1839] (new ed., Cambridge, MA: Harvard University Press, 2006), p. 193.

[9]   See, amongst many others, Samuel Clark and J.S. Donnelly, Jr, *Irish Peasants: Violence and Political Unrest* (Manchester: Manchester University Press, 1983) and M.R. Beames, *Peasants and Power: The Whiteboy Movements and their Control in Pre-Famine Ireland* (Brighton: Harvester Press, 1983).

[10]   Samuel Clark, *Social Origins of the Irish Land War* (Princeton, NJ: Princeton University Press, 1979), p. 66.

[11]   S.J. Connolly, *Priests and People in Pre-Famine Ireland* (2nd ed. Dublin: Four Courts Press, 2001), p. 208.

[12]   J.S. Donnelly, Jr, 'Factions in Pre-Famine Ireland' in A.S. Eyler and R.F. Garratt (eds),

immediately preceding the Famine, 'violence and crime remained at what was undoubtedly a higher level than in any other area of Western Europe.'[13] Others have linked such violent activity to a longer-term and more pervasive propensity for violence on the part of Irish people. Writing in the mid-1970s, A.T.Q. Stewart argued that there was a long-standing culture of violence in Ireland, claiming that 'violence would appear to be endemic within Irish society, and this has been so as far back as history is recorded.' Moreover, he noted that 'for the last two hundred years, it is only when one turns to the newspapers that the sheer intensity and continuity of disturbance becomes apparent. There can hardly be a square inch of earth anywhere in Ireland that has not been at some time stained with blood.'[14]

In contrast to historians of eighteenth- and nineteenth-century Britain and Europe who have identified and sought to explain declining rates of interpersonal violence at this time,[15] a number of historians in Ireland have identified this period as one of increased and increasing violent activity. Connolly points to the 'relative infrequency of lethal violence' in the eighteenth century; this is in contrast to the nineteenth century where, he argues, the 'threshold of violence, in disputes of all kinds, became significantly lower'.[16] Neal Garnham, while noting 'some decline in levels of violence' in the eighteenth century also believes that whatever changes were underway were 'largely obscured' by 'new economic, political, and sectarian tensions' in the later part of the century.[17] For Stanley Palmer, 'an era of

The Uses of the Past: Essays on Irish Culture (Newark, DE: University of Delaware Press, 1988), pp. 113–30.

[13] Galen Broeker, *Rural Disorder and Police Reform in Ireland, 1812–36* (London: Routledge & Kegan Paul, 1970), p. 239.

[14] A.T.Q. Stewart, *The Narrow Ground: Aspects of Ulster, 1609–1969* (2nd ed., Belfast: Blackstaff Press, 1997), p. 113.

[15] See, among others, J.S. Cockburn, 'Patterns of Violence in English Society: Homicide in Kent, 1560–1985' *Past & Present*, 130 (1991), pp. 70–106; J.M. Beattie, *Crime and the Courts in England, 1660–1800* (Oxford: Clarendon Press, 1986), pp. 132–9; John Carter Wood, *Violence and Crime in Nineteenth-Century England: The Shadow of our Refinement* (London: Routledge, 2004); J.R. Ruff, *Violence in Early Modern Europe* (Cambridge: Cambridge University Press, 2001); Manuel Eisner, 'Modernization, Self-Control and Lethal Violence: The Long-Term Dynamics of European Homicide Rates in Theoretical Perspective', *British Journal of Criminology*, 41.4 (2001), pp. 618–38; Eisner, 'Long-Term Trends in Violent Crime' in Michael Tonry (ed.), *Crime and Justice: A Review of Research, Vol. 30* (Chicago, MI: University of Chicago Press, 2003), pp. 83–142.

[16] S.J. Connolly, *Religion, Law and Power: The Making of Protestant Ireland 1660–1760* (Oxford: Clarendon Press, 1992), p. 221 and pp. 314–16. Connolly, it should be noted, also warns against exaggerating the extent of violence in pre-Famine Ireland.

[17] Neal Garnham, *The Courts, Crime and the Criminal Law in Ireland, 1692–1760* (Dublin: Irish Academic Press, 1996), p. 185.

apparently low violence, at least by Irish standards, came to an end in the early 1790s.'[18] More starkly, J.S. Donnelly, has claimed that the 'culture of popular violence born of economic crucifixion, sectarianism, and repression' in the late eighteenth century was 'only a pale shadow of the nightmare that it would soon become' in the nineteenth.[19]

A number of historians have, however, challenged or at least qualified the view of Ireland in this period as a particularly violent society. Cormac Ó Gráda, for instance, has argued that the belief in 'endemic violent criminality' in the early to mid-nineteenth-century 'was almost certainly exaggerated'.[20] Similarly, David Fitzpatrick has suggested that Irish society at this time, 'in certain regions and for prolonged periods, was not endemically or abnormally violent'.[21] K.T. Hoppen has also warned that 'the violence of pre-Famine Ireland was both less constant and less universal than has often been supposed.'[22] D.J. McCabe has concluded that Ireland was 'merely rowdier than elsewhere in the British Isles'.[23] Perhaps the main area of broad agreement on the extent of violence in the first half of the nineteenth century is that it was worse than in more recent times. Ó Gráda, for example, points out that Ireland in this period was simply 'a violent place by the standards of the 1990s'.[24]

Was Ireland in the first half of the nineteenth century a violent society? Two approaches can be employed in assessing whether a society is a 'violent society'. The first is both quantitative and comparative; that is, a violent society is one in which the extent of violence is greater (often much greater) than at other periods and in other places. The second approach is both contextual and comparative. This examines the wider role of violence and what it reveals about the nature of a given society and how it compares to experiences at other times and in other places. From this perspective, a violent society is one in which the use of violence is accepted as a part of everyday living and can also be integral to the operation and regulation of

---

[18]   S.H. Palmer, *Police and Protest in England and Ireland, 1780–1850* (Cambridge: Cambridge University Press, 1988), p. 46.

[19]   J.S. Donnelly, Jr, 'The Rightboy Movement, 1785–8', *Studia Hibernica*, 17–18 (1977–8), p. 202.

[20]   Cormac Ó Gráda, *Ireland: A New Economic History, 1780–1939* (Oxford: Clarendon Press, 1994), p. 332.

[21]   David Fitzpatrick, 'Unrest in Rural Ireland', *Irish Economic and Social History*, 12 (1985), p. 100.

[22]   K.T. Hoppen, *Elections, Politics and Society in Ireland 1832–1885* (Oxford: Clarendon Press, 1984), p. 342.

[23]   D.J. McCabe, 'Law, Conflict and Social Order: County Mayo, 1820–45' (PhD thesis, University College Dublin, 1991), p. 56.

[24]   Ó Gráda, *Ireland: A New Economic History*, p. 332.

social life. In this sense, a violent society is one which not only experiences high levels of violence but one in which social relations are characterised by violence. Both factors, quantitative and contextual, will be considered in this book in the particular context of a study of homicide.

The study of homicide cannot, of course, offer a complete or definitive account of violent activity. It does, however, have a number of advantages. To begin, and as Eric Monkkonen has pointed out, homicide is undoubtedly a significant form of violence which is worthy of study in its own right and without which any study of violence would be incomplete.[25] It is also generally regarded as perhaps the only violent offence for which it is possible to offer a viable statistical analysis.[26] Moreover, while a study of homicide does not reveal the levels of violent activity in a given society, it can aid in discerning the difference between a society in which the extent and nature of violence might be carefully limited and controlled and one in which such controls are substantially weaker or even non-existent.

The study of homicide also serves to fill a gap in the historiography of pre-Famine and Famine Ireland. There has, with a few notable exceptions, been little detailed examination of the incidence and nature of particular violent offences, such as assault, rape, robbery, and homicide in pre-Famine and Famine Ireland outside of their relevance to debates concerning the character of wider rural unrest and popular protest.[27] By studying the incidence of a single offence such as homicide in different areas of the

---

[25] E.H. Monkkonen, 'New Standards for Historical Homicide Research', *Crime, Histoire & Sociétés/ Crime, History & Societies*, 5.2 (2001), p. 6.

[26] Julius R. Ruff, for example, claims that 'only the crime of homicide, which many scholars regard as an important indicator of a society's overall level of violence, seems to be a valid object of statistical analysis'. See Ruff, *Violence*, p. 120.

[27] The main quantitative analyses of homicide in pre-Famine and Famine Ireland are provided by S.J. Connolly and D.J. McCabe. See S.J. Connolly, 'Unnatural Death in Four Nations: Contrasts and Comparisons' in Connolly (ed.), *Kingdoms United? Ireland and Great Britain from 1500: Integration and Diversity* (Dublin: Four Courts Press, 1998), pp. 200–14; McCabe, 'Law, Conflict and Social Order', chapter three. These studies will be discussed in chapter one. The main contextual studies of homicide in this period are provided by D.J. McCabe and M.R. Beames. See McCabe, 'Law, Conflict and Social Order', chapter three and M.R. Beames, 'Rural Conflict in Pre-Famine Ireland: Peasant Assassinations in Tipperary, 1837–1847', in C.H.E. Philpin (ed.), *Nationalism and Popular Protest in Ireland* (Cambridge: Cambridge University Press, 1987). For longer-term trends, see Ian O'Donnell, 'Lethal Violence in Ireland, 1841–2003: Famine, Celibacy and Parental Pacification', *British Journal of Criminology*, 45 (2005), pp. 671–95; O'Donnell, 'Unlawful Killing Past and Present', *The Irish Jurist*, 37 new series (2002), pp. 56–90. See also Mark Finnane, 'A Decline in Violence in Ireland? Crime, Policing and Social Relations, 1860–1914', *Crime, Histoire & Sociétés/ Crime, History & Societies*, 1.1 (1997), pp. 51–70.

country we can avoid some of the problems inherent in the studies of rural unrest and collective violence. Such studies have, understandably, tended to focus on areas of the country that were particularly disturbed by rural unrest. As a result, rural areas of north Munster, west Leinster and east Connacht have largely dominated our understanding of violence in this period and, in consequence, levels and experiences of violence in other parts of the country have too often been overlooked. Studies of rural unrest have also tended to focus on directly economic and, to a lesser extent, political and sectarian disputes and, as a consequence, more personal and familial disputes have not received the attention they merit. Thus, by studying the incidence of a single offence such as homicide rather than focusing exclusively on violence arising directly from economic or political conflict, it is possible to glean a broader view of the causes of violence in Irish society at the time. It also offers a greater insight into interpersonal as opposed to group or collective violence.

The examination of this offence also allows us to compare Irish experiences to those in other societies. The last thirty years or so have seen a burgeoning interest in the historiography of crime and criminal justice in the extent and nature of homicide in early modern and modern Europe. Drawing inspiration from Ted Robert Gurr's ground-breaking study of long-term homicide rates from the late middle ages to the latter half of the twentieth century,[28] historians have increasingly sought to map and to explain long-term patterns in lethal interpersonal violence and, in particular, the reasons behind the apparent decline in homicide rates in many areas of Europe over the course of this period.

For some, the apparent decline in homicide rates reflects considerable and perhaps even fundamental change in cultural attitudes towards violent activity. A number of historians, particularly those working on early modern Britain and Germany, have understood the shifts in patterns of violent activity as a consequence of changes in perceptions of male honour and the rise of individualism. They argue that, as community influence waned and new norms surrounding individual behaviour emerged, violence, over the course of the eighteenth century in particular, became less central to individual male identity and came increasingly to be the preserve of, often

---

[28]   Ted Robert Gurr, 'Historical Trends in Violent Crime: A Critical Review of the Evidence' in Michael Tonry and Norval Morris (eds), *Crime and Justice: An Annual Review of Research, Vol. 3* (Chicago, MI: University of Chicago Press, 1982), pp. 295–353. Gurr's article sparked off considerable debate within the English historiography. See Lawrence Stone, 'Interpersonal Violence in English Society, 1300–1900', *Past & Present*, 101 (1983), pp. 22–33; J.A. Sharpe, 'The History of Violence in England: Some Observations', *Past & Present*, 108 (1985), pp. 206–15; Lawrence Stone 'A rejoinder' *Past & Present*, 108 (1985), pp. 216–24.

marginalised, sections of the lower orders.[29] Greater state intervention and a wider process of social disciplining, often driven by church bodies, new work practices and the expansion in the number of schools have also been credited with contributing to a diminution in violent activity among individuals.[30]

Others have viewed the apparent decline in lethal interpersonal violence not simply as a product of greater state intervention, increased social discipline or changes in ideas surrounding personal honour, but rather have understood change in the context of a wider civilising process. Indeed, Norbert Elias's civilising process thesis has provided a prominent and highly influential interpretative framework for the apparent changes in patterns of homicidal violence. Pieter Spierenburg, drawing on Elias, argues, for instance, that patterns of violence have been profoundly altered not only by greater state intervention and changing conceptions of male honour, but also by the trickle down of increased levels of 'affect control' from the social elite to the mass of the people over several centuries. In this view, as the state became more active in prosecuting violence through the courts, as interdependence among individuals increased with the development of new economic forms and as new ideas concerning appropriate behaviour trickled down from the elite, individuals became less likely to resort to acts of interpersonal violence to resolve conflicts.[31] Steven Pinker, using

---

[29] Robert Shoemaker, 'Male Honour and the Decline of Public Violence in Eighteenth-Century London', *Social History*, 26 (2001); Joachim Eibach, 'The Containment of Violence in Central European Cities, 1500–1800' in Richard Mc Mahon (ed.), *Crime, Law and Popular Culture in Europe 1500–1900* (Cullompton: Willan Publishing, 2008), pp. 52–73. See also Gerd Schwerhoff, 'Social Control of Violence, Violence as Social Control: The Case of Early Modern Germany' in Herman Roodenburg and Pieter Spierenburg (eds), *Social Control in Europe, 1500–1800* (Columbus, OH: Ohio State University Press, 2004), pp. 220–46.

[30] Eisner, 'Modernization'.

[31] See Norbert Elias, *The Civilizing Process: Sociogenetic and Psychogenetic Investigations* [1939] (revised ed., Oxford: Blackwell Publishing, 2000) and Pieter Spierenburg, 'Faces of Violence: Homicide Trends and Cultural Meanings, Amsterdam, 1431–1816', *Journal of Social History*, 27 (1994), pp. 701–16; Spierenburg, 'Long-Term Trends in Homicide: Theoretical Reflections and Dutch Evidence, Fifteenth to Twentieth Centuries' in E.A. Johnson and E.H. Monkkonen (eds), *The Civilization of Crime: Violence in Town and Country since the Middle Ages* (Urbana, IL: University of Illinois Press, 1996), pp. 63–105; Spierenburg, *A History of Murder: Personal Violence in Europe from the Middle Ages to the Present* (Cambridge: Polity Press, 2008). For the debate between Spierenburg and Schwerhoff on the relative merits of their positions, see Pieter Spierenburg, 'Violence and the Civilizing Process: Does it Work?', *Crime, Histoire & Sociétés/ Crime, History & Societies*, 5.2 (2001), pp. 87–105; Gerd Schwerhoff, 'Criminalized Violence and the Process of Civilisation: A Reappraisal', *Crime, Histoire & Sociétés/ Crime, History & Societies*, 6.2 (2002), pp. 103–36; Pieter Spierenburg, 'Theorizing in Jurassic Park: a

a dazzling array of statistical evidence and a broad range of case studies, also draws on the concept of a civilising process to argue that the apparent decline in violence is a chief benefit and consequence of the impact of modernity on the western world and, in particular, the influence of enlightenment thought since the eighteenth century. For Pinker, the 'erosion of family, tribe, tradition, and religion' by the 'forces of individualism, cosmopolitanism, reason, and science' ultimately underpinned the decline in rates of interpersonal violence in western societies.[32] Pinker and others, most notably Gregory Hanlon and John Carter Wood, have also looked to evolutionary psychology to provide a broad cross-cultural framework within which the history of interpersonal violence can be understood. Recurrent patterns in interpersonal violence, particularly the predominance of men as both victims and perpetrators, are seen as being deeply rooted in a shared human psychology and explicable in the light of a general theory of human nature based on Darwin's theory of evolution by natural selection.[33]

Others have adopted a more sceptical approach to the evidence and have been suspicious of applying over-arching theories of socio-cultural change to explain the decline in homicide rates – preferring instead to emphasise changes in medical expertise and practice, in the age structure of the population and also the difficulties inherent in the use of the available sources.[34] Outside of a directly European context (but with clear implications for it) Randolph Roth has also proposed an alternative framework for understanding variations in homicide rates over time which emphasises the

reply to Gerd Schwerhoff', *Crime, Histoire & Sociétés/ Crime, History & Societies*, 6.2 (2002), pp. 127–8. For a good overview of the differing interpretations of the history of interpersonal violence in Europe, see Eisner, 'Modernization' and 'Long-Term Trends in Violent Crime'.

[32] For Pinker, the rise of the state, the development of webs of commerce, feminisation, cosmopolitanism and an increasing resort to reason as a means of resolving conflict, have all contributed to the decline in interpersonal violence. See: Steven Pinker, *The Better Angels of our Nature: The Decline of Violence in History and its Causes* (London: Allen Lane, 2011).

[33] See, for instance, Pinker, *Better Angels*; Martin Daly and Margo Wilson, *Homicide* (New York: A. de Gruyter, 1988); John Carter Wood, 'The Limits of Culture? Society, Evolutionary Psychology and the History of Violence', *Cultural and Social History*, 4.1 (2007), pp. 95–114; Manuel Eisner, 'Human Evolution, History and Violence: An Introduction', *British Journal of Criminology*, 51.3 (2011), pp. 473–8 (and accompanying articles); Gregory Hanlon, 'The Decline of Violence in the West: From Cultural to Post-Cultural History', *English Historical Review*, 128 (2013), pp. 367–400.

[34] See, for instance, Cockburn, 'Patterns of Violence in English Society', pp. 101–6 and Stuart Carroll, 'Introduction' in Carroll (ed.), *Cultures of Violence: Interpersonal Violence in Historical Perspective* (Basingstoke: Palgrave Macmillan, 2007).

importance of trust in government and, more broadly, the process of nation building in establishing low levels of interpersonal violence.[35]

With some exceptions, the Irish historiography of violence has remained largely untouched by such debates.[36] This is due, in part, to the paucity of available sources for a study of long-term trends, which means that it is practically impossible to trace long-term homicide trends before the early to mid-eighteenth century, and even then the available evidence is less than ideal. There is also undoubtedly a sense that Ireland is not exactly fertile ground for such theories. Historians have certainly been more concerned with explaining the distinctive causes of violence in Ireland than mapping any possible decline in its use or in seeking deep structures rooted in evolutionary processes which underpin individual action. Yet the difficulties with the available data and the seemingly distinctive elements of the Irish experience should not wholly discourage us from exploring the relevance and applicability of these theories to the Irish context, although it does perhaps force us to take a somewhat different approach. The focus of this study will not be on mapping long-term trends in homicide rates *per se*, but rather on providing an in-depth analysis of homicide in pre-Famine and Famine Ireland and how this might compare with other periods and places. In doing so, the book engages with, but also challenges, the dominant interpretations offered within the international historiography.

A diverse range of sources are employed, including parliamentary papers, newspapers, police reports and prisoners' petitions. The use of such sources is by no means unproblematic and their limitations will be discussed, where necessary, in the individual chapters, as well as in Appendix one, which explores the various methodological problems involved in a quantitative assessment of homicide rates and the potential pitfalls in the available sources for pre-Famine and Famine Ireland. The general approach is also not only to take account of national data, where it is available, but to look in detail at a number of counties for which there are adequate surviving sources. In

---

[35] Randolph Roth, *American Homicide* (Cambridge, MA: The Belknap of Harvard University Press, 2009). See also Pieter Spierenburg, 'American Homicide. What Does the Evidence Mean for Theories of Violence and Society?', *Crime, Histoire & Sociétés/ Crime, History & Societies*, 15.2 (2011), pp. 123–9; Randolph Roth, 'Yes We Can: Working Together Toward a History of Homicide that is Empirically, Mathematically, and Theoretically Sound', *Crime, Histoire & Sociétés/ Crime, History & Societies*, 15.2 (2011), pp. 131–45; Pieter Spierenburg, 'Questions that Remain: Pieter Spierenburg's Reply to Randolph Roth', *Crime, Histoire & Sociétés/ Crime, History & Societies*, 15.2 (2011), pp. 147–50.

[36] For an exploration of the relevance of the concept of the civilising process to Irish homicide rates, see O'Donnell, 'Lethal Violence in Ireland' and Ian O'Donnell, 'Killing in Ireland at the Turn of the Centuries: Contexts, Consequences and Civilizing Processes', *Irish Economic and Social History*, 37 (2010), pp. 53–74.

particular, there is a focus on the incidence of homicide in four counties: Co. Armagh and Co. Fermanagh in the north, and Queen's Co. and Co. Kilkenny, both in the south of the country. These counties have been selected primarily because there is viable source material available for all four areas. Fortunately, as we shall see, they also provide an insight into areas of the country that had somewhat contrasting rates and experiences of homicide.

In the context of this study, the term 'homicide' refers to two forms of unlawful killing: manslaughter and murder. I also adopt the definitions of these offences as they applied in Ireland at the time.[37] I exclude, however, cases of infanticide from the study. The reason for this is that the study of infanticide raises distinct questions, such as the social value of children, issues of sexuality, female honour and welfare provision, which warrant separate investigation and which, while by no means unrelated to, are quite distinct from the primary concerns of this book.[38] This study also focuses on patterns of violent activity rather than the prosecution of violence. The latter will be dealt with in a forthcoming book.[39]

The first chapter engages in a quantitative analysis of homicide rates while those that follow investigate the nature and character of lethal violence in Irish society. This is achieved through an exploration of the part played by lethal violence in personal and familial relationships (chapters two and three). Though homicides arising from familial disputes have received scant attention within the historiography, they constituted a significant proportion of all incidents of homicide. Following this, the part played by violence in land and sectarian disputes is examined (chapters four and five). In contrast

[37] Blackstone defines manslaughter as 'the unlawful killing of another without malice either express or implied; which may be either voluntarily, upon a sudden heat; or involuntarily, but in the commission of some unlawful act.' Murder, in contrast, 'is when a person, of sound memory and discretion, unlawfully killeth any reasonable creature in being, and under the king's peace, with malice aforethought, either express or implied'. See William Blackstone, *Commentaries on the Laws of England, Book the Fourth* (15th ed., London: Strahan, 1809), pp. 190 and 195.

[38] There has been some discussion within the historiography as to whether or not infanticide should be included in more general studies of homicide. See, for instance, Cockburn, 'Patterns of Violence in English Society' and Spierenburg, 'Long-Term Trends'. For an account of infanticide in nineteenth-century Ireland, see Elaine Farrell, "Infanticide of the Ordinary Character': An Overview of the Crime in Ireland, 1850–1900', *Irish Economic and Social History*, 39 (2012), pp. 56–72. See also Dympna McLoughlin, 'Infanticide in Nineteenth-Century Ireland' in Angela Bourke, Siobhán Kilfeather, Maria Luddy, Margaret MacCurtain, Gerardine Meaney, Máirín Ní Dhonnchadha, Mary O'Dowd and Clair Wills (eds), *Field Day Anthology of Irish Writing: Irish Women's Writing and Traditions Vol. 4* (New York: New York University Press, 2002), pp. 915–19.

[39] See Richard Mc Mahon, *Violence, the Courts and Legal Cultures in Ireland, 1801–1850* (forthcoming).

to more personal and familial conflicts, disputes arising from land and sectarian animosity have received considerably more attention within the historiography and are often seen as primary and significant causes of violent conflict in Ireland at this time. But they were by no means the primary causes of lethal violent conflict and this study places the role of violence in such disputes within their proper context.

1

Homicide rates in Ireland, 1801–1850

How common was homicide in Ireland in the first half of the nineteenth century?[1] Between 1841 and 1850, the decade for which the most consistent data is available, there were 2,792 reported cases of homicide in Ireland.[2] This figure comprises all incidents of alleged murder, manslaughter and infanticide reported by the police in the country throughout the decade. Of the total number of incidents reported, 1,230, or forty-four per cent, were alleged cases of infanticide, while the remaining 1,562, or fifty-six per cent, were alleged murders or manslaughters. The rate of homicide (excluding infanticide), therefore, was 1.97 per 100,000 of the population.[3]

Is the Irish rate unusually high when compared to other countries? Given the widely recognised dangers involved in international comparisons of crime rates, this is a difficult question to address. Differences in the efficiency of criminal justice systems, the definitions of offences and the

---

[1] For a discussion of the methods and sources employed in this chapter, see Appendix one.

[2] This figure is derived from the *Return of outrages reported to the constabulary office* for the years 1841 to 1850 (these returns are available in the *Irish crime records* held at the National Archives of Ireland) and the *Return of the number of offences reported as having been committed in the Dublin police district* for the years 1841 to 1850 (available in the National Library of Ireland).

[3] The rate of reported homicides per 100,000 of the population was calculated using the 1821, 1841 and 1851 census figures for the country. I have calculated an average annual growth rate between the 1821 and 1841 censuses and have extended this growth rate up to 1845. I then calculated an annual average decrease in population in the famine years of 1846–50 using my estimated figure for 1845 and the 1851 census. By calculating an average annual increase up to 1845 and then an annual average decrease between 1846 and 1850, I have been able to arrive at an average population figure for the ten-year period between 1841 and 1850. For the national population figures for 1821, 1841 and 1851, see W.E. Vaughan and A.J. Fitzpatrick (ed.), *Irish Historical Statistics: Population, 1821–1971* A New History of Ireland: Ancillary Publications II (Dublin: Royal Irish Academy, 1978). It should be noted that my rates differ slightly to those provided by Ian O'Donnell. This is due to minor differences in population estimates. See O'Donnell, 'Lethal Violence in Ireland'.

differing methods employed in the compilation of crime statistics all render comparison difficult. Perhaps the most reliable comparison that can be made is with England and Wales, given the broad similarities between both the criminal law and criminal justice systems. Even here, the situation is complicated by the fact that comparable national data based on reported incidents for England and Wales is not available before the late 1850s, which means that a direct comparison can only be made with English and Welsh figures from later in the century.[4]

There is already a degree of confusion in the historiography as to how Irish rates in the pre-Famine and Famine periods compare with those found in England and Wales in the latter half of the nineteenth century. Connolly, in his general survey of homicide in modern Ireland, suggests that the country endured a 'high level of violence relative to other parts of the United Kingdom', with homicide rates in the 1830s and 40s 'two-and-a-half times that recorded in England and Wales in the 1850s and 1860s'.[5] In contrast, McCabe's analysis of the rates, based on the same Irish sources, suggests that homicide rates in Ireland before the Famine, while higher, were not markedly different from those recorded for England and Wales in the 1860s and 1870s.[6] The main reason for the difference is that Connolly includes cases of infanticide in his figures while McCabe, in making his comparison, excludes them. Given that the English and Welsh figures, certainly from the late 1870s onwards, include cases of infanticide, it is clear that Connolly's comparison is the more viable. The overall homicide rate of 3.52 per 100,000 in 1840s Ireland is, for instance, more than double that recorded for England in the early 1880s, where the rate of reported homicide (including infanticide) known to the police was 1.6 per 100,000.[7]

Were the higher Irish rates in the 1840s determined by higher levels of reported infanticide? Connolly has argued that higher Irish levels of infanticide cannot explain the difference between Irish and English 'murder' rates in the nineteenth century. In support of this, he points to the fact

---

[4]   There are homicide figures based on indictments available for England and Wales in the early to mid-nineteenth century, but these are a less satisfactory source for comparison as they are based on the numbers prosecuted for an offence rather than the number of offences. For a discussion of these kinds of sources in Ireland, see Appendix one. For a consideration of how the English indictment figures compare with the Irish police reports in the 1840s, see below, p. 15.

[5]   Connolly, 'Unnatural Death in Four Nations', p. 206.

[6]   McCabe, 'Law, Conflict and Social Order', p. 55.

[7]   V.A.C. Gatrell, 'The Decline of Theft and Violence in Victorian and Edwardian England' in V.A.C. Gatrell, Bruce Lenman and Geoffrey Parker (eds), *Crime and the Law: The Social History of Crime in Western Europe since 1500* (London: Europa Publications, 1980), p. 287.

that the murder rate in the later part of the century (excluding cases of infanticide) is much higher in Ireland than in England (a rate of just over 2:1 in the 1880s, for instance).[8] While this may be the case for the *murder* rates in the latter part of the century, in the context of the overall *homicide* rate recorded in Ireland in the 1840s the situation is quite different.

The higher Irish rate of homicide in the 1840s can be explained, partially at least, by higher levels of reported infanticide. Reports of infanticide account for forty-four per cent of all reported homicides in 1840s Ireland whereas, in England, as Gatrell has pointed out, infanticides accounted for twenty per cent of known homicides in the late nineteenth century.[9] Thus, the level of reported infanticide in 1840s Ireland, as a proportion of all reported homicide, is more than double that of late nineteenth-century England.

This has serious implications for how we compare and, indeed, understand the rates of reported homicide in both countries. As Connolly points out, while 'infanticide can hardly be left out of any discussion of violence' it does belong to 'a different category to the violence of one adult against another'.[10] Thus, it is more appropriate, when comparing rates of homicide in both countries, to separate the rate of infanticide from the rate of homicide of persons aged over one year. If we exclude the reported infanticides from our figures we get a rate of reported homicide of 1.97 per 100,000 in Ireland in the 1840s compared with an estimated rate of 1.28 per 100,000 in England. Thus, the rate of reported homicide (excluding infanticide) in 1840s Ireland was just over one and a half times that of England in the early 1880s.[11] While certainly higher, the Irish figures indicate that, in the

---

8   Connolly, 'Unnatural Death in Four Nations', p. 206.
9   Gatrell, 'The Decline of Theft and Violence', p. 342.
10   Connolly, 'Unnatural Death in Four Nations', p. 206.
11   As noted in the introduction, I have not included cases of infanticide in this study. The figures cited above would, however, indicate that rates of this offence in Ireland were higher than in England. Yet, we also need to be exceedingly careful when comparing infanticide rates between different countries. Calculating rates of infanticide per 100,000 of the population can, for instance, be misleading. A more satisfactory measure would be to examine the incidence of this offence per birth. Adopting this methodology, my preliminary investigations suggest that the rate of infanticide for the country as a whole in the five years preceding the Famine, 1841–5, was 3.82 per 10,000 births (one infanticide per 2,617 births). This would mean that a relatively large parish with, perhaps, around 400 births annually, would have had one case of reported infanticide every six or seven years. Indeed, even if the rate of undetected cases was ten times the rate of reported cases, an average parish would probably have had 'only' around one or two cases a year from an average of 400 births. This, moreover, would be working on the assumption that every case of infanticide recorded by the police was genuine. These figures are, of course, high compared to the present day, but they do little to suggest that infanticide was a

context of homicide at least, 1840s Ireland was by no means unusually or remarkably violent in comparison with late nineteenth-century England. To draw a modern-day parallel, the difference between Ireland and England in the nineteenth century is less than the difference between modern-day Belgium (1.2 per 100,000) and France (2 per 100,000).[12] Moreover, if we compare the Irish figures from the 1840s with the admittedly much less reliable homicide indictment rates for England and Wales in the 1830s and 1840s, the difference in rates between the two countries is even less pronounced. The national homicide indictment rates for England and Wales were, for instance, 1.8 per 100,000 in the 1840s – broadly similar to rates of reported homicide in Ireland at the same time. The English and Welsh rates do admittedly include some infanticides which inflate the rate, but they only accounted for a small fraction of recorded indictments.[13] On the whole, it is likely that 1840s Ireland was probably not exceptionally violent by the standards of the day and was certainly nowhere near the highest rates recorded in Europe at this time.[14]

Even in comparison with rates in the present day, 1840s Ireland was not particularly prone to high rates of homicide. The 1840s homicide rate of 1.97 per 100,000 is somewhat, but by no means exceptionally, higher than the rate of 1.2 per 100,000 recorded in the Republic of Ireland in the 1990s, a society with 'one of the lowest rates of homicide in the world'.[15] The rate is actually lower than the rate of 2.1 per 100,000 recorded for Northern Ireland in the mid-1990s.[16] It is also lower than that of modern-day Dublin

---

common occurrence. The figures for the incidence of infanticide were derived from the *Irish crime records* (NAI) and the *Return of the number of offences reported as having been committed in the Dublin police district* for the years 1841 to 1845.

[12] *Criminal Statistics England and Wales 1996* cited in Enda Dooley, *Homicide in Ireland 1992–1996* (Dublin: Stationery Office, 2001), p. 9.

[13] See Cockburn, 'Patterns of Violence in English Society', p. 78; Gatrell, 'The Decline of Theft and Violence', pp. 342–3. Drawing on evidence from London, Peter King estimates that infanticides accounted for only six per cent of murder indictments in the early nineteenth century. See Peter King, 'The Impact of Urbanization on Murder Rates and on the Geography of Homicide in England and Wales, 1780–1850', *Historical Journal*, 53.3 (2010), p. 682. It should be noted that the Irish homicide indictment rates were higher at this time but these, as highlighted in Appendix one, are highly unrepresentative of the actual number of homicide cases. See below, pp. 188–89. See also W.E. Vaughan, *Murder Trials in Ireland, 1836–1914* (Dublin: Four Courts Press, 2009), pp. 21–34.

[14] The highest rates recorded for Europe in this period are probably those of Corsica, where rates of sixty-four per 100,000 were recorded in the late 1840s. Stephen Wilson, *Feuding, Conflict and Banditry in Nineteenth-Century Corsica* (Cambridge: Cambridge University Press, 1988), p. 16.

[15] Dooley, *Homicide in Ireland*, p. 9.

[16] Ibid.

with its rate of 2.19 per 100,000 in the period 1998–2000.[17] Moreover, in a wider European context, Irish rates in the 1840s compare quite favourably with those recorded for modern-day Europe. The Irish rate of 1.97 is, for instance, lower than rates recorded for modern-day France (2.0 per 100,000) and Austria (2.2 per 100,000).[18] 1840s Ireland also compares very favourably with jurisdictions outside of Europe. Its rate is around one quarter of that in the United States, one tenth of that in Russia and one thirtieth of that for South Africa in the 1990s.[19]

In comparing rates from Ireland in the 1840s with those of nineteenth-century England and those in the present day it is important, of course, not to rely too heavily on the available figures without, to some extent at least, exploring the contexts from which they emerge. The police in 1840s Ireland, under strict government supervision, played a very active role in investigating suspicious deaths in their localities.[20] In contrast, there is strong evidence to suggest that the English police in the late nineteenth century were somewhat less vigorous in their efforts. The most compelling critique of the English statistics is that put forward by Howard Taylor, who claims that 'it was an open secret that most murders and suspicious deaths went uninvestigated' in late nineteenth-century England. This was due, he argues, to pressures on police budgets, which meant that the police, with the connivance of coroners' inquests, were selective in the cases they chose to investigate and record as murder.[21]

Taylor's position is certainly not without its critics. R.M. Morris, for instance, has argued that Taylor both overstates the extent of budgetary constraints on police investigations and unnecessarily diminishes the independent role of the coroner's inquest in determining the cause of death. Yet, while rejecting Taylor's argument of a deliberate 'conspiracy' to under-record cases of murder, Morris does accept that the evidence Taylor produces 'convincingly demonstrates a lack of effectiveness and an unacceptable degree on occasion of complacency' in the recording and investigation of murder cases by both the police and coroners.[22]

We seem, therefore, to be comparing figures produced by systems with

---

[17] Ian O'Donnell, 'Unlawful Killing', p. 75.

[18] Dooley, *Homicide in Ireland*, p. 9.

[19] *Homicide Statistics*, House of Commons research paper 1999/56, p. 37.

[20] For a discussion of the part played by the police in investigating homicides, see Appendix one below.

[21] Howard Taylor, 'Rationing Crime: The Political Economy of Criminal Statistics since the 1850s', *Economic History Review*, 51.3 (1998), p. 588.

[22] R.M. Morris, 'Lies, Damned Lies and Criminal Statistics: Reinterpreting the Criminal Statistics in England and Wales', *Crime, Histoire & Sociétés/ Crime, History & Societies*, 5.1 (2001), pp. 117–19. See also King, 'The Impact of Urbanization', pp. 675–8.

quite different *modi operandi*. Given that the Irish police were probably more conscientious and vigorous in investigating cases of suspicious death, it seems likely that even the relatively small difference between the English and Irish figures may serve to exaggerate the degree to which homicide was more prevalent in Ireland.

Factors other than the propensity of people to resort to acts of lethal violence and the ability and/or willingness of the authorities to record such acts can have an impact on homicide rates. The medical attention given to victims, for instance, may also have a bearing on the rates. This may be of particular significance when comparing rates from the early nineteenth century with those of the present day. Could it be that the main difference between rates of lethal violence in pre-Famine and Famine Ireland and the present day lies not in the propensity of people to resort to acts of lethal violence, but in the standard of medical care and attention given to victims of violent attacks?

Crucial to any examination of the effect of improved medical care is an assessment of the time between the initial injury and the death of the victim. Monkkonen, in an examination of homicide in nineteenth-century New York, draws on expert medical evidence, which suggests that 'many' of those deaths that occurred twenty-four hours after the initial assault 'could have been prevented with today's medicine'. Moreover, a reasonable proportion of those deaths that occurred one hour after the initial assault may also have been preventable with modern medical techniques.[23]

The extent of the time difference between the occurrence of an assault and the death of the victim in homicide cases in nineteenth-century Ireland is somewhat difficult to assess. The police reports of serious crime are, perhaps, the most viable source. Such reports are not, however, always consistent or precise in offering information on the time difference between an alleged assault and the death of the victim. Moreover, the diligence of the police in recording such details varied from place to place.

The limited evidence that is available, however, raises the very distinct possibility that the difference between homicide rates in the 1840s and those of the late twentieth century lies not in a greater propensity for violence, but is largely rooted in the different standards of medical care available to victims of violent acts.

[23] Monkkonen, 'New Standards', pp. 16–18.

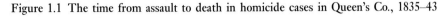
Figure 1.1 The time from assault to death in homicide cases in Queen's Co., 1835–43

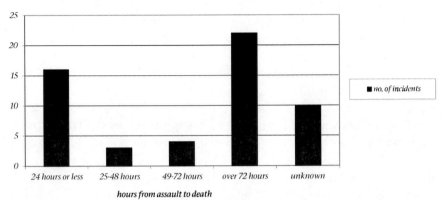

The chart above sets out the time differences between the initial alleged attack and the death of the victim in fifty-five cases that occurred in Queen's Co. over a nine-year period between 1835 and 1843. In just under 30 per cent of cases the victim died within twenty-four hours of the initial violent attack, while in over fifty per cent of cases the victim died after the initial twenty-four hour period, the overwhelming majority of these dying over three days after the initial assault.[24]

There were certainly some cases in our sample where it is not difficult to imagine that if adequate medical attention and care were given to the victim of the violent attack then he or she would have survived. In Queen's Co. in 1836, at a coroner's inquest on the body of John McDowell, who died on 13 March of that year, the jury found that the deceased died 'from the effects of a fractured leg inflicted by Thomas McEvoy on 24 January [...] by blow of a stone or stones inflicted on [McDowell's] right leg'.[25] It is unlikely, given modern techniques, that someone would die as a consequence of a broken leg in the present day or at least not over six weeks after the initial attack. The risk of death from an untreated infection was also obviously far higher than in the present day. In Armagh, in 1848, for instance, a man died as a consequence of lockjaw after being 'wounded in the thumb by [a] butcher's knife' by a man called Fitzpatrick.[26]

The conditions in which victims of violent attacks lived probably also contributed to their deaths. For instance, in 1840, Bridget Bryan, an elderly woman 'probably [aged] between 60 and 70' died six weeks after having

---

24   This data is based on information gleaned from the Queen's Co. outrage papers, 1835–43 (NAI) and the *Leinster Express*, 1835–43.
25   NAI, outrage papers, Queen's Co., 1836/18 and 1836/31.
26   *Armagh Guardian*, 17 Jul. 1848.

been beaten by her son. In this case, Bryan's 'arm was broken, her face, legs, and thighs, in fact her whole body was blackened' as a consequence of the beating. Despite these injuries she was left lying in her cabin in an area that 'was wet, [due to] being exposed to the rain, and the straw under her was wet'. She seems to have had limited medical attention in the aftermath of the attack and was only moved to better lodgings seven or eight days after the beating. Even then, according to her daughter, she was 'in great want, and before her death was literary [sic] starving'.[27] Medical doctors at the time could also be critical of the treatment given to those whose lives were thought to be in danger. George Nixon, esq. M.D., the 'surgeon to the county of Fermanagh' admitted, under cross-examination at the trial for the murder of Owen Drum in 1835, that 'under different treatment the man might have recovered'.[28] Similarly, at the trial for the manslaughter of Frank Wynne at the Fermanagh spring assizes of 1850, Surgeon Wilkins gave his opinion that 'the deceased might have lived longer had better care been taken of him'.[29]

It may be, of course, that improvements in medical care could be offset, as Monkkonen suggests, by the greater availability and sophistication of weaponry in the present day.[30] There is certainly evidence that some homicides in the present day are facilitated by the availability of hand guns, particularly in cases related to organised crime.[31] Such cases accounted for 7.3 per cent of cases in Ireland between 1992 and 1996 and the proportion of such cases has probably increased since that time.[32] Yet, outside of these 'gangland' crimes, the effect on homicide rates of the greater availability of sophisticated weaponry to the general public should not be exaggerated. Unlike the present-day United States of America, gun laws in modern Ireland remain relatively strict, particularly relating to hand guns, and firearms are not readily available to the general public outside of gun clubs. Moreover, the primarily rural inhabitants of pre-Famine and Famine Ireland probably had a wider range of potentially lethal implements at their disposal

---

27 *Leinster Express*, 25 Jul. 1840.

28 *Enniskillen Chronicle and Erne Packet*, 19 Mar. 1835. Drum had been operated on by a Dr McNeece who had performed 'the operation of trepanning' while Nixon thought that if the 'suppuration [had] been punctured and allowed to come away the man might have lived'.

29 *Enniskillen Chronicle and Erne Packet*, 14 Mar. 1850.

30 Monkkonen, 'New Standards', pp. 18–19.

31 See Ian O'Donnell, 'Violence and Social Change in the Republic of Ireland', *International Journal of the Sociology of Law*, 33 (2005), p. 110.

32 Dooley, *Homicide in Ireland*, p. 16.

Figure 1.2   Reported incidents of homicide in Ireland, 1831–1850

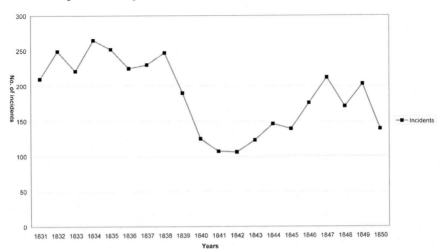

(scythes, spades, reaping hooks) than the urban dweller of modern-day Ireland.[33]

Thus, if we accept Monkkonen's thesis that 'many' of the deaths that occurred after twenty-four hours and a significant proportion of those occurring within twenty-four hours would have been preventable with modern medical care and attention, then serious question marks must hang over any claims, based on homicide rates, that Ireland in the 1840s was necessarily a much more violent place than the present day. It should also be taken into consideration that Ireland in the second half of the 1840s endured severe Famine conditions throughout the country, which led to an increase in homicide rates (see Figure 1.2).

It is not unreasonable to speculate that if the Famine had not occurred, and if the conditions of the early 1840s had persisted, then the already quite low rate of homicide may have been even lower.

This, however, is evidence from only one decade. The admittedly less reliable police statistics from the 1830s suggest that rates were higher.[34] A total of 2,214 cases of homicide (excluding infanticide) were reported between 1831 and 1840.[35] This gives us a rate of 2.83 per 100,000, which

---

33   The highest homicide rates in modern-day Ireland are in urban areas, particularly Limerick and Dublin. See Dooley, *Homicide in Ireland*, p. 13.

34   For a discussion of the homicide figures from the 1830s, see Appendix one.

35   This finding is based on the following sources: *A return of the number of offences against the law, which have been committed in Ireland, during the years 1831–32, so far as returns*

is somewhat, although it has to be said not much, higher than that found in the 1840s.[36] This figure is also much more in line with Connolly's assertion that homicide rates in the pre-Famine period were more than double those in late nineteenth-century England. Yet, the extent of the differences should not be exaggerated. The difference between the countries is not much greater than that between Ireland (1.2 per 100,000) and Scotland (2.7 per 100,000) in the mid-1990s.[37] We should not underestimate these differences, but it is probable that they reflect a difference of degrees rather than any fundamental difference of practice or outlook when it came to violent activity. The Irish rate also compares favourably to other European jurisdictions in the first half of the nineteenth century – it is certainly lower than the rate of 4.1 per 100,000 estimated for Germany and Switzerland between 1825 and 1850 or that of 15 per 100,000 estimated for Italy over the same period. Indeed, the rate of 2.83 per 100,000 is only slightly above the estimated European average of 2.6 per 100,000 for the whole of the nineteenth century.[38]

The Irish rate from the 1830s is also by no means wholly out of line with rates in modern-day Europe, being comparable to rates in countries

of such offences have been made to the Irish government; specifying the general nature of the offences, and the counties or places in which they have occurred, H.C. 1833 (80), xxix, 411; summary of outrages for Ulster, Leinster, Munster and Connacht, official papers, 1833/153, 154, 154a and b; summary of outrages for Ulster, Leinster, Munster and Connacht, official papers, 1834/385, 386, 387, 388, 389, 525, 526, 527, 528; summary of outrages for Ulster, Leinster, Munster and Connacht, official papers, 1835/351, 352, 353, 354, 355; summary of outrages for Ulster, Leinster, Munster and Connacht, January to June, official papers, 1836/116, 117, 118, 119; A return of all crimes and outrages reported by the stipendiary magistrates and officers of police in Ireland, to the inspector general of police, or to the Irish government, as having been perpetrated in their respective districts from the 1st of January 1836 to the 12th December 1837; distinguishing such crimes and outrages as were contained in the usual monthly reports, and such as were specially reported, H.C. 1837–38 (157), xlvi, 427; A return of outrages reported to the constabulary office, Dublin, as having occurred during the five months commencing September 1836, H.C. 1837 (212), xlvi, 293; A return of outrages reported to the constabulary office, Dublin, as having occurred during the months of January and February last, H.C. 1837–38 (214), xlvi, 457; Return of outrages reported to the constabulary office for the years 1837–40 in NAI, Irish crime records.

[36] It should be noted that the rate from the 1830s does not include homicides from the Dublin metropolitan area. It is unlikely, however, that the addition of cases from Dublin would significantly increase the rate given that homicides in the city accounted for less than three per cent of all reported homicide cases in the country in the 1840s and probably did not account for much more than this in the 1830s.

[37] This is based on a comparison of rates in the two countries in 1995. See *Homicide Statistics*, p. 29.

[38] Eisner, 'Long-Term Trends in Violent Crime' p. 99. See also Eisner, 'Modernization', p. 629.

in Eastern Europe such as Poland and Hungary and countries on the outer edge of Europe such as Finland, Scotland and Spain. The rate in the 1830s is also much lower than the national rates found in jurisdictions outside of Europe such as the United States, Russia or South Africa in the present day.[39]

The figures from the 1830s were, however, not wholly reliable and underestimate the homicide rate as the police were not always diligent in reporting cases at that time.[40] This would push the rate even higher, yet the rates in other jurisdictions in the nineteenth century were also likely influenced by a lack of diligence in reporting and recording cases. This was, as we have seen, certainly the case in late nineteenth-century England. Moreover, if improvements in medical care are taken into consideration this would offset any downward bias in the rates when compared to those of the modern day. On the whole, the homicide rate in 1830s Ireland was not radically different from rates found in other jurisdictions at the time and in some areas of present-day Europe. It might be argued, of course, that in comparing rates from such disparate and different societies we are not quite comparing like with like. This, however, is what makes the study of patterns of violence across societies significant – it allows us to explore to what extent different societies might or might not produce similar patterns of violence.

Regional variations

There are dangers in relying too heavily on national figures in reaching conclusions about the extent of homicide in the country as a whole in the first half of the nineteenth century. We must be careful, for instance, not to place too much emphasis on the national average. It is necessary to examine to what degree there were regional variations in these rates. As Zehr has pointed out, 'national averages [...] only have meaning if regional rates tend to be grouped around the national mean; if local rates are highly dispersed, national averages are at best mathematical abstractions.'[41]

Were there regional variations in these rates? Table 1.1 provides a county-by-county breakdown of rates of homicide (excluding infanticide) in Ireland in the period 1841–50. Twenty-six of the thirty-two counties were within 1 per 100,000 of the national average, which suggests that regional

---

[39] *Homicide Statistics*, p. 37.
[40] See Appendix one.
[41] Howard Zehr, *Crime and the Development of Modern Society: Patterns of Criminality in Nineteenth-Century Germany and France* (Totowa, NJ: Rowman and Littlefield, 1976), p. 14.

variations were not all that great. There was some variation, however. Counties in Connacht, western areas of Leinster and Munster were generally above the national average, while the majority of counties in Leinster and all the counties in Ulster were below it.[42] Western areas of Leinster and north Munster tended to produce the highest rates of reported homicide in this period. The most obvious deviation from the national average is the rate recorded for Co. Tipperary, which had a rate of 6.1 per 100,000, at least double that of every other county (except Limerick) and over eight times the lowest rate in the country, Donegal's 0.72 per 100,000.[43] The neighbouring counties of Limerick and Clare also exhibited higher than average rates of reported homicide.

Table 1.1   Rates of homicide per 100,000 in Irish counties, 1841–50[44]

County	Rate per 100,000	County	Rate per 100,000	County	Rate per 100,000
Tipperary	6.1	Sligo	2.03	Monaghan	1.38
Limerick	3.6	Longford	1.7	Londonderry	1.25
King's	3.05	Carlow	1.66	Wicklow	1.23
Clare	2.84	Armagh	1.63	Tyrone	1.1
Mayo	2.78	Down	1.57	Westmeath	1.1
Kilkenny	2.75	Louth	1.53	Fermanagh	1
Roscommon	2.62	Antrim	1.47	Meath	0.97
Galway	2.42	Cavan	1.46	Wexford	0.88
Cork	2.2	Dublin	1.42	Kildare	0.75
Waterford	2.15	Queen's	1.41	Donegal	0.72
Leitrim	2.07	Kerry	1.41		

[42] The majority of counties were below the national average. Of the thirty-two counties, twenty were below the national average and only twelve were above.

[43] Such disparities were also not unusual in England and Wales. King, for instance, has found that the highest murder rate for an individual county in England in the mid-nineteenth century was 'more than eight times the lowest figure'. See King, 'The Impact of Urbanization', p. 685.

[44] NAI, official papers, 1842/83; NAI, chief secretary's office, monthly returns of outrages, specially reported to the constabulary office, 1841–49; NAI, *Irish crime records*.

The lowest rates in the country were recorded in mid and west Ulster and in the eastern areas of Leinster. Donegal, as already noted, had the lowest rate in the country, while neighbouring Fermanagh, Tyrone and Londonderry all feature among the counties with the ten lowest rates. The eastern seaboard also figures quite prominently among the counties with the lowest rates with Meath, Wicklow and Wexford being represented along with the inland counties of Westmeath and Kildare.[45]

The extent of regional differences should not, however, be exaggerated. Tipperary was exceptional in its high rate of homicide. For a county that contained just over five per cent of the population of the country as a whole, it accounted for close to sixteen per cent of all reported homicides in the period 1841–50. Its rate was also high compared to rates found in other jurisdictions in nineteenth-century and present-day Europe. If anything, its rate is comparable to rates found in the late twentieth century United States of America.[46] Other counties in the south and west of the country were, however, far closer to the northern counties than to Tipperary in terms of the actual rates of homicide and are by no means wholly out of line with rates found in modern-day Europe.

The regional variations in the rates were more pronounced in the 1830s than in the 1840s. While twenty-six of the thirty-two counties in our sample were within 1 per 100,000 of the national average between 1841 and 1850, only fourteen counties were this close to the national average between 1831 and 1840. Tipperary was, as in the sample from the 1840s, the most obvious deviation from the national average, with a rate of 8.38 per 100,000 – again over ten times that of the county with the lowest rates, Donegal, with a rate of 0.8 per 100,000. A further five counties had rates which were more than 1 per 100,000 over the national average. All but one of these shared a border with Tipperary and accounted for just over forty per cent of all homicides in the country at this time while accounting for around twenty per cent of the population.

45 These rates are similar, and in some cases compare favourably, to those identified by Cockburn for Kent in the 1840s. See Cockburn, 'Patterns of Violence in English Society', p. 78.
46 The rate in Tipperary in the 1840s actually compares favourably to many of the states in the modern-day United States of America – it is lower than rates recorded for twenty-three states in 1997. See *Homicide Statistics*, p. 36.

Table 1.2   Rates of homicide per 100,000 in Irish counties, 1831–40[47]

County	Rate per 100,000	County	Rate per 100,000	County	Rate per 100,000
Tipperary	8.38	Carlow	3.21	Meath	1.76
Queen's	6.01	Sligo	3.01	Kildare	1.7
Kilkenny	5.62	Antrim	2.64	Wexford	1.7
Limerick	4.77	Mayo	2.61	Wicklow	1.7
Clare	4.22	King's	2.46	Armagh	1.3
Roscommon	3.87	Kerry	2.41	Londonderry	1.16
Galway	3.55	Cork	2.39	Fermanagh	1.14
Waterford	3.53	Cavan	2.31	Down	0.99
Westmeath	3.43	Monaghan	2.26	Tyrone	0.87
Longford	3.36	Leitrim	2.19	Donegal	0.8
		Louth	1.81		

There is also a level of consistency with the figures from the 1840s, with certain counties, particularly in north Munster and west Leinster, having relatively high rates while counties along the eastern seaboard and in the north of the country generally had lower rates. The majority of counties were actually below the national average. Indeed, eleven of the thirty-one counties were more than 1 per 100,000 below the national average. The national average for the 1830s is then less representative of rates in the country as a whole than those from the 1840s, reflecting as it does particular periods of unrest in certain areas of the country.[48]

Homicide over time

What then of longer-term rates of homicide in Ireland over the first half of the nineteenth century? A longer-term view of homicide trends in pre-Famine and Famine Ireland is only available through the court records. Table 1.3 shows the homicide rate for the three counties for which there are adequate surviving court records for the period 1801–50.

[47] See the sources cited in n. 35 above. This table does not include rates from Dublin as there are no figures available for the Dublin metropolitan area at this time.
[48] These periods of unrest will be discussed in more detail in chapter four.

Table 1.3 Homicide prosecutions per 100,000 in three Ulster counties, 1801–50[49]

Decades	Co. Armagh	Co. Fermanagh	Co. Tyrone
1801–10	2.24	2	1.89
1811–20	2.0	1.09	1.22
1821–30	1.80	1.47	2
1831–40	1.71	1.34	1.5
1841–50	2.11	0.80	1.8

The most reliable and consistent court record available for the entire first half of the nineteenth century is the grand jury book of Co. Fermanagh. It is clear from Table 1.3 that there was no marked increase in Fermanagh for the period 1801–50. Indeed, if anything, there was an overall decrease in the rates. It could be, of course, that there was simply a failure in bringing cases before the courts. The authorities, however, seem to have been quite successful in getting cases to court. The ratio of detected homicides to prosecuted homicides was, for instance, quite low in the 1830s and 1840s.[50]

There is also little evidence that these rates mask a substantial or significant 'dark figure'. The presiding judge at the 1832 Fermanagh summer assizes addressed this issue directly. He admitted that the calendar of prisoners at the assizes was 'often a fallacious criterion of the peace of a county; for it frequently happened in other parts that the apparent absence of crime was occasioned by the presence of intimidation'. In Fermanagh, however, he was 'happy to say [this] was not the case'. The state of the county, in fact, 'presented a picture which it was delightful to rest the eye upon. When other parts exhibited disorder and outrage, it was [...] delightful to find a place where justice could be impartially administered without dread, where the person was safe and property secure'.[51]

Fermanagh was also repeatedly praised throughout this period for its peaceful and stable state by the judges who presided at the assizes in the county. Addressing the grand jury at the summer assizes of 1844, the judge congratulated them and 'the county at large, on the continued tranquillity which had characterised the county for nearly half a century that he [had]

---

[49] The pre-1821 population figures utilised in this study were derived from Stuart Daultrey, David Dickson, and Cormac Ó Gráda, 'Hearth Tax, Household Size and Irish Population Change 1672–1821', *Proceedings of the Royal Irish Academy*, series c., 82/6 (1982), pp. 125–82. The population figures for 1821 and beyond were calculated using the same sources as in n. 3 above.

[50] See Mc Mahon, *Violence, the Courts and Legal Cultures*, chapter one.

[51] *Enniskillen Chronicle and Erne Packet*, 19 Jul. 1832.

known it, in travelling the circuit both as counsel and judge'.[52] Even in the 1820s, when the rates were relatively high, a judge expressing concern at recent developments in the county also declared that if he required 'a place to fix his residence he knew of none so likely to be the object of choice as the celebrated county of Fermanagh'.[53]

The admittedly less reliable figures for Armagh provide a somewhat different picture to that of Fermanagh.[54] There was certainly an increase in the homicide rates in the 1840s, which probably reflects greater unrest in the county at that time.[55] Yet it is also clear that there was no overwhelming or consistent rise in the rates over this period. The county also won praise from the judiciary for its peaceful state at the assizes. For instance, in 1824 Judge Torrens remarked at the Armagh summer assizes that 'in a county of such immense population, great trade, flourishing commercial intercourse, the state of the calendar [which included only one homicide] denoted a degree of civilization not exceeded by any county in the Empire.'[56] The figures from Tyrone are probably the least reliable,[57] yet they also suggest that there was no dramatic rise in the rates of lethal violence. The figures from all three counties, despite their flaws, seem to indicate, therefore, that rates of lethal violence did not rise markedly in the first half of the nineteenth century. The relatively low incidence of homicide also seems to reflect a low level of social unrest generally in the three counties.

Table 1.4   Responses from Co. Armagh, Co. Fermanagh and Co. Tyrone to inquiries by the 1835 Poor Law Commission[58]

County	Perfectly tranquil	Peaceable	Not disturbed	Occasionally disturbed	Very much disturbed	Total
Armagh	3	50	2	3	0	58
Fermanagh	2	19	3	3	1	28
Tyrone	7	36	1	10	0	54

52 Ibid., 18 Jul. 1844.
53 Ibid., 19 Aug. 1824.
54 See Appendix one.
55 Armagh was somewhat more disturbed in the 1840s and particularly so during the Famine years. See Select committee on outrages, *Minutes of evidence* 1852.
56 *Northern Whig*, 12 Aug. 1824.
57 See Appendix one.
58 *Poor inquiry (Ireland): appendix (E) containing baronial examinations relative to food, cottages and cabins, clothing and furniture, pawnbroking and savings' banks, drinking and supplement containing answers to questions 13 to 22 circulated by the commissioners*, H.C. 1836, xxxii, [37], 1 (hereafter cited as Poor Law Commission, *appendix e*).

Table 1.4 outlines the responses of 140 men (mainly clergy and justices of the peace) to the parliamentary commission survey in 1835 on the incidence of disturbances in their parishes since 1815. These responses do little to suggest a society in the midst of violent conflict.

It may even be that this was a time of decline in the rates of lethal violence in these northern counties. There is some evidence to support this if we combine the nineteenth-century figures with those compiled by Garnham for the eighteenth century (see Figure 1.3). These figures are not wholly reliable,[59] yet it is difficult to see how the flaws in the statistics could account for such an obvious downward trend in the overall rates of homicide.

The fact that the same broad trend is evident in all three counties would also suggest that the decline in the rates was somewhat more than a mere statistical mirage. These figures probably serve to exaggerate the extent of the downward trend, but they certainly call into question any notion that rates of violence were increasing in Ulster at this time. We are, however, dealing with evidence from Ulster, which, as we have seen, was probably the area of the country least prone to homicide in the first half of the nineteenth century.

The evidence from the court records of Kilkenny and Queen's Co. suggest that rates of homicide in southern areas of the country were markedly higher than in their northern counterparts. Rates of prosecuted homicide in both counties were certainly higher in the 1830s.

Table 1.5   Rates of homicide prosecutions per 100,000 in Co. Kilkenny and Queen's Co., 1821–50

Years	Co. Kilkenny	Queen's Co.
1821–30	—	4
1831–40	4.44	5.54
1841–50	1.86	1.7

This is further emphasised by the responses of ninety-one men (again mainly clergy and justices of the peace) to a parliamentary commission survey in 1835 on the incidence of disturbances in their parishes since 1815.

Both counties experienced considerable social unrest in this period and many respondents cited the early 1830s as a period of particular disturbance.

---

[59] It is likely that the rates from the eighteenth century exaggerate the extent of homicide cases before the courts in Ireland at that time. For a discussion of the reasons for this, see Appendix one.

Figure 1.3 Homicide prosecutions in Ulster, 1732–1850

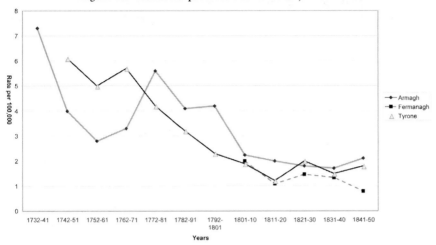

Table 1.6   Responses from Co. Kilkenny and Queen's Co. to inquiries by the 1835 Poor Law Commission[60]

County	Perfectly tranquil	Peaceable	Not disturbed	Occasionally disturbed	Very much disturbed	Total
Kilkenny	0	12	0	31	2	45
Queen's Co.	1	4	0	22	19	46

Kilkenny experienced considerable unrest in the early 1830s and was subject to the Coercion Act in 1833.[61] Areas of the county had also experienced occasional outbursts of rural unrest and a spate of (generally land-related) homicides in earlier decades, most notably, perhaps, in the early 1820s.[62] Queen's Co. also suffered from high levels of rural unrest in the early 1830s. As Stephen Randolph Gibbons points out, while Queen's Co. 'had often previously had its share of such agrarian crime [...] it is clear that 1831–32 saw the phenomenon reach a new, local peak', so much so that by 1833 Queen's Co. had 'become the most disturbed county in Ireland'.[63] It

60 Poor Law Commission, *appendix e*.

61 *An act for the more effectual suppression of local disturbances and dangerous associations in Ireland* (3 & 4 Will. 4, c. 4). See Virginia Crossman, *Politics, Law and Order in Nineteenth-Century Ireland* (Dublin: Gill & Macmillan, 1996), pp. 58–66.

62 See, for instance, Pádraig Ó Macháin, *Six Years in Galmoy: Rural Unrest in County Kilkenny, 1819–1824* (Dublin: Poodle Press, 2004).

63 S.R. Gibbons, 'Captain Rock in the Queen's Co.' in William Nolan and Pádraig Lane

should be noted, however, that the extent of the unrest in the early 1830s was unprecedented and was not representative of earlier experiences. At the 1834 spring assizes, Judge Torrens could reflect on the fact that he 'was acquainted with the Queen's County long before he entered it in his judicial capacity; and if there was a place in which peace and prosperity had fixed their abode, their favoured Queen's Co. was the spot'. He went on to express regret at the unrest 'this formerly peaceable county' had experienced in the preceding few years.[64]

Much of the testimony given before the Poor Law Commission of 1835 also suggests that the responses gleaned from the northern counties of Armagh and Fermanagh were more typical of conditions in the country as a whole than those from Queen's Co. and Kilkenny. Sixty per cent of the parishes visited indicated that there had been no unrest in their area since 1815, while a further thirty-eight per cent reported only occasional or periodic disturbances. Only two per cent of the parishes in the whole country were regarded as 'disturbed' during this period.[65] This is also consistent with the police statistics on homicide in the 1830s, which indicate that both Queen's Co. and Co. Kilkenny had rates of homicide which were considerably higher than the national average. There is also much evidence to suggest that the trends observable in Ulster were far more representative or indicative of future trends than those found in Tipperary and in some other areas in the 1830s. Ian O'Donnell, for instance, has demonstrated that the generally low homicide rates evident in our sample from Ulster can be found on a national level into the second half of the nineteenth and the twentieth centuries. He points out that after the Famine there was 'a persistent, if somewhat erratic, decline [in homicide rates] over the next one hundred years'.[66] Indeed, his data from the nineteenth century points to low rates of homicide from the 1840s onwards, which show limited variation and are consistently below the European average of 2.6 per 100,000 detected by Eisner.[67]

In sum, at certain times and in certain areas in pre-Famine and Famine Ireland there were high rates of lethal violence relative to those found in

(eds), *Laois: History and Society: Interdisciplinary Essays on the History of an Irish County* (Dublin: Geography Publications, 1999), p. 487 and p. 503.

[64]   *Leinster Express*, 15 Mar. 1834.

[65]   Ó Gráda, *New Economic History*, p. 332.

[66]   O'Donnell, 'Unlawful Killing', p. 63 and Figure 2, p. 64. See also William Wilbanks, 'Homicide in Ireland', *International Journal of Comparative and Applied Criminal Justice*, 20.1 (1996), pp. 59–75. For a discussion of the implications and meaning of the decline in homicide rates in Ireland and the post-Famine statistics, see O' Donnell 'Lethal Violence' as well as chapter two and the conclusion below.

[67]   O' Donnell 'Lethal Violence', p. 677.

the present day in Ireland and much of Europe – comparable, at their very worst, to those found in some areas of the United States of America in the 1990s. The extent of such activity should not be lightly dismissed or ignored. It is also clear, however, that such activity was not wholly representative of experiences of lethal violence in Irish society over the course of the first half of the nineteenth century. Rather, what is striking about the above study of homicide is the degree to which the rates were not much greater than those found in nineteenth-century England and, in the present day, in Ireland, north and south, and in Europe generally. There is, indeed, little statistical evidence, in the context of a study of homicide at least, to support the view that Ireland was a 'remarkably' violent society at this time.[68]

A quantitative analysis can, however, only take us so far. It is also necessary to look beyond the figures and to explore the wider part played by homicide in Irish society at this time. In doing so, I will argue that while violence was prominent and significant at certain times and in certain contexts, this was a society in which the use of violence was contained and controlled and in which violence was not central to the regulation of social, cultural or economic life.

[68] The statistical analysis of non-lethal violence is far more problematic. Research on non-lethal offences does reveal that the rates of such violence could be lower in the pre-Famine period, but they have not been included here due to reservations about the reliability and comparability of the data.

2

'Do you want to pick
a fight out of me?':
Homicide and personal relations

Studies of violence in Ireland in the first half of the nineteenth century have generally focused on conflicts arising from the rural economy and, to a lesser extent, from religious divisions and popular, or more particularly, Catholic alienation from the existing political and legal order. Indeed, it has been often assumed that these were the primary causes of violent activity in Ireland at that time.[1] There can be little doubt that such studies have added immeasurably to our understanding of Irish society in the nineteenth century. The problem with this emphasis, however, is that more personal and less directly economic, political and religious disputes have not received the attention they merit. This chapter redresses this imbalance by exploring the part played by lethal violence in what I term personal disputes. Any wider understanding of patterns of violent activity in Ireland at this time depends on a study of such cases. This is not least because, as Carolyn Conley has noted for the late nineteenth century, 'the bulk of Irish violence was personal'[2] and 'agrarian, political and sectarian violence constituted only a small part of Ireland's criminal violence'.[3] This assertion holds true for the pre-Famine and Famine period too.

---

[1] Oliver MacDonagh has, for instance, claimed that 'land and religion were for long the primary sources of violence in Ireland.' Oliver MacDonagh, *States of Mind: A Study of Anglo-Irish Conflict 1780–1980* (London: Harper Collins, 1983), p. 71.

[2] Carolyn A. Conley, *Melancholy Accidents: The Meaning of Violence in Post-Famine Ireland* (Lanham, MA: Lexington Books, 1999), p. 215.

[3] Conley, *Melancholy Accidents*, pp. 216–17. Sean Connolly, in his study of long-term homicide trends in Ireland, also points out that 'agrarian' violence 'accounted for only a small part of total Irish deaths by violence'. See Connolly, 'Unnatural Death in Four Nations', p. 207.

Table 2.1 The incidence of homicides arising from personal disputes in
pre-Famine and Famine Ireland[4]

	Ireland 1843–5	Ireland 1847–9	Armagh 1835–50	Fermanagh 1811–50	Kilkenny 1835–50	Queen's Co. 1835–50
Homicides arising from personal disputes	112	53	23	21	25	19
Percentage of all homicide cases	26.85	20.30	25.27	28	21.92	24.35
Rate per 100,000	0.44	0.62	0.63	0.36	0.88	0.8

This is evident from reports of homicide cases in national samples for
Ireland from 1843 to 1845 and between 1847 and 1849, as well as a more
long-term study of four counties – Co. Armagh and Co. Fermanagh in
the north, and Queen's Co. and Co. Kilkenny in the south of the country.
Personal disputes were the single largest cause of homicide in all the above
samples.[5] Despite the fact that violence arising from personal disputes
constituted such a significant element of violent activity in the nineteenth
century, it has received relatively little attention. There are two main
exceptions to this. Desmond McCabe has examined the role of violence
in personal relationships in pre-Famine Mayo, while Carolyn Conley, in
her study of late nineteenth-century Ireland, has also focused on the more
personal origins of violence.

For McCabe, the use of violence was linked to a sense of personal
and familial honour, the attainment and achievement of which was central
to the maintenance of personal and familial security and status within
communities.[6] Much of the violence, he argues, was informed by a need or
desire to protect or even promote both individual and family honour which
was, in turn, rooted in the economic and political realities of the communities
in which people lived.[7] McCabe's position also chimes with debates about
the role of male honour and 'constructions of masculinity' which play a
prominent part in the wider historiography of violence. Shoemaker, in his
study of homicide in eighteenth-century London claims, for instance, that

---

[4] For sources and methods, see Appendix two.
[5] See Appendix two.
[6] See, for instance, McCabe, 'Law, Conflict and Social Order', p. 65. McCabe points
out that 'the moral value which is bound up with the continual striving for household
security, which obtains in [peasant] societies, is that of honour, that of the individual
and kingroup.'
[7] Ibid., pp. 151–2. For McCabe 'the dictates of honour guided behaviour less stringently
than among Mediterranean societies, but to a marked degree nonetheless.'

the 'most common theme' in accounts of homicide in this period was that they were 'prompted by perceived threats to male honour'. Men, he argues, 'could not allow themselves to be verbally insulted or physically jostled without responding'.[8] Such studies have also linked the apparent decline in rates of homicide observable in many European countries to a decline in the use of violence by men as a means of upholding personal honour and the rise of individualism.[9] These developments have also been linked, more broadly, to a wider civilising process and viewed, by some, as a manifestation of the benefits of modernity underpinned by greater state intervention and increasing levels of individual self-control.[10]

A different view of violence in nineteenth-century Ireland is provided by Carolyn Conley, who argues that most violent activity in Ireland was not bound by an 'honour culture', but was, in fact, recreational in nature. Recreational violence, for Conley, was deeply rooted in Irish culture (although not unique to it) and followed patterns of behaviour which 'had continued as fundamental parts of Irish life over the centuries'.[11] She stresses that most cases arose from petty disagreements at social gatherings where drink had been taken and in which no serious grounds for malice existed. For Conley, such patterns of violent activity closely resembled those evident in pre-industrial societies. Such violence was 'expressive' rather than 'instrumental', 'rational' or 'goal-orientated'. The reasons for this in an Irish context, according to Conley, were twofold. First, she argues that people in Ireland, as in other agrarian societies, 'were forced to find their own forms of entertainment and amusement and fighting often was their chosen activity'. Second, she contends that 'status connected with physical strength was often the only sort of status attainable by the people of rural Ireland'.[12] Conley also explicitly rejects the characterisation of Ireland at this time as an honour culture. She argues that while late nineteenth-century Ireland 'meets some of the criteria [of an honour culture], there are also significant differences'. Noting that 'one of the identifying characteristics of most honor cultures is a high level of interpersonal violence and a very high homicide rate', she points out that Ireland at this time 'had neither'.[13]

Did interpersonal violence arising from personal disputes simply reflect

8   Shoemaker, 'Male Honour and the Decline of Public Violence', p. 193.
9   See Eisner, 'Modernization', pp. 632–3 and Eibach, 'The Containment of Violence in Central European Cities, 1500–1800'. See also Gerd Schwerhoff, 'Social Control of Violence, Violence as Social Control'.
10   See, for instance, Spierenburg, *A History of Murder* and Pinker, *The Better Angels*.
11   Conley, *Melancholy Accidents*, p. 18.
12   Ibid., p. 217.
13   Ibid., p. 2.

a desire for 'recreation' on the part of the protagonists? Was violence used to express or uphold a sense of male honour and, more broadly, can changes in patterns of such violence be understood in the context of a wider civilising process or fundamental changes in perceptions of male honour? While engaging with these questions as well as prominent theories of cultural change in the international historiography, a different approach to understanding interpersonal violence is adopted here. This approach warns against the dangers of understanding interpersonal violence in this period as simply a product of a distinctive culture of recreational violence or of an honour culture peculiar to traditional societies. It also questions whether we can understand the nature and extent of such violence in the nineteenth century as fundamentally different to that of the present day and queries the applicability of broad theories of cultural change to the Irish case. Instead, parallels are drawn with patterns of violence in other countries and also with those in late twentieth-century Ireland in order to show how such violence might be more appropriately understood as part of a wider cross-cultural pattern of violent activity among men and, in particular, young men.

I

The first factor that needs to be acknowledged in our discussion of these cases is that they were overwhelmingly male affairs.

Table 2.2   Sex of the protagonists in homicides arising from personal disputes in four Irish counties

Sex	Armagh 1835–50	Fermanagh 1811–50	Kilkenny 1835–50	Queen's Co. 1835–50
Exclusively male	21	14	24	14
Male and female	2	6	1	4
Exclusively female	0	1	0	1

In all four counties in the sample at least two-thirds of homicides arising from personal disputes were all-male affairs. This pattern is also largely confirmed by the national samples. Of the 112 homicides arising from personal disputes reported between 1843 and 1845, the victim was male in 105, or 93.75 per cent of cases. In our sample from the Famine years forty-nine of the fifty-three victims were male – accounting for 92.45 per cent of victims in these cases.[14]

[14]   It is more difficult to identify the perpetrators in the national sample, but the overall

While those accused could be drawn from all age groups, more often than not the protagonists were males in their late teens or twenties. In all four counties the vast majority of the men accused of homicide were aged between sixteen and forty; the majority being drawn from the sixteen to thirty age group.[15] Many of the protagonists in personal disputes were also drawn from this age group. In May 1838, John Grant, a sixteen-year-old cooper, stabbed John Dunne, also a cooper, in the side with a cooper's knife during a fight in Kilkenny.[16] In Queen's Co. in 1834, John Dunphy, described as 'a very fine young man, apparently 20 years of age; well-formed, and being about 14 stones weight' was convicted of the murder of William Lalor.[17]

Those involved were drawn from all sections of society. Many were from its lower ranks. At the Queen's Co. spring assizes of 1835, John Bergin, who was indicted for the murder of John McGrath in February of that year, was a labourer who had been employed to kill pigs on the day before the murder.[18] In Armagh in 1849, Patrick Ward, described as a poor farmer,

---

impression is that they were generally men.

[15] In Armagh, fifty-nine per cent of those suspected of homicide between 1841 and 1850 were aged between sixteen and thirty; in Fermanagh, sixty-nine per cent were drawn from this age group; in Kilkenny the figure was somewhat lower at fifty-nine per cent, while in Queen's Co. the figure was sixty-nine per cent. These figures are derived from the following sources: *Twentieth report of the inspectors general on the general state of the prisons of Ireland, 1841, appendix no. 2*, H.C. 1842 (377), xxii, 117; *Twenty-first report of the inspectors general on the general state of the prisons of Ireland, 1842, appendix no. 2*, H.C. 1843 (462), xxvii, 83; *Twenty-second report of the inspectors general on the general state of the prisons of Ireland, 1843, appendix no. 2*, H.C. 1844 (535), xxviii, 329; *Twenty-third report of the inspectors general on the general state of the prisons of Ireland, 1843, appendix no. 2*, H.C. 1845 (620), xxv, 231; *Tables showing the number of criminal offenders committed for trial or bailed for appearance at the assize and sessions in each county in the Year 1845, and the result of the proceedings*, H.C. 1846 (696), xxxv, 81; *Tables showing the number of criminal offenders committed for trial or bailed for appearance at the assize and sessions in each county in the year 1846, and the result of the proceedings*, H.C. 1847 (822) xlvii, 189; *Tables showing the number of criminal offenders committed for trial or bailed for appearance at the assize and sessions in each county in the year 1847, and the result of the proceedings*, H.C. 1847–48 (953), lii, 361; *Tables showing the number of criminal offenders committed for trial or bailed for appearance at the assize and sessions in each county in the year 1848, and the result of the proceedings*, H.C. 1849 (1067), xliv, 129; *Tables showing the number of criminal offenders committed for trial or bailed for appearance at the assize and sessions in each county in the year 1849, and the result of the proceedings.* H.C. 1850 (1271), xlv, 529; *Tables showing the number of criminal offenders committed for trial or bailed for appearance at the assize and sessions in each county in the year 1850, and the result of the proceedings.* H.C. 1851 (1386), xlvi, 97.

[16] NAI, Convict Reference Files/1838/Grant/107 (hereafter cited as CRF).

[17] *Leinster Express*, 29 Mar. 1834.

[18] Ibid., 28 Mar. 1835.

was killed by his neighbour, Neal Farnham.[19] Others, however, were middle ranking farmers. Thomas Shortal, a 'farmer in comfortable circumstances' was accused of the killing of Robert Becton in a pub in the city of Kilkenny in January 1838.[20] In Armagh, John Pillow, a 'very respectable farmer', died as a consequence of a violent confrontation with Robert Hooey in September 1847.[21]

The gentry could be involved in such disputes. There were, for instance, two cases in Co. Fermanagh in which members of the gentry stood accused of a homicide arising from a personal dispute. In January 1836, Mr Arthur Irvine and Mr Arthur Forster were accused of the murder of Robert Farnan in Brookeborough, following a drunken altercation with the man in his cabin.[22] In May 1817, William Griffith, a magistrate, was implicated in the murder of James Duffy, who was beaten outside a pub after an argument arising from a cockfight.[23] Such involvement should not be exaggerated, however. In the other three counties in our sample, there were no cases arising from personal disputes where the gentry stood accused of homicide between 1835 and 1850.[24] In both cases in Co. Fermanagh it may also be the fact that they were young males rather than their social status that had a greater influence on their actions. At the trial of Irvine and Forster, Judge Moore regretted that 'youthful indiscretion and folly should have brought gentlemen of their station in life into their present situation'.[25] William Griffith was also described by one witness at his trial as 'young Mr Griffith'.[26] There was only one case arising from a personal dispute in which a member of the landowning classes was a victim. In Kilkenny in 1839, Thomas Willoughby and John Shoar, who were caretakers to the Hon. Mr Wandesforde, were accused of the killing of a Henry O'Reilly esq., the twenty-year-old son of a surgeon and landowner from Co. Kildare. The accused were, however, unaware of the social status of O'Reilly when they shot at him.[27]

19 *Armagh Guardian*, 11 Mar. 1850.
20 NAI, outrage papers, Kilkenny, 1838/1.
21 *Armagh Guardian*, 28 Sept. 1847.
22 *Enniskillen Chronicle and Erne Packet*, 21 Jul. 1836.
23 Ibid., 19 Mar. 1818.
24 The rarity of gentry involvement in such cases is also reflected in a comment made by the *Leinster Express* in its report of the trial of a Mr Feale, whose 'dress and appearance unequivocally bespoke the gentleman', at the Kilkenny spring assizes of 1834. The report noted that 'this case was attended with marked and peculiar features of interest, in consequence of the highly respectable sphere of life the prisoner at the bar moved in.' *Leinster Express*, 22 Mar. 1834.
25 *Enniskillen Chronicle and Erne Packet*, 21 Jul. 1836.
26 Ibid., 19 Mar. 1818. It should also be noted that the evidence against Griffith was not very strong and he seems at most to have been an accomplice to the perpetrator.
27 NAI, outrage papers, Kilkenny, 1838/110.

What was the relationship between the parties involved? Some incidents involved individuals unknown to each other. On Sunday 13 November 1836 in Freshford, Co. Kilkenny, James McGee was killed during a dispute in a pub. The deceased in this case was said to be a 'total stranger' in Freshford.[28] There were also cases where the victims at least claimed that they did not know their attackers. In Queen's Co. in May 1836, William Campion 'was struck with a stone on the left ear in the fair green of Cullihill [...] which knocked him down'; Campion had 'no knowledge of the person who struck him'. He died two days later.[29] Such cases were, however, not all that common.

Where the relationship between the protagonists is known, it is clear that, in most cases, the parties involved were acquaintances (see Table 2.3).

Table 2.3 Relationships between the accused and the deceased in homicides arising from personal disputes in four Irish counties

Offender–victim relationship	*Armagh 1835–50*	*Fermanagh 1811–50*	*Kilkenny 1835–50*	*Queen's Co. 1835–50*
Acquaintances	12	13	13	11
Strangers	0	1	1	2

In a number of cases it is possible to discern the nature of the relationship. In some, the parties involved were neighbours. In Fermanagh in 1828, at the trial of three men for the murder of James Fagan, the accused and the deceased were said to be 'near neighbours'.[30] In the same county in 1836, Simon Cross was indicted for the murder of his neighbour, Bernard Morris.[31] There were also cases where the parties were friends. George Irvine, who was tried at the Fermanagh summer assizes of 1814 for the murder of James Stafford, was described by one witness as an 'intimate acquaintance' of the deceased. Another witness claimed that the 'prisoner and deceased had been friends for a good while before the death of the deceased'.[32] In the case of Thomas Pembroke, who was convicted of manslaughter at the Co. Kilkenny spring assizes of 1837, it was noted that 'the deceased man and himself was the best friends always and always went together.'[33] Some could even be friends after a violent confrontation. At the trial of Patrick

28   NAI, outrage papers, Queen's Co., 1836/236.
29   Ibid., 1836/56.
30   *Enniskillen Chronicle and Erne Packet*, 31 Jul. 1828.
31   Ibid., 23 Mar. 1837.
32   Ibid., 11 Aug. 1814.
33   NAI, CRF/1837/Pembroke/49.

Kennedy for the manslaughter of Charles Kelly at the Queen's Co. spring assizes of 1839, one witness gave evidence that he saw the two men on the night after their fight 'when all appeared to be good friends'. Kelly did not die for another 'fourteen or fifteen days' after the incident.[34] In other cases, those involved came into contact through their work. At the spring assizes of 1812, Thomas Maguire, a blacksmith, was accused of the murder of a man called Loughran, who had been in his employment 'for upwards of six years'.[35]

II

In what circumstances did these cases arise? The disputes tended to occur in public, often in front of a number of witnesses. In three of the four counties in our sample over seventy per cent of disputes occurred in public.[36] In Armagh, twenty of the twenty-three cases occurred in a public area, and of these seven occurred either in, just outside or on the way home from a pub, while other cases occurred on the street or a public road or in a place of work. Of the twenty-one cases in Fermanagh, fifteen occurred in a public area, the pub again being the location in five, while other disputes arose at or after social gatherings such as weddings, fairs and dances. In Kilkenny, twenty of the twenty-five personal disputes occurred in a public area. The pub was, however, less prominent here, providing the location for only three cases. Other social gatherings figure prominently in the sample: three cases occurred at a fair, three on the way home from a funeral and one returning from a race meeting.[37] In Queen's Co., nine of the nineteen cases occurred in public areas (with five of these occurring in or outside a pub, accounting for over one in four of all the disputes).

In many cases, one or more of those involved had been drinking. Of the 112 cases in our national sample, 1843–5, that I have classified as 'personal

---

[34] Ibid., 16 Mar. 1839. Such reconciliations are by no means unique to Ireland. See Pinker, *Better Angels*, p. 516.

[35] *Enniskillen Chronicle and Erne Packet*, 12 Mar. 1812.

[36] It is more difficult to establish the location of these incidents in the national samples. The evidence that is available, however, also suggests that these were largely public affairs. Of the 112 homicides arising from personal disputes reported between 1843 and 1845, it is possible to identify sixty-four which occurred in a public area. One case seems to have arisen on the perpetrator's property, while it has not been possible to identify the location in the remaining forty-seven cases. Of the twenty-seven cases in our Famine sample where the location could be identified, twenty-four took place in a public place while only three occurred in private. In twenty-six cases the location could not be identified.

[37] Other public locations included a street (four cases) or a public road (five cases).

disputes', over a third arose directly from drunken arguments.[38] In Cork in January 1843, William Hennessy died as a consequence of 'being struck on the head with stones, all the parties being at the time intoxicated'.[39] During the Famine years, the proportion of such cases fell somewhat (as might be expected) but even at this time a sizeable number still arose from drunken disputes – accounting for 28.30 per cent of personal disputes and 5.7 per cent of all cases.

The part played by alcohol is also evident in the county-based samples. Of the twenty-three personal disputes recorded in the Armagh sample, nine (or thirty-nine per cent) of cases arose from drunken arguments. In Fermanagh, the influence of drink was even more pronounced. In fourteen of the twenty-one cases (66.6 per cent) at least one of the parties had consumed alcohol, and in most of these cases one of them was drunk. The evidence of alcohol consumption is less obvious in the southern counties, but here too drink certainly had an influence. In October 1847, an engineer named Henry Knight died after being hit on the temple 'with a pint bottle filled with porter [...] during a drinking dispute' in a pub in Kilkenny.[40]

Many of these confrontations were sparked by the utterance of a direct insult and/or acting in an insulting manner. In September 1845, John McAnally was killed in Armagh by Felix Brangin after using 'very insulting language' towards him and, in particular, referring to him as a 'bastard'. Initially, Brangin did not respond, but told McAnally to go about his business. McAnally persisted and 'told Brangin that he might thank his father for being what he was'. This was too much for Brangin and a fight broke out between the two, as a result of which McAnally was killed.[41]

Insults directed at other members of the family could also provoke a violent reaction. In Fermanagh in 1831, Alexander Johnston was killed during a fight after he referred to the brother-in-law of someone he was dining with as a 'beggar man'.[42] Before the killing of Patrick Ward by Neal Farnham in Armagh in August 1849, the latter was, according to the deceased's wife, 'casting up things to my husband, about himself or his people'. This provoked Ward to push Farnham and a fight ensued, during which Ward was stabbed.[43]

---

38 Forty-two or 37.5 per cent of these cases were drunken disputes – just over ten per cent of the total number of cases.
39 NAI, chief secretary's office, constabulary returns, monthly returns of outrages, 1843–45, 3/7/2 (hereafter cited as *Returns of outrages, 1843–45*).
40 NAI, chief secretary's office, constabulary returns, monthly returns of outrages, 1847–49, 3/7/2 (hereafter cited as *Returns of outrages, 1847–49*).
41 *The Banner of Ulster*, 6 Mar. 1846.
42 *Enniskillen Chronicle and Erne Packet*, 15 Mar. 1832.
43 *Armagh Guardian*, 11 Mar. 1850.

Insults directed at the place in which the perpetrator lived could also lead to violence. On 11 August 1838 in Stradbally, Queen's Co., Patrick Salmon was killed following a somewhat obscure exchange outside a pub. The dispute arose when Salmon declared that 'there was not a man from the end of the ash trees to the green that he cared for in fairity.'[44] Two men who were outside the pub took offence at this and one of them 'asked [Salmon] had he anything to say to the ash tree fellows'. Salmon then replied that 'he never had anything to say to any man but in fairity'. This led to a violent confrontation in which Salmon was killed.[45]

At other times, insults relating to occupations provoked violence. At the Queen's Co. summer assizes of 1836, John Deevy of the 71st regiment was indicted for the manslaughter of Edward Hyland on 27 December 1835. In this case, Deevy and a number of fellow soldiers were making their way on the public road when they passed Hyland. The soldiers bid Hyland good night and said they were 'going to serve the king' and asked Hyland if he would join them. Hyland responded by saying that 'he would not go into a ragged regiment'. Deevy took offence at this and there was a further exchange of words between them before a fight broke out in which Hyland received a blow from a stone, which killed him.[46]

There was also a willingness to resort to violence if it was felt that someone had acted inappropriately towards or insulted another, unrelated, member of the community. Loyalty to an employer could, for instance, prompt violent action. At the spring assizes of 1837 in Co. Kilkenny, three men were convicted of the murder of Edward Madden. In this case, the three accused were labourers employed by a man called Brophy. On the day the incident occurred, Brophy was drunk and insulting people on the road as they passed. Madden, a 'Connaughtman', who had been hired as a labourer in the area, took offence at this and challenged Brophy, but was restrained by the three accused. After this initial confrontation, they followed Madden along the road and beat him to death.[47] In some cases, it was not what was said but rather the manner in which it was said that provoked the violent act. In Kilkenny in March 1842, Daniel Ryan, an elderly man, stabbed a young man called Lacey during a fight after the latter had criticised Ryan for his 'aggressive' behaviour in demanding money from an employer.[48]

---

[44] The word 'fairity' seems to be a colloquialism variously employed to mean 'fairness', 'truth' or 'justice'.

[45] *Leinster Express*, 23 Mar. 1839.

[46] *Leinster Express*, 16 Jul. 1836. The sister of the deceased denied that he said a 'ragged regiment' but rather that they should have 'got a good regiment'.

[47] NAI, outrage papers, Kilkenny, 1836/171.

[48] *Kilkenny Moderator*, 19 Mar. 1842.

In other cases, it could simply be a general feeling that someone had acted in an inappropriate or insulting manner towards a third party. These cases often constituted an attempt, however misplaced, to control the behaviour of others and to impose norms of appropriate behaviour. At the Queen's Co. summer assizes of 1838, James Delaney was tried for the murder of Thomas and Denis Delaney. This dispute arose in a pub where the victims 'got up and endeavoured to take the chair from an old man'. This produced a reaction from a number of those present in the pub and a fight broke out. The pub owner was able to quell the fight, but when Thomas and Denis went outside they were attacked again and James Delany was seen to hit Denis Delany with a poker, which caused his death.[49]

Disputes could also arise when someone felt their reputation had been called into question. At the Armagh spring assizes of 1846, Michael Flanagan, a reaper, was indicted for the manslaughter of a fellow reaper, Henry Convere. In this case, Flanagan had accused Convere of telling lies about another man in front of their employer. This provoked an angry reaction from Convere, who 'lifted a stone and said he would dash it into [Flanagan] if he told lies on him'. There was then a confrontation between the two men in which Flanagan cut Convere with a reaping hook which caused his death half an hour later.[50] Similarly, in the case of James Canavan, a labourer, who was killed by fellow labourer Daniel McCabe in Kilkenny in May 1841, the original dispute arose when Canavan accused McCabe of telling lies about him.[51]

At times, although it has to be said not very often, these disputes were rooted in problems within intimate relationships. Extra-marital affairs could, for instance, provoke a violent reaction. In Antrim in June 1844, William McElree was 'found murdered at the back of a ditch, where, it is reported, he was surprised in the act of illicit intercourse with the offender's wife'.[52] Personal rejection and jealousy also led to acts of lethal violence. In Queen's Co. in 1849, schoolmaster Robert Wright was convicted of the manslaughter of Michael Moloney. According to a report in the *Enniskillen Chronicle and Erne Packet*, the incident 'arose out of jealousy. Wright had been rejected by a female to whom he had been paying his addresses, and the deceased was his favoured rival'.[53]

Issues of status and reputation could also arise from marriage arrangements. As has been noted in a somewhat different context, 'marriage

---

49   *Leinster Express*, 21 Jul. 1838.
50   Ibid., 10 Mar. 1846.
51   *Kilkenny Moderator*, 11 Aug. 1841.
52   *Returns of outrages, 1843–45.*
53   *Enniskillen Chronicle and Erne Packet*, 15 Mar. 1849.

was an expression of a family's social status, and the refusal of a woman's family to accept a marriage proposal could be interpreted as a statement of social superiority.'[54] At the Queen's Co. spring assizes of 1835, four men were tried for the murder of John McGrath. One of them, John Bergin, was a rival suitor to McGrath for the hand of Mary Howe, the daughter of a local farmer. Bergin had asked to marry Mary but her father, John Howe, refused permission. Bergin, in response, led a group of men in an attack on Howe's house, in which they beat him and attacked McGrath 'most unmercifully [and] fractured his skull very extensively'. He died on the spot.[55]

Disputes between families over the paternity of children led to violent conflict too. This is evident in the case of Henry Gillespie, who died in Armagh in October 1836 as a consequence of a violent confrontation with Thomas Todd after 'a daughter of Todd's had processed one of the Gillespies for the maintenance of an illegitimate child, which she had by him.' She was unsuccessful in her claim before the court of quarter sessions and the Gillespies gloated over their success on their return home, thereby provoking Todd's violent reaction. He struck Henry Gillespie over the head with a reaping hook.[56]

Violent activity could also emerge from seemingly petty disagreements. The police reports for the whole country between 1843 and 1845 contain a number of such incidents. In January 1843, Rody Monahan died in Tipperary as a 'result of injuries inflicted in consequence of a dispute respecting a Black Bird'.[57] In September 1844, Bartholomew Curren was 'quietly returning from Dungarvan fair' in Waterford when he was struck with a stone for 'having spoken favourably of a man who was disliked by his assailant'.[58] It is also possible to find examples of such cases in the more long-term study of the four counties. In Fermanagh in December 1836, Bernard Morris was fatally injured by his neighbour Simon Cross in a dispute over a pipe.[59] In Armagh in September 1847, John Pillow died as a consequence of a violent confrontation with Robert Hooey after they 'began to argue and scold about [a] *half-penny* in dispute for four years'.[60] In some cases there was no pretext whatever for violence. As Conley has noted,

---

[54] J.D. Rogers, *Crime, Justice and Society in Colonial Sri Lanka* (London: Curzon Press, 1987), p. 140.

[55] *Leinster Express*, 28 Mar. 1835. See also Michael Huggins, *Social Conflict in Pre-Famine Ireland: The Case of County Roscommon* (Dublin: Four Courts Press, 2007), pp. 121–2.

[56] NAI, outrage papers, Armagh, 1836/72. See also *Belfast Newsletter*, 21 Mar. 1837.

[57] *Returns of outrages, 1843–45*. Unfortunately, the report of this incident does not provide any further information on this case.

[58] Ibid.

[59] *Enniskillen Chronicle and Erne Packet*, 23 Mar. 1837.

[60] *Armagh Guardian*, 28 Sept. 1847.

'violence did not always require a grievance.'[61] In Queen's Co., Charles Kelly and Patrick Kennedy were returning from a funeral in February 1838 at about eleven o'clock at night in the company of two women, one of whom was a cousin of Kennedy's. According to her account of the incident, 'Kelly's hat was knocked off by Kennedy without any previous dispute whatever and a boxing match commenced which the females were unable to prevent.' Kelly died as a consequence of his injuries two weeks later.[62]

III

What were the characteristics of these acts of lethal violence? Some cases reveal an extraordinary degree of premeditation. This is evident in the killing of Thomas Murnane in Tipperary in January 1843. The police believed that Murnane was murdered in revenge for the murder of a man called Burke exactly five years beforehand. Murnane was killed at the same hour and within forty yards of the same place where Burke was killed. Burke's three sons were arrested in connection with the case.[63]

In other cases, evidence of premeditation could be implied from the lapse of time between the initial confrontation or disagreement and the actual killing itself. On 8 May 1841, Daniel McCabe and James Canavan, both farm labourers in Co. Kilkenny, had an argument and agreed to fight the next morning. They then slept in a barn with two fellow labourers. Early the next morning, however, McCabe woke early and hit Canavan on the head with a stick. One of the men who was sleeping in the barn with McCabe was woken by this and told McCabe to desist. McCabe, however, ignored him and proceeded to hit Canavan again, administering a fatal blow.[64]

At other times, there was a matter of minutes between the initial confrontation and the actual killing. In such cases, there is evidence of premeditation but the act of violence seems to emerge within the context of the specific situation in which the parties found themselves, rather than stemming from any long-term or well-thought-out plan to kill. At the Armagh summer assizes of 1846, Thomas Neal was tried and convicted for the murder of John Simmington. In this case, there was a fight between the two men in a pub. Those present, however, managed to separate them and Simmington was taken outside. Neal remained inside for a further fifteen

61 Conley, *Melancholy Accidents*, p. 27.
62 NAI, outrage papers, Queen's Co., 1840/24.
63 *Returns of outrages, 1843–45.* Revenge killings in medieval Europe were, on occasion, also carried out on the anniversary of the original homicide, see Spierenburg, *A History of Murder*, p. 36.
64 *Kilkenny Moderator*, 11 Aug. 1841.

minutes while Simmington waited outside for him. When Neal came out they started to fight again and Simmington had the upper hand. During the course of the fight, however, Neal pulled out a knife and was seen to stab Simmington with it, causing injuries from which he later died.[65]

The majority of homicides arising from personal disputes did not even have this minimum level of premeditation, but rather occurred 'in the heat of the moment'. The pattern these cases could follow can be seen in a case at the Armagh summer assizes of 1801 when Hugh Williamson was indicted for the murder of James Patterson on 13 June of that year. In this case, Williamson was 'making mortar on the flag-way of Thomas street Armagh' when Patterson passed by and 'some splashes reached him, upon which [he] remonstrated saying "you are an uncivil man to give offence to any one passing the parade". The accused replied: "if you do not pass smart, you may get more of the splashes you complain of."' There was a further exchange of words between the two and then Patterson 'advanced towards the [accused] with his stick raised, [Williamson] threw some of the mortar at him, for the purpose of keeping him back, [Patterson] then struck the prisoner once or twice with his stick; [the accused] then struck [Patterson] a blow on the right side of the head, which knocked [him] down, and of which he died in about an hour and an half'.[66]

At the Co. Fermanagh spring assizes of 1812, blacksmith Thomas Maguire was accused of the murder of an employee called Loughran who, it seems, entered Maguire's forge 'in a state of intoxication'. The accused took umbrage at this and 'reprimanded [Loughran] for getting drunk and absenting himself from his business'. Loughran then used 'improper language', called Maguire a liar and approached the accused 'as if to strike'. Maguire responded by putting down the bellows he had in his hand and prepared to fight. At this point, Loughran backed down and moved towards the door, but then turned and approached Maguire again 'using bad language' and acting as if he was about to strike his employer. Maguire, who had a nail-rod in his left hand, responded by pushing the nail-rod into Loughran's body. Loughran died two days later.[67]

The unplanned nature of these incidents is also emphasised to some degree by the means employed to carry them out. Most cases of homicide, as Table 2.4 makes clear, involved a beating with fists and/or feet or was carried out with some blunt instrument.

[65] *Armagh Guardian*, 14 Jul. 1846.
[66] *Dublin Evening Post*, 18 Aug. 1801.
[67] Ibid., 12 Mar. 1812.

Table 2.4   Means employed in homicides arising from personal disputes in
pre-Famine and Famine Ireland

Means	Ireland 1843–5	Ireland 1847–9	Armagh 1835–50	Fermanagh 1811–50	Kilkenny 1835–50	Queen's Co. 1835–50
Beating	54	14	10	6	3	4
Blunt instrument	37	23	5	7	18	12
Sharp instrument	11	5	5	4	2	1
Shot	2	1	0	2	2	2
Other	2	1	3	2	0	0

The relatively high proportion of deaths resulting from beatings indicates that acts of lethal violence emerged in the context of the specific situation rather than being carefully planned (assuming that if one were to plan a murder the use of an appropriate weapon would be important in giving an advantage to the attacker in the confrontation). The use of blunt instruments also reflects the often unplanned nature of these cases as people reached for what was to hand when the dispute arose. Among the blunt instruments employed were spades, sticks, tongs, iron bars, shovels and stones. Stones were somewhat more popular weapons in the southern counties than in the north. In Queen's Co. they were used in five of nineteen cases, while in Kilkenny the stone was by far the most commonly used weapon (eleven of twenty-five cases). The use of stones may reflect the difficulty of procuring more sophisticated weapons, thereby forcing people to resort to the use of more *ad hoc* and widely available weapons. It is also likely, however, that the use of stones reflects the unplanned nature of many of these killings – they were close to hand when the parties felt aggrieved.

Even where firearms were employed, there is little evidence of premeditation on the part of the accused. In Kildare in July 1845, Joshua Macklin, 'who was at the time under the influence of liquor', fired into a group of people, killing one man. The police attributed this incident to 'momentary excitement' on the part of the accused.[68] The relative rarity of cases in which sharp instruments (in particular, knives) were used also suggests that the use of lethal weapons to deal with personal quarrels was not considered legitimate and/or that it was not common for men to carry weapons such as knives with them. The overall impression then is that most acts of lethal interpersonal violence arising from personal disputes were unplanned and that lethal intent was largely absent.

[68]   *Returns of outrages, 1843–45.*

IV

What does this reveal about the role of violence in personal relationships in the pre-Famine and Famine period? Is it indicative of an honour culture or does it reflect a propensity to resort to violence as a form of recreation? More broadly, can we understand these cases in the light of changes in ideas of male honour and even a wider civilising process, or do they reflect pronounced continuities in behaviour, particularly among men, over time?

While many of the cases in the sample meet Conley's criteria for 'recreational violence' (unplanned acts arising from petty disagreements at social gatherings where drink had been taken) it does not appear to be a wholly appropriate description of these cases. For Conley, 'recreational violence includes incidents in which a challenge was issued and a fight agreed upon but no serious grounds for malice existed.'[69] It is not entirely clear, however, how we judge whether or not serious grounds for malice existed. It seems a somewhat dubious proposition to say that no serious grounds for malice existed between the parties just because the substantive issue in these cases appears trivial to us.

It is possible that what might appear to be a relatively trivial incident was, for those involved, very serious indeed. It is possible also that these apparently 'trivial' disputes might mask a more 'serious' quarrel between the parties. It may be, for instance, that rather than simply reflecting a desire for recreation, the trivial dispute served as a pretext to vent long-standing animosities. At the trial of Thomas Neal for the murder of John Simmington in Armagh in 1846 it was revealed by one witness that there was 'some animosity [...] between Simmington and Neal for they had fought before'.[70] Indeed, the dispute had its origins in 'an old grudge of four years standing'.[71] This is further emphasised if we take into account the fact that in many cases the parties were acquaintances who knew each other through work or were neighbours or friends. It could also be, as McCabe argues, that 'the background to any conflict probably lay in village economics and politics but this was ostensibly ignored in choosing to react, in drink, to veiled or imagined slights of a trivial kind.'[72] There may, indeed, have been an underlying economic issue at stake in some of these incidents. For example, in the abovementioned case of the murder of Edward Madden it is, perhaps, no coincidence that the deceased was a labourer from Connacht who may have been working in Kilkenny for a lower wage. Resentment towards men

---

69 Conley, *Melancholy Accidents*, p. 17.
70 *Armagh Guardian*, 14 Jul. 1846.
71 NAI, CRF/1846/Neal/5.
72 McCabe, 'Law, Conflict and Social Order', p. 97.

who came to work in the county and undercut the wages of those from the local area may have fuelled the incident, which was ultimately sparked off by an insult uttered by a drunken employer.[73] McCabe's interpretation might then seem more plausible in that it takes seriously the sense of grievance involved in many of these cases and the degree to which it may have been rooted in a sense of honour which was, in turn, a product of prevailing socio-economic conditions.

An acute sense of honour certainly played a part in many of these cases. Petty disagreements, insults directed towards others or aspersions cast on their reputations, their families, occupations and localities, and even unrelated third parties, could all provoke acts of lethal violence. Such disputes arose, moreover, where there was a perceived threat to a man's standing and reputation and/or where there was an opportunity to enhance it.[74] It is likely that in some of these disputes men were provided with, or indeed created, an opportunity not only to defend their reputations but also to assert their manliness. As McCabe has pointed out, 'proof of valour would assure men of a standing of strength in practical terms. Adversaries would know not to underestimate those whose fury could rise so terribly.'[75]

There were also probably cases where those involved took the opportunity that arose from personal disputes or, indeed, created such disputes in order to assert control over another. In such cases, the issue at stake was not so much the cause of but was rather the pretext for violence. This would certainly go some way towards explaining the often petty and trivial nature of the disputes that gave rise to homicide. In this sense, violence and sometimes lethal violence was clearly employed to uphold and sometimes advance position, status and reputation within the wider community.

Yet there are also problems with interpreting this violence simply in the light of a culture of honour. First, these cases were rarely premeditated

---

[73] See above p. 41. It should be noted too that Conley acknowledges that 'economic, social and psychological factors' should also be taken into account when trying to understand interpersonal violence. See Carolyn Conley, 'The Agreeable Recreation of Fighting', *Journal of Social History*, 33.1 (1999), p. 68.

[74] That these incidents involved a defence of manliness is also explicit in a number of cases. For instance, at the spring assizes of 1847 in Queen's Co., Richard Malone, 'a peasant upwards of 70 years of age, was indicted for the willful murder of Patrick Brennan on the 18th day of October 1810.' When arrested, the accused declared 'I never will deny that when I was attacked in an open fair, that *I acted like a man*, the same man brought a party on me' (*Leinster Express*, 20 Mar. 1847 [my italics]). In the case of Neal and Simmington, Neal also responded to Simmington's provocation by declaring 'Do you want to pick a fight out of me, or what do you want? *If you do I'm the man for you, any time*' and 'if you assault me again, in the same manner I'll put my fist through you' (*Armagh Guardian*, 14 Jul. 1846 [my italics]).

[75] McCabe, 'Law, Conflict and Social Order', p. 97.

– while some may have taken the opportunity to vent long-standing grievances and tensions, there is little sense that these were planned or well-thought-out attempts to kill. There were also very few revenge killings of the kind found in some cultures where honour is central to violent activity.[76] Second, the use of violence was not restricted to the protection of personal and familial honour, but rather could be used when it was thought a third party had been insulted and, more generally, to impose wider norms of social interaction. Third, there is Conley's objection that while 'one of the identifying characteristics of most honor cultures is a high level of interpersonal violence and a very high homicide rate', Ireland in the nineteenth century 'had neither'. This also holds true, as we saw in chapter one, for our study of pre-Famine homicide rates.[77] Thus, while lethal violence could be used as a means of upholding status and of imposing norms of behaviour, it is far more problematic to link these cases to a wider culture of honour or to understand them as central to a culture that simply accepted violence as a primary means of recreation.

Why, then, if men were willing to react so violently to such apparently minor slights and ostensibly trivial infringements, was the rate of homicide relatively low? To address this question, two possibilities need to be explored. First, there is a need to examine whether the homicide rates reflect the growing influence of effective controls on the behaviour of individuals and if the cases we have examined are simply the remnants of an older tradition of violence under pressure from the emergence of new ideas surrounding appropriate behaviour among men. Second, and alternatively, we need to explore the extent to which these cases reflect certain continuities in patterns of behaviour among men which transcend the specific contexts of pre-Famine and Famine Ireland and persist to the present day. Both need to be explored in order to reach a viable understanding of personal violence in Ireland.

This period did witness greater attempts at state intervention in and control of aspects of social life in Ireland. The state became active in a variety of different areas including public health, education and welfare. There were also crucial developments in the areas of law and order. Among these changes may be cited the introduction of professional or stipendiary magistrates, a nationwide system of petty session courts and, most crucially

---

[76] See, for instance, Wilson's study of nineteenth-century Corsica, *Feuding, Conflict and Banditry*.

[77] There are, it should be noted, some societies, the mid-eighteenth-century plantation American South, for instance, in which honour played a central role, but which did not necessarily produce high homicide rates. See Roth, *American Homicide*, p. 13. This points to the highly complex relationship between personal honour and violent activity.

perhaps, a centrally-controlled national police force.[78] It may be that these innovations served to inhibit violent activity. A number of historians have, for instance, pointed to the efficacy of the police in suppressing faction fights at fairs in the late 1830s.[79]

Other developments point to an even wider process of social disciplining similar, in some respects, to that found in other European countries.[80] There were a number of developments in Ireland in the first half of the nineteenth century which have been cited as indicating a move towards a more disciplinary society.[81] There was certainly an attempt by the Catholic Church, in the years preceding the Famine, to impose more rigid and orthodox practices on the Catholic population.[82] This found expression in clerical opposition to wakes, gatherings at holy wells as well as faction fighting at fairs and agrarian violence.[83] The Fr. Mathew-inspired temperance movement which sought to and was quite successful in getting sizeable numbers of people to pledge to abstain from alcohol was also part of this wider trend.[84] The high point of the temperance movement, 1839–42, also coincided with low rates of homicide in the country generally. It might be that these factors and forces combined and marshalled by church and state led to an overall decrease in violent activity as violence became an

[78] For an overview of these developments, see, among others, Oliver MacDonagh, *Ireland: The Union and its Aftermath* (London: Allen and Unwin, 1977); MacDonagh, 'Ideas and Institutions, 1830–45' in W.E. Vaughan (ed.), *A New History of Ireland, V: Ireland Under the Union, I. 1801–70* (Oxford: Oxford University Press, 1989), pp. 193–217; Patrick Carroll-Burke, *Colonial Discipline: The Making of the Irish Convict System* (Dublin: Four Courts Press, 2000), chapter two.

[79] See, for instance, Broeker, *Rural Disorder*, pp. 226–7; J.S. Donnelly, Jr, 'Factions in Pre-Famine Ireland', pp. 126–7.

[80] See Eisner, 'Modernization', p. 631.

[81] See Carroll-Burke, *Colonial Discipline*.

[82] There is a considerable body of work on changes in church practice and popular religion in nineteenth-century Ireland. Perhaps the most pertinent of which is Connolly, *Priests and People in Pre-Famine Ireland*. Such efforts were also by no means an exclusively Catholic phenomenon. For a discussion of attempts by evangelical Protestants to reform the manners of ordinary people in this period, see David Hempton and Myrtle Hill, ''Godliness and Good Citizenship': Evangelical Protestantism and Social Control in Ulster, 1790–1850' in *Saothar: Journal of the Irish Labour History Society*, 13 (1988), pp. 68–76.

[83] For an example of the attempts to regulate the activities of ordinary people at fairs, see the controversies surrounding the Donnybrook fair in the first half of the nineteenth century. Fergus D'Arcy, 'The Decline and Fall of Donnybrook Fair: Moral Reform and Social Control in Nineteenth-Century Ireland' in *Saothar: Journal of the Irish Labour History Society*, 13 (1988), pp. 7–21.

[84] On the temperance movement, see Elizabeth Malcolm, *Ireland Sober, Ireland Free: Drink and Temperance in Nineteenth-Century Ireland* (Dublin: Gill and Macmillan, 1986).

increasingly unacceptable means of asserting, maintaining or advancing social status.

It may be, then, that these cases do not represent an honour culture so much as an honour culture in decline – a society in which violence was becoming increasingly marginalised, under pressure from the forces of church and state, as a means of resolving disputes. This would also be consistent with James Kelly's findings on the history of duelling. Kelly notes that the second quarter of the nineteenth century marked a decline in the incidence of duelling in Ireland. In the eighteenth century, many of the duels also arose from 'insult' or 'argument'.[85] Could it be that there was a similar decline in the propensity of the middling and lower orders to resort to violence over apparently trivial slights or minor disagreements? This would certainly fit Kelly's view that it was in fact the middle classes who were driving this social change at the time.[86] It would also be consistent with findings in other parts of the United Kingdom and Europe where the decline in rates of homicide observable in many countries is linked to a change in the use of violence among men as a means of upholding and asserting personal honour.[87]

This view would also complement the alternative but not necessarily contrary interpretation of the pattern of homicide in early modern and modern Europe offered by, among others, Pieter Spierenburg and inspired by the work of Norbert Elias.[88] Spierenburg claims that the apparent decline in homicide rates reflects and is explained by a long-term trend in interpersonal violence whereby there was a move away from public, impulsive violence with an often ritual or 'expressive' function (of the kind we have encountered in Ireland) towards a more 'civilised' form of violence, which is more clearly planned and the function of which is often 'instrumental' in nature. This shift, he argues, was the product of the wider development of greater levels of individual self-control on the part of the mass of the people, who gradually

---

[85] From a sample of 249 cases Kelly identifies ninety-three (or 37.34 per cent) that arose from 'insult' or 'argument'. See James Kelly, 'That Damn'd Thing Called Honour': Duelling in Ireland, 1570–1860 (Cork: Cork University Press, 1995), pp. 83 and 120.

[86] See Kelly, 'That Damn'd Thing Called Honour', chapters six and seven.

[87] See Shoemaker, 'Male Honour and the Decline of Public Violence' and Schwerhoff, 'Social Control of Violence, Violence as Social Control'.

[88] See Spierenburg, 'Long-Term Trends' and Elias, The Civilizing Process. It should be noted that some scholars have been highly critical of any attempt to locate changes in perceptions of male honour within a wider civilising process and are sceptical of using homicide data from before the early modern period. See, for instance, Schwerhoff, 'Social Control of Violence, Violence as Social Control'. Spierenburg argues, however, that the studies of the central place of honour in medieval and early modern Europe can be integrated into a wider framework rooted in Elias's theory.

came to emulate the more civilised manners of their social superiors. This process evolved throughout Europe over several centuries underpinned by the process of state formation and was reinforced by greater state intervention in the early modern and modern era. The Irish experience might also be seen by some to fit Steven Pinker's view that violence decreases when more modern forms of social organisation and cultural expression begin to take hold. This was a time when Ireland was becoming more integrated into a wider market economy, in which ordinary people were becoming increasingly engaged with political ideas and in political activity and in which the population was becoming increasingly literate.[89]

O'Donnell has also acknowledged the utility of the concept of a civilising process in explaining changing patterns of lethal violence in nineteenth- and twentieth-century Ireland and has demonstrated the degree to which Irish homicide rates followed broader European trends – reaching an all-time low in the mid-twentieth century and only increasing within the last few decades to levels which, while higher than earlier in the century, remain among the lowest in the world.[90] O'Donnell also argues that a broad civilising process can be traced through changes in the locations of violence from the countryside to the city, in a decrease in homicides arising from brawls involving young men and in the more punitive attitude of the courts towards those convicted of homicide in the present day.[91]

In this view, the relatively low homicide rate reflects an exponential growth in external and internal controls on the behavioural patterns of the mass of the people and the cases in our sample may simply be viewed as a hangover from earlier and outmoded cultural forms and practices. If correct, this would safely place Ireland within broader trends (albeit as a somewhat late entrant) which have been identified for other parts of the United Kingdom and Europe – whether interpreted in the light of a change in ideas of male honour, the outcome of a civilising process and the adoption of modern forms of social interaction and organisation, as a product of a process of social disciplining instigated by church and state, or as a combination of all of the above.

There are, however, serious problems with this analysis. The reasons for this are two-fold. First, it exaggerates the impact of both church and state intervention as well as broader social and cultural change on patterns of lethal violence. Second, it serves to underestimate the continuities evident in the extent and practice of lethal interpersonal violence over time.

While there was undoubtedly a greater level of state intervention and

---

[89] Pinker, *Better Angels*.
[90] O' Donnell 'Lethal Violence', p. 667.
[91] O'Donnell, 'Killing in Ireland at the Turn of the Centuries'.

control, this did not fundamentally re-shape patterns of lethal violence in pre-Famine Ireland. The apparent decline in homicide rates which dated from the late eighteenth century largely predated the major law and order reforms of our period and there is little or no evidence of a radical decline in rates following their introduction. Indeed, homicide rates undoubtedly increased in some areas following the introduction of criminal justice reforms, most notably in the early 1830s. Too much can also be made of the effectiveness of police patrols at fairs as a means of preventing violent confrontations, particularly faction fights. There was certainly a decline in the number of reported incidents of faction fights at this time: by 1840, the number fell to one quarter of reported levels in the mid-1830s. This, however, was from a very low base: in 1836 there were only eighteen reported cases of faction fighting.[92] This, of course, is likely to be an underestimate of the real incidence of such fights and it is probable that faction fighting was more prevalent in earlier decades. Yet, even if this number was twenty times higher than reported and assuming around one hundred participants on either side, those involved in such activity would still amount to less than one per cent of the population of the island. Moreover, the level of reported incidents of faction fighting actually rose in the mid-1840s to higher levels than were reported in the 1830s, which suggests that policing was not wholly effective in inhibiting what remained a consistent but, it seems, by this time at least, a relatively rare practice in much of the country.[93]

It is possible also to overstate the influence of the Catholic clergy on the activities and attitudes of the mass of the people. As Connolly has pointed out, the influence of the clergy was by no means total. Indeed, the efforts of the church authorities to reform popular behaviour were, he

---

[92] By 1840, this had fallen to four cases. McCabe, 'Law, Conflict and Social Order', p. 514.

[93] The practice of faction fighting also persisted into the late nineteenth century. See Conley, *Melancholy Accidents*, pp. 20–4. It is probable also that these encounters, where engaged in, served to keep the extent of violent activity within certain bounds and limits by allowing for the expression of aggression in a relatively controlled environment. They may, indeed, have been a method of conflict control – a means of restricting the expression of conflict within controlled environments. This, however, requires further study. The phenomenon of faction fighting has received surprisingly little attention within the existing historiography. See, however, Patrick O'Donnell, *The Irish Faction Fighters of the Nineteenth Century* (Dublin: Anvil Books, 1975) and Donnelly, 'Factions in Pre-Famine Ireland'. See also Huggins, *Social Conflict in Pre-Famine Ireland*, pp. 81–3, 120–1. Huggins suggests that faction fights may have been 'rather more complicated than merely recreational set-pieces for the playing out of pre-modern or vertical loyalties' and points to the fact that, on occasion, they were 'non-violent ritual confrontations'. He also argues persuasively that while factions were a part of life in rural Ireland, it was as 'one characteristic, rather than a paradigm, of the customary consciousness of the rural poor'.

argues, 'remarkably unimpressive' before the Famine.[94] Likewise, the effect of developments such as the temperance movement on homicide rates should not be exaggerated. In Cork, which was very much at the epicentre of the temperance movement, there was admittedly a decline in the levels of homicide in those years, 1839–42, when the movement was at its height. Yet the overall decrease in the county and city between the 1830s and 1840s was minimal – from a rate of 2.39 per 100,000 in the 1830s to 2.2 per 100,000 in the 1840s. This would indicate that if the temperance movement did have an impact it was more of a temporary blip than any fundamental shift in practice. Moreover, the temperance movement had less impact in other counties, which showed a similar, and in some places a considerably more pronounced, drop in homicide rates in these years, which indicates that other factors besides the temperance movement were influencing the decline in homicide rates at that time.[95]

It is also doubtful whether we can see the low rates of homicide in pre-Famine and Famine Ireland as a product of the emergence of a more 'modern' Ireland in the early nineteenth century. There may have been higher levels of literacy, but any claim that modernisation contributed to lower levels of violent activity is hard to sustain. The impression is certainly that some of the most popular reading material available in pre-Famine Ireland (such as chivalric romances and criminal biography) was more likely to promote violent action than to offer a critique.[96] It has also been argued that violence played a minimal part in more 'traditional' forms of expression such as folksongs and poetry in the pre-Famine period, in which violence was portrayed as 'noble but futile' and the Irish peasant as a victim rather than perpetrator of violence.[97] The encroachment of the market economy, as will be discussed in chapter four, is often seen as a force which was more likely to produce a violent reaction than to contribute to a process of pacification.[98] Any crude association of the spread of new political ideas with an increase in violent action is unwarranted, yet it is also hard to argue that an increased awareness of political ideas, particularly from the continent,

---

[94] Connolly, *Priests and People*, p. 250.

[95] See chapter one, Tables 1.1 and 1.2.

[96] This was certainly the view of concerned commentators of the day. Whitley Stokes, writing in 1799, claimed that the romances that were popular among ordinary people did much to 'keep alive a false admiration of courage, a spirit of war and revenge, and a love of adventure so incompatible with the happiness of mankind'. See Niall Ó Ciosáin, *Print and Popular Culture in Ireland, 1750–1850* (2nd ed., Dublin: Lilliput Press, 2010), p. 16.

[97] Mary Thuente, 'Violence in Pre-Famine Ireland: The Testimony of Irish Folklore and Fiction', *Irish University Review*, 15.2 (1985), p. 132.

[98] See below, chapter four.

necessarily contributed to a decline in violent activity in pre-Famine and Famine Ireland.

The evidence for a fundamental downward trend in patterns of violence from the eighteenth century is also weak. The available quantitative data for long-term trends in Ireland before 1837 is certainly very limited and we should be wary of applying wide-ranging and all-encompassing explanations for cultural change on such limited evidence. While the available statistics demonstrate that there was no marked increase in the rate of homicide, it would be somewhat riskier to declare that they reflect a fundamental decline in the rate of violent activity and a corresponding growth in levels of individual self-control.[99]

Most crucially, perhaps, it would also be a mistake to see the cases in our sample as simply remnants of older and outmoded cultural practices. What is striking about them is not necessarily that they are consistent with older forms of violent activity (of which we know relatively little in Ireland), but rather that they closely resemble many aspects of homicide in the present day. Enda Dooley, in his examination of homicide in 1990s Ireland, reveals that 'in the majority of cases the victim and perpetrator were known to each other and the incident occurred in the context of an argument or quarrel.'[100] Indeed, over fifty per cent of cases arose from what he refers to as 'anger/quarrel/rage'.[101] Moreover, he notes that 'frequently one or more of the parties will have been intoxicated and the incident will not have been premeditated'.[102] Studies of violence in present-day England also consistently reveal that such 'trivial altercations' among men are the mainstay of homicidal violence. In England between 1992 and 2003, 45.6 per cent of known homicides arose from 'quarrel, revenge or loss of temper'. Such cases were, moreover, more likely to emerge among those who knew each other before the incident while homicides 'in furtherance of theft or gain' or more 'instrumental' violence accounted for only 7.25 per cent of cases.[103] Marvin Wolfgang, in his study of homicidal violence in mid-twentieth-century Philadelphia, also identified 'altercations of relatively trivial origin; insult, curse, jostling etc.' as the single largest cause of

---

[99] See chapter one and Appendix one.

[100] Dooley, *Homicide in Ireland*, p. 23.

[101] Ibid., p. 16.

[102] Ibid., p. 23. For an analysis of homicide in Ireland in the latter half of the twentieth century, see John D. Brewer, Bill Lockhart and Paula Rodgers, *Crime in Ireland 1945–95: Here Be Dragons* (Oxford: Clarendon Press, 1997), esp. 34–40; Ian O'Donnell, 'Violence and Social Change', pp. 101–17; Wilbanks, 'Homicide in Ireland'.

[103] David Povey (ed.), *Crime in England and Wales 2002/2003: Supplementary Volume 1: Homicide and Gun Crime* (London: Home Office, 2004).

homicide in the city in that period.[104] These cases represent not so much the remnants of former cultural practices but rather a continuity of certain aspects of behaviour, particularly although not exclusively among young men, which are still evident in the present day. It is likely, of course, that these modern-day cases may reveal a strong sense of personal honour or even in some cases a desire for recreation among the parties involved. Yet, we would be reluctant to describe modern-day Ireland or England as an 'honour culture' or, indeed, to explain violence in the present as indicative of a wider cultural outlook which accepts the recreational value of violence. Why, then, should we apply such an analysis to nineteenth-century Ireland where the character and circumstances of interpersonal lethal violence, although by no means identical, were not radically different from those of the present day?

The only real argument for doing so would be that there was a greater propensity among men to react violently to apparently trivial slights than in the present day. As was noted earlier, rates of homicide were higher in the pre-Famine and Famine period than in the Republic of Ireland in the late twentieth century. The difference in rates is, however, by no means overwhelming. The 1840s homicide rate of 1.97 per 100,000 is, as noted in chapter one, somewhat, but by no means exceptionally, higher than the rate of 1.2 per 100,000 recorded in the Republic of Ireland in the 1990s and is lower than the rate of 2.1 per 100,000 recorded for Northern Ireland in the mid-1990s.[105] It is also lower than rates in modern-day Dublin,[106] while rates from the 1830s are also not that much higher than those found in late twentieth-century Dublin.

The differences in rates suggest more a difference of degrees rather than a fundamental difference in attitudes to the use of lethal violence. Moreover, as was noted in the previous chapter, changes in living conditions as well as medical expertise must raise the distinct possibility that much of the difference in the rates reflects the fact that men are simply less likely to die as a result of violent confrontations and not necessarily that they are less willing to engage in them. The differences in homicide rates, such as they are, may not, therefore, simply reflect a diminution in the propensity of men to resort to individual acts of violence, but rather a reduction in the number of fatalities which arise from such confrontations.

There have, of course, been other changes in patterns of violence between the early nineteenth century and the present day. There has been a shift in the location of homicide from the countryside to the city. This, however, does not indicate any significant or notable increase in levels of self-control.

---

[104] Cited in Daly and Wilson, *Homicide*, p. 174.
[105] Dooley, *Homicide in Ireland*, p. 9.
[106] O'Donnell, 'Unlawful Killing', p. 75.

An increase in urban violence is, in fact, a peculiar argument in support of a civilising process. Surely, the forces imposing greater levels of self-control would have been at their most effective in cities.[107] The shift in lethal violence from rural to urban Ireland is more likely to reflect the fact that the underlying points of conflict have shifted from a rural to an urban setting. In this sense, it has less to do with increased levels of self-control in rural Ireland and more to do with clear conflicts arising from economic and social conditions in parts of cities such as Limerick and Dublin, in the south, and a range of conflicts arising from circumstances in such urban areas as Derry and Belfast, in the north, in the late twentieth century and early twenty-first century. Similarly, in the pre-Famine period, the much higher rates found in areas such as Tipperary were related to the development of particular conditions within that county rather than lower levels of self-control than in other areas of the country.

There have also been changes in the attitudes of the courts in the sentencing of those convicted of homicide with longer prison sentences being imposed on convicts in the present day than in the nineteenth century. This, O'Donnell argues, reflects a growing intolerance for violent action in Irish society.[108] There does not, however, appear to be any clear or definitive relationship between high levels of violence and either a low conviction rate or a relatively lenient sentencing policy. There were areas of pre-Famine Ireland which had low rates of conviction, and when convictions for homicide were secured, short sentences were often imposed and yet these areas also had very low homicide rates and, in the case of a county like Fermanagh, had a general reputation as peaceful counties.[109] This would suggest that a punitive attitude towards lethal interpersonal violence is not a necessary condition for the achievement of low rates of lethal interpersonal violence or, indeed, wider stability within an area. Nor should we underestimate the impact that even short sentences could have on convicts and their families. Given that those who were involved in these cases were often young men in their twenties, the removal of their labour and earning power from their families, even for a few months, could potentially have a very detrimental effect. Lighter sentences may also reflect a greater emphasis on the ability of communities to regulate and control disruptive individuals than is found in the present day. It might be remembered also that the death sentence, the ultimate in punitive punishments, was utilised

---

[107] On the link between urbanization and the apparent decline in interpersonal violence, see E.A. Johnson and E.H. Monkkonen (eds), *The Civilization of Crime: Violence in Town and Country since the Middle Ages* (Urbana, IL: University of Illinois Press, 1996).

[108] O'Donnell, 'Killing in Ireland at the Turn of the Centuries'.

[109] See Mc Mahon, *Violence, the Courts and Legal Cultures*, chapter four.

in the pre-Famine period, which suggests that tolerance towards serious acts of lethal violence could, on occasion, be very limited indeed. The less punitive prison sentences imposed in the nineteenth century may then reflect an alternative approach to the control of violent activity rather than reflecting a fundamentally different attitude towards serious acts of violence.

On the whole, although interpersonal violence could play a significant role in Irish society in the first half of the nineteenth century it does not appear to be much more central to interpersonal relationships or, indeed, individual male identity than in the present day. While these homicides reflect a desire on the part of the protagonists to maintain, assert or enhance their status within the community, it is by no means clear that the perpetration of individual acts of violence was considered a more (or a less) valid or legitimate way of achieving this aim in much of the country in the nineteenth century than it is today. Indeed, the gender and age profile of the perpetrators and victims, the use of serious violence to respond to trivial altercations, and the underlying concern with personal position and status within a wider community, all have clear parallels within other societies and cultures across time and space. The case study of pre-Famine and Famine Ireland simply adds to the clear evidence from a myriad of other societies and cultures that the predominance of male homicide perpetrators appears 'resistant to all cultural and economic change'.[110]

---

[110] Eisner, 'Human Evolution, History and Violence: An Introduction', p. 473. The reasons behind such continuities are explored, along with continuities in family violence, in the conclusion to the following chapter.

3

'Sending them to heaven':
Homicide and the family

The role of the family in pre-Famine and Famine Ireland, let alone the role of violence within it, has received little attention within the historiography. There are, however, exceptions. Fitzpatrick, in an article on the role of the family in rural unrest, suggests that 'intra-family conflict was unusually prevalent in nineteenth-century Ireland, with its extensive kinship networks, its scarcity of resources and its lack of clear criteria for disposing of property.'[1] Fitzpatrick's main concern, however, is with the wider issue of 'rural unrest' and his study of intra-family conflict focuses largely on economic disputes among families over the control of land and other resources. Such cases are undoubtedly significant, and they will be discussed in greater detail in the next chapter, but they by no means constituted the sum total of cases of intra-family violence in this period. Rather, violence within the family often stemmed from more personal motives.[2] The only sustained analysis of these personal family disputes in pre-Famine and Famine Ireland is provided by McCabe.[3]

As one might expect in a study that sees the protection of family honour

---

[1]   David Fitzpatrick, 'Class, Family and Rural Unrest in Nineteenth-Century Ireland' in P.J. Drudy (ed.) *Ireland: Land, Politics and People* (Cambridge: Cambridge University Press, 1982), p. 59.

[2]   Most intra-family homicides arose from personal disputes. Between 1843 and 1845, personal disputes in Ireland accounted for 76.19 per cent of all intra-family homicides; in our sample from the Famine years the proportion of cases fell somewhat to 68.62 per cent. The proportion of these cases in the county-based samples was also high. In Armagh, they accounted for 83.33 per cent of cases, in Fermanagh 93.33 per cent, in Kilkenny 76.47 per cent and in Queen's Co. 91.66 per cent.

[3]   There has also been some discussion of domestic violence in the latter half of the nineteenth century. See, for instance, Conley, *Melancholy Accidents*, chapter three and Elizabeth Steiner-Scott, "To Bounce a Boot off her now & then...': Domestic Violence in Post-Famine Ireland' in M.G. Valiulius and Mary O' Dowd (eds), *Women and Irish History* (Dublin: Wolfhound Press, 1997), pp. 125–43. Both authors are, however, concerned primarily with attitudes towards and reactions to domestic violence rather

and kin solidarity as a key feature of social life, McCabe stresses the relative infrequency of intra-family homicide. Spousal homicides, although the most common form of family homicide, were, he points out, relatively few in number. He suggests that this may have been due to strict definitions of gender roles in Irish society, where 'female inferiority' was broadly accepted.[4] He also stresses the rarity of cases involving other family members claiming that the 'moral solidarity of the family ensured that conflict between siblings and between parents and children was kept below extreme levels'.[5] While agreeing with McCabe that the use of violence within the family, although often severe, was clearly controlled and limited, a somewhat different interpretation will be offered. The relative rarity of family homicide cases was not necessarily rooted in the acceptance of notions of 'female inferiority' or the 'moral solidarity' inherent in or peculiar to 'peasant societies', but rather reflects a continuity of behaviour within the family which persists to the present day. Such continuities are evident not only in the rates of family homicide but also in the contexts in which such cases emerge. This chapter also explores whether insights derived from evolutionary theory can shed light on the continuities in violent behaviour both inside and outside the family.

I

Of all the contexts in which violence occurs, violence within the family is the most difficult to quantify with any confidence. As Cockburn has noted, 'the true dimensions of domestic violence in earlier times are irretrievably lost behind a veil of domestic privacy, societal reticence and the common-law doctrine which sanctioned the "moderate" correction of wives, children and servants by heads of households'.[6] Even in cases of homicide there are considerable difficulties with the data.[7] The fact that such cases often did not occur in public but were of a more private nature meant that actual witnesses

---

than the violence itself, although Conley does note similarities between the patterns of violence within and outside the family.

4   For McCabe, the 'relative fewness of domestic homicides may lie in the sharp definition of gender roles, and in peasant acceptance of the idea of female inferiority'. McCabe, 'Law, Conflict and Social Order', p. 123.

5   Ibid., p. 152.

6   Cockburn, 'Patterns of Violence in English Society', pp. 93–5.

7   Homicide is, however, regarded as one of the more reliable indices of domestic violence. See, for instance, J.A. Sharpe, 'Domestic Homicide in Early Modern England', *The Historical Journal*, 24.1 (1981), pp. 29–48.

to the event were limited and many cases were based on circumstantial evidence rather than eyewitness accounts.[8]

There are also particular problems with cases in which the use of poison was suspected.[9] For instance, in Fermanagh in 1835, Thomas Maguire and his mother Phoebe were suspected of poisoning Thomas's wife, Catherine. In this case, the body of the deceased was only exhumed five weeks after the death because of a disagreement between Thomas and his wife's friends, who suspected the accused of poisoning her. The body was brought to Dublin by local surgeons and examined, but no poison was found.[10] Were these cases in which it was particularly difficult to find evidence or were they cases where people were willing to intervene and accuse a suspect even when the evidence was unsustainable? This is obviously a difficult, if not impossible, question to address and such considerations should make us wary of the reliability of our data.[11]

Yet, as Spierenburg has quite correctly argued, they should not cause us to give up on the exercise altogether.[12] We should be wary of reaching any conclusions in cases of poisoning (much as contemporary juries were), but we can reach some firmer conclusions about cases where other means were used. Conclusions must be qualified by the possibility of the prevalence of poisoning cases which did not appear in our sample, but this should not cause us to wholly abandon the possibility of reaching some conclusions about the role of lethal violence within the family.

Table 3.1   The incidence of family homicide in pre-Famine and Famine Ireland

	Ireland 1843–5	Ireland 1847–9	Armagh 1835–50	Fermanagh 1811–50	Kilkenny 1835–50	Queen's Co. 1835–50
All homicides arising within the family	66	51	18	15	17	12
Percentage of all homicide cases	15.82	19.54	19.78	20	14.91	15.38
Rate per 100,000	0.26	0.59	0.49	0.26	0.6	0.51

[8]   See Richard Mc Mahon, 'For Fear of the Vengeance': The Prosecution of Homicide in Pre-Famine and Famine Ireland' in *idem* (ed.), *Crime, Law and Popular Culture*.
[9]   The use or suspected use of poison is mainly restricted to family cases.
[10]   *Enniskillen Chronicle and Erne Packet*, 17 Mar. 1836.
[11]   On poisoning cases in Britain at this time, see Ian Burney, *Poison, Detection, and the Victorian Imagination* (Manchester: Manchester University Press, 2006) and Katherine Watson, *Poisoned Lives: English Poisoners and their Victims* (London: Hambledon and London, 2004).
[12]   Spierenburg, 'Long-Term Trends', p. 75.

Figure 3.1 Rates of family homicide in four Irish counties

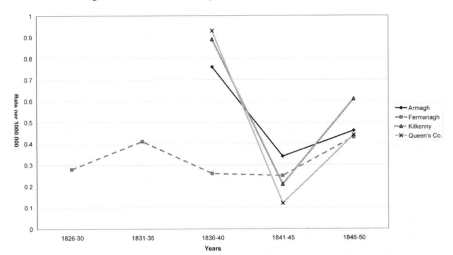

Rates of intra-family homicide were less than 1 per 100,000 in both our national samples and in the samples from the four counties. There is, though, a degree of variation in the samples. This is particularly apparent in our national samples. In our sample from 1843–5 the rate of intra-family homicides was 0.26 per 100,000, while there was a rate of 0.59 per 100,000 in the sample from the Famine period – more than double that before the Famine. This would suggest a marked increase in family homicides during the Famine. We need to be careful, however, as this increase is less evident in the county-based samples where rates in the 1830s were, with the exception of Fermanagh, higher than those during the Famine.

It is likely that levels of intra-family homicide were lower in the period from 1843 to 1845 than at other times. It should be noted, however, that such variations are all within a narrow band of between 0.1 and 1 per 100,000, suggesting that violence within the family was generally kept within definite limits and rarely reached the level of homicide.

It is difficult to compare these figures with those from other countries due to the lack of comparable studies. The most viable comparison that can be made is with Dooley's study of homicide in 1990s Ireland. Even here, however, there are difficulties. Dooley only offers data relating to married couples and blood relations, while our sample also includes non-blood relations.[13] According to Dooley's figures, the rate of homicide within the family, excluding non-blood relatives, was 0.32 per 100,000 in the 1990s.[14] The rate at which homicide arose

[13]   It is difficult to determine, in some cases, whether the relatives mentioned in these reports were blood or non-blood relatives.
[14]   Dooley, *Homicide in Ireland*, p. 16.

within the family, including cases involving non-blood relatives, in our sample of cases from between 1843 and 1845 (0.26 per 100,000) was lower than this. The more long-term studies of the four counties and the sample from the Famine years suggest that rates were somewhat higher, but, given that these figures also include non-blood relatives, and taking account of the fact that the higher homicide rates in the nineteenth century may also be influenced by a lack of medical expertise and poorer living conditions, it does not seem unreasonable to assume that the use of lethal violence within the family was not much greater in the first half of the nineteenth century than in the present day. Indeed, at certain times and in certain places, it was actually lower.[15]

This impression is further confirmed if we look at one form of intra-family homicide for which there is comparable published data for the 1990s – spousal homicide. These rates (see Table 3.2) are, with the exception of Queen's Co., broadly in line with the rates of 0.13 or 0.2 per 100,000 adults recorded for the Republic of Ireland in the 1990s.[16] This is especially so if we take account of the fact that improvements in medical care and living conditions have probably served to depress the rates in more recent times.[17] The spousal homicide rates are also, again with the exception of Queen's Co., generally below the rate of 0.24 per 100,000 recorded for England and Wales at the turn of the twenty-first century.[18]

Table 3.2   The rates of spousal homicide in pre-Famine and Famine Ireland

Cause	Ireland 1843–5	Ireland 1847–9	Armagh 1835–50	Fermanagh 1811–50	Kilkenny 1835–50	Queen's Co. 1835–50
Spousal homicides	21	14	5	7	5	7
Rate per 100,000	0.08	0.16	0.13	0.12	0.16	0.29
Rates per 100,000 adults	0.12	0.24	0.2	0.18	0.24	0.44

[15]   It should be noted also that homicides in the present day are generally a good deal more likely to involve family members than in the nineteenth century. Intra-family homicides, including cases involving non-blood relatives, accounted for circa fifteen to twenty per cent of cases in both the national and county-based samples from the nineteenth century. In the present day, homicides among married couples and blood relations alone account for 28.29 per cent of cases. See Dooley, *Homicide in Ireland*.

[16]   Dooley, *Homicide in Ireland*, p. 16.

[17]   It is more difficult to compare other forms of family homicide with rates in the present day. The rates for these other forms of homicide will, however, be noted throughout the chapter and, where possible, comparisons will be drawn with other jurisdictions.

[18]   This rate is based on the number of cases in which men and women were killed by their partners or ex-partners in England and Wales between 1997 and 2003. See Povey (ed.), *Crime in England and Wales 2002/2003*.

The lack of comparable data for the nineteenth century makes it difficult to assess how the Irish rates compare to those in other countries. Rates from the United States in the mid-nineteenth century indicate, however, that Irish spousal homicide rates were relatively low when compared to both rural and, more particularly, urban areas of North America. The national rates per 100,000 adults in Ireland in the 1840s are, for instance, around a third of those found in rural Ohio and around one-sixth of those in New York City in the mid-nineteenth century.[19] Moreover, these American rates were not especially high and family homicides in the United States were, as Roth observes, a very rare phenomenon, which again serves to emphasise that rates of family homicide in Ireland were relatively low in the 1840s.

A low rate of homicide, of course, does not imply that rates of domestic violence were necessarily also low. It would also be wrong to underestimate the impact of domestic violence. When and where it occurs, it is undoubtedly a disturbing, disruptive and coercive phenomenon within the family and, at times, in the wider community. There can also be little doubt but that violence and the credible threat of violence played, and continues to play, a prominent role in the lives of many families. Indeed, it can be taken as a certainty that, as in the present day, rates of non-lethal violence were considerably higher than is suggested by these homicide rates. Yet it is probably also a mistake to exaggerate the role that violence plays in family relationships. While it is significant in the present day, affecting a disturbingly high proportion of families, the evidence available also indicates that a sizeable majority report that violence or abuse are not a feature of domestic relations. In a 2005 study it was found that eleven per cent of the respondents surveyed had experienced domestic abuse which had 'an actual or potential impact on their lives'. This included 'physical, emotional and sexual abuse'. A further seventeen per cent 'experienced one or perhaps two physical or emotional incidents, but without these having a severe impact on them'. The 'largest group' of respondents, seventy-two per cent, consisted, however, of those who had 'never in their lives experienced any of these incidents'.[20] It is obviously impossible to engage in similar research for the nineteenth century. More in-depth and comparative research also needs to

---

[19]   Roth, *American Homicide*, pp. 254–55. Curiously, Irish migrants made a considerable contribution to the high rates of spousal homicides in New York City – accounting for nearly sixty per cent of all victims in a sample of 134 cases from the nineteenth century. See Eric H. Monkkonen, *Murder in New York City* (Berkeley and Los Angeles, CA: University of California Press, 2001), p. 76. Tracing the reasons for these changes in patterns of violence following migration is the focus of my current research.

[20]   Dorothy Watson and Sara Parsons, *Domestic Abuse of Women and Men in Ireland: Report on the National Study of Domestic Abuse* (Dublin: Stationery Office, 2005), p. 50.

be done in this area, particularly into non-lethal forms of violence, before more solid conclusions can be reached. Yet, given the similarities in the rates identified in this study between the first half of the nineteenth century and the present day, it is not unreasonable to suggest that a similar situation may have prevailed in the nineteenth century.[21]

II

A quantitative analysis can, of course, only take us so far. It is also necessary to look in greater detail at the cases themselves and the contexts in which they emerged. Within the family, some relationships were somewhat more likely to give rise to homicide than others. The majority of cases in our

---

[21] There is, of course, one area where there is a marked difference between the first half of the nineteenth century and the present day, namely the offence of infanticide – rates of which were higher then than they are today (see chapter one, n. 11). Yet comparisons with the present day need to be tempered somewhat by the fact that women in the nineteenth century did not have the same range of options available to them either in terms of contraception and abortion (albeit in other countries) as women in Ireland today. If such options had been available, it is not hard to imagine that the rate of infanticide would have been markedly lower in Ireland. Of course, as O'Donnell has convincingly argued, there are probably other reasons aside from the greater availability of contraception and abortion which influenced the decreasing rates of infanticide between the nineteenth and twentieth centuries. Emigration, for instance, may have become more of a practical option for women who became pregnant outside of marriage in the post-Famine period and, of course, in the twentieth-century. O'Donnell also refers to the possibility that the incidence of pre-marital sexual activity declined in Ireland in the post-Famine period. While this is obviously a difficult phenomenon to quantify, it is also by no means an implausible theory, though one which probably requires further investigation. O'Donnell's further argument that higher rates of infanticide in the nineteenth-century may also have stemmed from the low social value placed on infant life is, however, less convincing. The more qualitative evidence given to the Poor Law Commission in 1835 certainly suggests that women with illegitimate children, despite there being clear hostility towards them, could make great efforts on behalf of their offspring. In the parish of Drumaul, Co. Antrim, for instance, it was claimed that 'mothers do not destroy or desert their illegitimate children, but, on the contrary, generally, make great exertions for them' (*First report of His Majesty's commissioners for inquiring into the condition of the poorer classes of Ireland*, app. a, p. 100, H.C. 1835, xxxii, (369), 1). Moreover, the belief that the mother's actions stemmed from a lack of respect for infant life rather than perhaps a sense of misguided altruism (as is, as we shall see, the case in some non-infant child homicides) remains to be fully explored. The assumption that in 'an environment in which death was omnipresent, arguments for the sanctity of human life carried little weight' is also open to question as it might just as easily be argued that familiarity with and proximity to death might heighten the sense of importance attached to human life. The whole topic, as noted in the introduction, undoubtedly requires a dedicated study for the pre-Famine period. See O'Donnell, 'Lethal Violence', pp. 685–90.

national and county-based samples arose within the immediate family.[22] Spousal relations were, as in the present day, the most likely to give rise to homicide. They accounted for around thirty per cent of all homicides involving family members in the national samples.[23]

Table 3.3   The relationship of the accused to the deceased in homicides arising from all family disputes

Family relationship	Ireland 1843–5	Ireland 1847–9	Armagh 1835–50	Fermanagh 1811–50	Kilkenny 1835–50	Queen's Co. 1835–50
Spouse	21	14	5	7	5	7
Parent–child	12	14	4	2	2	2
Sibling	5	9	1	2	4	1
Other[23]	1	0	2	0	1	0
Relatives outside the immediate family	27	14	6	4	5	2
Total	66	51	18	15	17	12

In the county samples such cases also accounted for a sizeable proportion of cases – ranging from around thirty per cent of cases in Armagh and Kilkenny to nearly half those in Fermanagh and nearly sixty per cent in Queen's county. Homicides involving parents and their children also accounted for a considerable proportion of these cases. Between 1843 and 1845, just under one in every five reported homicides within the family involved parents and their children, while during the Famine such cases accounted for over one in every four cases in our national samples. In our county-based samples, such cases ranged from around eleven per cent of cases in Kilkenny to around twenty-two per cent of those in Armagh. Homicides involving siblings were less common than parent-child homicides in the national samples. Between 1843 and 1845, sibling homicides accounted for only 7.57 per cent of cases within the family. During the Famine, the proportion of such cases rose to 17.64 per cent of incidents. The higher rate during the Famine was due, to

22   Of homicides arising from family disputes in Ireland between 1843 and 1845, 59.09 per cent occurred within the immediate family; in our sample from the Famine years, the proportion rose to 72.54 per cent. In our county-based samples, the proportion varied from 66.66 per cent in Armagh to 83.33 per cent in Queen's Co. In Kilkenny, the proportion was 70.58 per cent while in Fermanagh it was 73.33 per cent.

23   In Dooley's study of homicide in the 1990s just over forty per cent of cases within the family arose among married couples. Dooley, *Homicide in Ireland*, p. 16.

24   These were cases where it was suspected that the deceased had been killed by a number of family members.

a large degree, to an increase in disputes over property among siblings. In both Co. Armagh and Queen's Co., over the sixteen-year period 1835–50, cases involving siblings accounted for less than ten per cent of cases involving family members. In Fermanagh, they accounted for only 13.33 per cent of family homicides between 1811 and 1850 and in Co. Kilkenny 23.52 per cent of family cases between 1835 and 1850.[25]

Spousal homicides

In the majority of cases of spousal homicide, the husband was, as in the present day, the alleged aggressor.

Table 3.4   The accused in cases of spousal homicide in pre-Famine and Famine Ireland (%)

Accused	Ireland 1843–5	Ireland 1847–9	Fermanagh 1811–50	Kilkenny 1835–50	Armagh 1835–50	Queen's Co. 1835–50
Husband	80.95	78.57	85.71	80	80	71.42
Wife	19.05	21.43	14.29	20	20	28.58

It is often difficult to determine the social background of those involved. Poverty and low economic status, however, were not determining factors in these cases. Some cases involved the lower orders. Lucy Keefe, accused of the murder of her husband in Co. Fermanagh in 1838 was a 'mat-maker'.[26] Catherine Moore, a collier's wife, was accused of the murder of her husband in Queen's Co. in 1850.[27] Others, however, were drawn from the middle and more respectable or 'comfortable' sections of Irish society. In Kilkenny in 1850, Patrick Costello, a fifty-year-old 'comfortable farmer' holding 'between fifty and sixty acres of land', was tried for the murder of his wife.[28] In Armagh in 1844, Francis Devlin, a shopkeeper and publican, was tried for the manslaughter of his wife, Ellen Devlin.[29] This indicates that such homicides could arise among the middle classes as well as the lower orders of Irish society, and it is unlikely that intra-family homicide was disproportionately prevalent among any one social group or class. This

---

[25]   The higher rate in Co. Kilkenny is due to a higher number of disputes between brothers over land than in the other counties.

[26]   *Enniskillen Chronicle and Erne Packet*, 15 Mar. 1838.

[27]   *Leinster Express*, 16 Mar. 1850.

[28]   *Kilkenny Journal*, 27 Jul. 1850 and NAI, CRF/1851/Costello/9.

[29]   *Northern Whig*, 7 Mar. 1844 and 25 Jul. 1844.

would also be consistent with findings from the present day, where spousal violence has an impact on people from a broad range of social backgrounds.[30] In what circumstances did these cases arise?

Table 3.5   The circumstances of spousal homicides

	General tension	*Jealousy*	*To take another partner*	*Other*
No. of cases	15	5	4	6

Table 3.5 outlines the main circumstances in which cases of spousal homicide arose in our national sample from 1843 to 1845, and in our four county-based samples.[31] Four cases arose from the desire to pursue another relationship. In all four, a wife was suspected, along with her lover, of poisoning her husband. In Kilkenny in 1844, Catherine Meaney, a servant woman, and Thomas Lannon, a horse trainer, were accused of the murder of Catherine's husband, Thomas Meaney.[32] In this case, Catherine was suspected of administering three grains of cantharides (or Spanish fly) to her husband in a raspberry cordial. Before passing away, Thomas Meaney gave evidence to the stipendiary magistrate that Catherine had poisoned him. Cantharides were also detected during a post-mortem examination of the deceased's body and another witness gave evidence that he had purchased this substance for Lannon who then supplied it to Catherine.[33]

There were also cases where a husband knew or suspected that his wife was having an affair. As in the present day, jealousy could lead to violent action.[34] All five cases of jealousy in our samples arose from jealousy on the part of the husband. Two of these five cases were attributed to insanity. In Kilkenny in March 1843, Nancy Lawless was killed by her jealous husband, who was also reputed to be insane.[35] In other cases, the actions of the husband were attributed to anger upon discovering an extra-marital affair. In the case of Samuel Smith, who was accused of murdering his wife in Armagh

---

[30]   A 2005 study of domestic abuse revealed that 'differences by socio-economic group are not statistically significant' in determining the risk of abuse in the domestic sphere (Watson and Parsons, *Domestic Abuse*, p. 147).

[31]   Table 3.5 is based on those cases where the circumstances of the homicide were clear from the reports. The data from the Famine years was generally not sufficiently clear to make an assessment of the circumstances in which the cases arose.

[32]   *Kilkenny Journal*, 19 Mar. 1845.

[33]   Ibid.

[34]   In a 2005 survey of domestic abuse, it was found that nine per cent of incidents of domestic abuse were 'triggered' by jealousy (Watson and Parsons, *Domestic Abuse*, p. 66).

[35]   *Returns of outrages, 1843–45.*

in 1843, it was reported to the police by James Williamson, a neighbour of the accused, that Smith came to his house on the night of the incident and said 'that he had caught James Devlin, the pensioner, in the act with his wife'. James's brother, William Williamson, also claimed that he had heard Smith 'that morning say that his wife was a whore'.[36]

Most cases, however, did not arise from a desire to pursue another relationship or to punish the attempt, or perceived attempt, to take another partner. More typically these homicides arose from a general hostility or tension between the parties. Such cases made up the single largest group of incidents of spousal homicide in our samples. At the spring assizes of 1838 in Co. Fermanagh, Lucy Keefe was tried and convicted for the murder of her husband, Hugh Keefe. Both parties were said to have lived on bad terms and were known to have 'frequent fights'. One witness, Mary Ker, a neighbour, testified that Lucy Keefe had complained to her 'of the disagreeable life [she and her husband] lived', and that they both 'appeared to be unhappy and give each other short answers' on the night before the alleged incident.[37]

In a number of these cases there was already a history of spousal abuse, and in most, if not all of these the husband was the alleged aggressor. In these circumstances, the homicide could represent a final and fatal culmination of previous violent action. In Limerick in November 1844, Ellen McCormick was killed by her husband. According to the police report, they had 'lived on bad terms, and he had ill-treated her on former occasions'.[38] In such cases, husbands may have used violence to exert control over the behaviour of their spouses. At the Kilkenny summer assizes of 1850, Patrick Costello was tried and convicted for the murder of his wife, Judith Costello. Patrick did not approve of his wife's drinking habits and, although reputed to be kind to her at other times, was 'particularly violent and ill-tempered' on those occasions when he thought she had been drinking.[39] On the night in question, he discovered that she had drunk some of his whiskey. This led to the dispute between them that culminated in Patrick beating her to death.[40] Such cases again arose from very similar circumstances to cases of domestic violence in the present day.[41]

---

[36]   NAI, outrage papers, Armagh, 1843/16211.

[37]   *Enniskillen Chronicle and Erne Packet*, 15 Mar. 1838.

[38]   *Returns of outrages, 1843–45*. McCabe also points out that in 'several' cases in pre-Famine Mayo 'the female victim had suffered much physical abuse from her husband before being murdered' (McCabe, 'Law, Conflict and Social Order', p. 123).

[39]   He was 'known to have beaten her with a pot-stick, shortly after her confinement of a child' (*Kilkenny Journal*, 27 Jul. 1850).

[40]   Ibid.

[41]   In a study of domestic violence in Northern Ireland, it was found that much of the evidence supported 'the view that men use violence to control their wives' or partners'

Alcohol abuse on the part of one or both of the marriage partners may have placed a strain on some relationships (and may, of course, have also been a reflection or expression of the problems within a relationship).[42] A number of cases do reveal a history of and propensity for alcohol abuse. In the abovementioned case of Patrick Costello, the accused was, according to counsel for the crown, 'addicted to the use of ardent spirits' and his wife was also 'not free from the same weakness'.[43] In the case of Robert Hoskins, a pensioner and sheriff's bailiff, who was tried at the Queen's Co. spring assizes of 1839 for the murder of his wife, Mary Hoskins, the police reported that Mary 'was greatly given to drinking & the [accused] in consequence had lived very unhappily with her'.[44] In the case of Francis Devlin in Armagh in 1844, Rose Quinn, a servant in his house, claimed that both Devlin and his wife were 'frequently in the habit of getting drunk'. Peter Graham, another servant, also pointed out that Ellen Devlin 'was always drunk when she could get the liquor' and that the accused 'was in the habit of getting drunk also'.[45] Tensions within the relationship could also intensify and give rise to violent action at times of particular stress. Pregnancy could be a time when relationships were put under severe pressure. In Armagh on the morning of 8 March 1836 at Newtownhamilton, Susan Kannon 'died from the effects of a beating she received from her husband James Kannon'. She was 'far advanced in pregnancy' at the time.[46]

Premeditation can be difficult to establish in spousal homicides. This

behaviour'. Monica McWilliams and Joan McKiernan, *Bringing it out in the Open: Domestic Violence in Northern Ireland* (Belfast: HMSO, 1993), p. 41. The use of violence to control behaviour is, of course, by no means unique to spousal relations. Indeed, all violent activity is, in some respects, about establishing or asserting control over another person.

[42] This again follows patterns found in late twentieth-century Ireland. In a study of domestic violence in Northern Ireland, McWilliams and McKiernan found that 'alcohol abuse was a relevant factor in a majority (66 per cent) of the relationships' in which violence occurred. They are, however, also keen to stress that while alcohol was a contributory factor in a high proportion of cases, it should not necessarily be seen as the primary or ultimate cause of such violence (McWilliams and McKiernan, *Bringing it out in the Open*, p. 40).

[43] *Kilkenny Journal*, 27 Jul. 1850.

[44] NAI, outrage papers, Queen's Co., 1838/141.

[45] *Northern Whig*, 7 Mar. 1844 and 25 Jul. 1844.

[46] Pregnancy seems to be a time of particular stress in marital relationships. In the present day, seven per cent of respondents to a 2005 survey of domestic abuse claimed that the abuse was 'triggered' by 'pregnancy'. Also 'research conducted amongst pregnant women attending the Rotunda Hospital [in Dublin] found that 16 per cent had been physically or sexually abused in the previous 12 months' (Watson and Parsons, *Domestic Abuse*, pp. 66–7).

is particularly true in those incidents where poison was suspected. The outcome of the case is known in three of the four cases involving poison in our sample. Of the three cases, a conviction was secured in only one – the above mentioned case of Catherine Meaney. Even in this case, however, the doctor admitted that the alleged poison had 'been used as a principal ingredient in what are called love-powders, [which] have been administered without the intention of destroying life'. Given that the accused, Catherine Meaney, was convicted on the lesser charge of manslaughter, it is likely that the jury gave the accused the benefit of the doubt and may have regarded it more as a case of negligence in administering a 'love-powder' than premeditated homicide.[47] In the other two cases where a wife was suspected of poisoning her husband, no concrete medical evidence of poisoning could be produced. Whether such cases were genuine must, as noted earlier, remain a matter of speculation. Premeditation was either very rare or the perpetrators were highly effective in avoiding detection in a large number of cases.

Aside from cases of poisoning, the majority of reported spousal homicides, similar to the personal disputes we examined in the previous chapter and to cases in the present day, were triggered by a minor incident or petty disagreement, often where one or both of the parties were drunk.[48] Of the cases drawn from the county-based sample, for instance, over half the cases, fourteen out of twenty-four, arose in the context of a quarrel. In the case of Catherine Connor in Queen's Co. in 1845, it was reported that Catherine's husband blamed her for allowing pigs to get into his potatoes, for which he gave her a kick in the side. She was pregnant at the time and died within an hour and a half of the attack.[49] Given the propensity for alcohol abuse noted earlier, it is perhaps unsurprising that alcohol could also play a part in a number of these disputes. In eight of the fourteen cases that arose from a quarrel in our county-based sample at least one of the parties was drunk. In the case of the murder of Mary Hoskins by her husband in Queen's Co. in December 1838, it was reported by the police that 'both were under the influence of liquor at the time.'[50]

---

47 *Kilkenny Journal*, 19 Mar. 1845.

48 In a 2005 survey of domestic abuse, it was found that thirty-six per cent of incidents of domestic abuse were 'triggered' by 'minor incidents' or 'nothing in particular'. This was the single most common 'trigger' for domestic abuse in the sample. A further thirty-four per cent of respondents claimed that abusive behaviour was 'triggered' by the 'use of alcohol (by either partner)', while eight per cent said that the abuse was triggered by a disagreement or row. See Watson and Parsons, *Domestic Abuse*, p. 66.

49 *Leinster Express*, 19 Jul. 1845. See also NAI, CRF/1845/Connor/35, which contains the depositions of Anne and Dennis Connor (the unmarried uncle and aunt of the deceased).

50 NAI, outrage papers, Queen's Co., 1838/141.

The preponderance of cases involving seemingly sudden and often drunken quarrels indicates that most of these cases were not premeditated. Some, however, were the culmination of previous acts of violence indicating a pattern of violence rather than a one-off encounter where tempers temporarily flared. There are also cases where the actions and statements of the accused certainly indicate lethal intent. In the case of Patrick Costello, after he had administered his beating, the accused remarked to a servant girl that '[his wife was] no more – she is a long time earning that, and it is all her own fault.' He also delivered a kick to her body as she lay on the ground.[51] In the case of the killing of Mary Hoskins, while both parties were drunk, her husband shot her at close range (claiming later that he did not know that the gun was loaded).[52] The nature of these acts indicates that such apparently sudden and drunken acts were, if not pre-planned, certainly rooted in long-standing tension and hostility within the marriage.

This pattern of abuse, of which homicide was, on occasion, the culmination, also indicates that non-lethal violence against women and the threat of such violence in pre-Famine Ireland was a significant problem. This is reinforced by studies of sexual violence against women which note how both the perpetration and threat of rape meant that women in Ireland were 'not able to function free of fear' of violence.[53] Violence and the threat of violence could clearly be used to control behaviour and restrict independence of action. The risk of violence for women also probably increased considerably when they could not rely on the support of family or acted independently of or contrary to their family's wishes. In this sense, women could face the threat of violence within the family but also run the risk of greater exposure to violence if they lost the support and protection of the family group. This situation could also be reinforced by the common law which allowed, as Cockburn notes, for the 'moderate' use of physical force by the head of the household. The law also failed to recognise rape within marriage as a criminal offence and conviction rates for rape outside the family were low relative to other serious offences. The position of women, and particularly wives, in such an 'undeniably patriarchal'[54] society was undoubtedly shaped, to some degree at least, by their vulnerability to violence.

Why then, given the nature of pre-Famine society, was the rate of spousal

---

51 *Kilkenny Journal*, 27 Jul. 1850.
52 *Leinster Express*, 23 Mar. 1839; NAI, outrage papers, Queen's Co. 1838/141.
53 James Kelly, "A Most Inhuman and Barbarous Piece of Villainy': An Exploration of the Crime of Rape in Eighteenth-Century Ireland', *Eighteenth-Century Ireland/ Iris an dá chultúr*, 10 (1995), p. 107.
54 Ibid.

homicide relatively low? It may be that the severity of violence was, in part, limited and controlled due to the ability of women to assert at least some kind of influence over the behaviour of men. This might be done in some cases through the use of violence. There were certainly cases where women used violence to counter male aggression or to impose control on their husbands. There are, for instance, a number of cases in our sample where women (on occasion acting with others) used violence against their spouses.[55] Other family members could also be called on, as we shall see, to try and prevent or avenge spousal violence.[56] Women, though by no means assured of a sympathetic hearing, could also make use of the law to defend themselves. There is certainly evidence that women could be assertive in bringing cases before the courts to prosecute violence and, more generally, to assert their legal rights.[57]

There is a sense also that, while some level of violence was tolerated within families, severe acts of violence against women were not regarded as legitimate.[58] Women may have been able to use or even subvert prevailing ideas of appropriate gender roles to impose certain standards of behaviour on men which could serve, with communal support and/or intelligent use of the law, to keep violence within certain bounds and limits. This would, moreover, be consistent with practices found elsewhere in Europe and in North America.[59] In this sense, it was less the acceptance of ideas of female inferiority but more the use of ideas of expected behaviour which inhibited acts of lethal violence against wives. Nor should we assume that men in this period were inherently violent towards women or were more violent towards women than men in other countries. The evidence suggests that the extent

---

55 Conley, in her study of the late nineteenth century, also notes that while 'some' women appear to have tolerated mistreatment, 'many Irish wives defended themselves'. See Conley, *Melancholy Accidents*, pp. 70–1.

56 See, for instance, the cases cited below of John Coleman in Cork in November 1844 and the case of Pat Gibbons in Mayo in November 1845 (*Returns of outrages, 1843–45*). See also Conley, *Melancholy Accidents*, p. 72.

57 See, for instance, Richard Mc Mahon, 'The Courts of Petty Sessions and Society in Pre-Famine Galway' in Raymond Gillespie (ed.), *The Re-Making of Modern Ireland: Essays in Honour of J.C. Beckett* (Dublin: Four Courts Press, 2003), pp. 101–37.

58 As Conley notes when discussing spousal violence, 'deliberate brutality towards an innocent victim was not acceptable, but casual violence was largely perceived as a private matter.' See Conley, *Melancholy Accidents*, p. 67.

59 See, for instance, Julie Hardwick, 'Early Modern Perspectives on the Long History of Domestic Violence: The Case of Seventeenth- and Eighteenth-Century France,' *The Journal of Modern History*, 78.1 (2006), pp. 1–36. In a North American context, see Laura F. Edwards, 'Women and Domestic Violence in Nineteenth-Century North Carolina' in Michael A. Bellesiles (ed.), *Lethal Imagination: Violence and Brutality in American History* (New York: NYU Press, 1999), pp. 115–38.

of lethal violence, at least, was limited and contained to a greater degree than in certain other countries. Whether women were at greater risk of domestic violence in the nineteenth century than in the present is difficult, if not impossible, to determine. It would, however, risk underestimating the impact of violence in later periods to assume the situation was necessarily worse in the pre-Famine era than in the present.[60] The similarity in spousal homicide rates also suggests that in both periods violence was generally kept within comparable limits, albeit probably in different ways.

Rates of spousal homicide are also obviously linked to wider economic, social and cultural contexts and can reflect the degree to which men feel comfortable with or threatened by wider societal developments. In particular, it is likely that where men feel their position within the family is threatened they will be more likely to resort to lethal violence.[61] Thus, within a continuum of domestic abuse, violence can, depending on circumstances, become more or less severe. The relatively low rates of spousal homicide in pre-Famine Ireland probably reflect the fact that women were able to impose limits on male violence and that the position or self-perceptions of men were not unduly or overtly threatened at this time.

Rather than being passive victims, then, women might draw on familial, communal and legal support to try to limit and control violence against themselves and probably other family members. This was done, however, in the face of considerable challenges and difficulties – a broader culture that tolerated some level of violence against women in the home, a sometimes unsympathetic court system and a society in which women who stepped outside of established norms of behaviour could be exposed to serious acts of violence. We should not, therefore, deny the patriarchal nature of Irish society, or be complacent about levels of spousal abuse in pre-Famine Ireland or about violence against women generally, but nor should we simply see women in this period as passive victims of male aggression. The relatively low rate of spousal homicide was more likely the product of a (profoundly unequal) negotiation of interests between husband and wife rather than a simple acceptance by women of a position of passive victimhood. Such

---

60 A similar point, albeit arising from very different contexts, emerges in Hardwick's discussion of domestic violence in early modern France. She notes that 'although a seventeenth-century woman was legally subject to her husband's discipline, wives themselves as well as individuals and institutions in local communities publicly negotiated the parameters of that discipline. A twentieth-century woman living in a community that valorized romantic, companionate, and privatized ideals of marriage was, by contrast, isolated and wary of public acknowledgment of her status as a battered wife' ('Early Modern Perspectives on the Long History of Domestic Violence', p. 1).

61 For an excellent discussion of the correlation between broader social and culture change and increasing levels of spousal homicide, see Roth, *American Homicide*, chapter six.

negotiations ensured that spousal violence, while undoubtedly prevalent, was, to some extent at least, controlled and not allowed to play a wholly disruptive role in pre-Famine and Famine Ireland.

Parricide

Within our samples there are a combined total of fifteen cases of parricide.[62] Parricide was a largely male phenomenon: sons were the main suspects in fourteen of the fifteen cases in which offspring killed their parents.[63] The sex of the victims was somewhat more balanced, however. In ten cases, it was the father who was the victim while the mother was the victim in the remaining five cases. In most instances of parricide the suspect also appears to have been an adult.[64]

Parricide arose in a variety of different circumstances. One in five arose from a dispute over property. These generally involved disputes between sons and fathers over property, in particular, land. These cases will be dealt with in the next chapter. The majority of cases, however, arose from more personal disputes. At times, the homicide was a response to abuse. In Cork in November 1844, the police suspected that John Coleman had been killed by his son in revenge for the ill-treatment of his wife (the perpetrator's mother).[65] On other occasions, there was a clear conflict of interests or clear difference of opinion between the parties. In Galway in August 1845, 'Thady Gannon, aged between 60 and 70, was strangled [...]

62 The parricide rate in Ireland between 1843 and 1845 was 0.02 per 100,000. In Fermanagh the rate between 1811 and 1850 was 0.01; in Kilkenny the rate was 0.03; in Queen's Co. the rate was higher at 0.08. There were no such cases in Co. Armagh. On a national level, the rate of parricide rose during the Famine to 0.04 per 100,000. These figures suggest that parricide was less common in pre-Famine and Famine Ireland than in some jurisdictions in the present day. The rate of parricide in the United States between 1977 and 1988 was 0.14 per 100,000. See Thomas J. Young, 'Parricide Rates and Criminal Street Violence in the United States: Is there a Correlation?' in *Adolescence*, 28.109 (1993), pp. 171–2.

63 The majority of those accused of parricide in the present day are also male. Charles Patrick Ewing, *Fatal Families: The Dynamics of Intrafamilial Homicide* (Thousand Oaks, CA: Sage Publications, 1997), p. 103.

64 In Queen's Co., in 1840, for instance, the forty-year-old collier Mathew Bryan was charged with the murder of his mother, Bridget Bryan (*Leinster Express*, 7 Mar. 1840). The high proportion of adult perpetrators, again, follows the modern-day pattern, where the majority of perpetrators of parricide are over the age of eighteen. See Ewing, *Fatal Families*, pp. 103–4. There was only one case where a parent seems to have been killed by a non-adult offspring. This occurred in Cork in August 1849, when Catherine Barry 'died from the effects of a shot fired by her son (aged 14 years)'. In this case, it was believed that the 'shot was intended for a man who he thought was in bed with his mother at the time'. *Returns of outrages, 1847–49*.

65 *Returns of outrages, 1843–45*.

by his son.' In this case, it was believed that the act had been carried out 'to prevent the deceased's intended marriage'.[66] A considerable degree of premeditation and lethal intent was a feature of such cases. In other cases the accused was mentally ill. There are three such cases in our samples and in all three the victim was the mother of the accused. In Queen's Co. in July 1837, for instance, a woman called Anne Fitzpatrick 'was murdered by her son Edward Fitzpatrick who had been a lunatic for some years'.[67] In such cases, great uncertainty must surround the extent of premeditation on the part of the perpetrator.

The most common cause of such cases was a petty dispute between the parties with little apparent premeditation on the part of the perpetrator.[68] In Mayo in March 1844, for instance, Pat Fahy was killed at his daughter's wedding during a drunken affray in which he was hit on the head with a pot hanger by his son.[69] In Queen's Co. in 1840, Bridget Bryan died after being beaten by her son, Mathew, following a dispute over some bread which Mathew believed had been stolen from the house. Similar in some respects to spousal homicides, there was little overt evidence of any well-thought-out plan to kill, but there does seem to have been long-standing tensions between the parties in this case. Bryan, although reputed to be kind to his mother when sober, was alleged to have beaten her on former occasions when drunk.[70]

Filicide

Within our samples there are a combined total of twenty-one cases of filicide.[71] In the majority, the father was a suspect. In eleven of the

---

[66] Ibid.

[67] NAI, outrage papers, Queen's Co., 1837/139.

[68] Such cases are also by no means unheard of in the present day. See, for instance, the case of Timmy Joe Murphy, who was found guilty of the manslaughter of his father at Tralee circuit criminal court in July 2005 (*Irish Times*, 29 Nov. 2005).

[69] See McCabe, 'Law, Conflict and Social Order', p. 90.

[70] *Leinster Express*, 25 Jul. 1840. See also Bryan's petition to the lord lieutenant requesting a commutation of his sentence. The petition makes a forceful case that he did not plan to kill his mother, but rather that she had died as a result of inadequate and incompetent medical treatment. See NAI, CRF/1840/Bryan/50.

[71] The rate of filicide in Ireland between 1843 and 1845 was 0.01 per 100,000. In Fermanagh between 1811 and 1850 the rate was 0.01; in Kilkenny the rate was 0.03 between 1835 and 1850; in Queen's Co. there were no such cases. The only exception to these generally low rates is Co. Armagh, where the rate was somewhat higher at 0.11. On a national level, the rate of filicide rose markedly during the Famine, to 0.11 per 100,000. These figures suggest that, with the exception of the Famine years and Co. Armagh, homicides of non-infant children by their parents were less common than in the present day. Between 2000 and April 2005 there were fifteen homicides of children by their parents

twenty-one cases, the father was the sole suspect, while in three cases, all of which occurred during the Famine, both parents stood accused of killing their child. In seven cases the mother was the only suspect.[72] There was no significant gender bias in the profile of the victims – out of a sample of twenty-one cases where children were killed by their parents the victim was male in eleven cases, female in nine cases, and in one case the sex was not recorded.

Almost invariably the victims were young children.[73] The overwhelming majority of children in these cases were the 'natural-born' offspring of the accused rather than stepchildren.[74] Similar to our study of spousal homicide, there are some striking similarities between the circumstances of the cases in our sample and those found in modern-day studies of filicide. There were those cases, for instance, where the parent became angry or irritated at the actions of the child and resorted to violence as a form of discipline.[75] In Co. Tipperary in October 1845 'Mary Barrett, aged 12 years, received a blow on the head from her father, with a piece of rod iron, which caused her death.' There was, according to the police, 'no premeditated intention, on the part of the accused, to inflict bodily injury' but rather the case stemmed from 'momentary irritation'.[76] Mental illness and/or drunkenness could also be

---

in Ireland – a rate of 0.07 per 100,000. Moreover, while this figure is lower than that for the Famine years and for Co. Armagh, if we take advancements in medical care and improvements in living conditions into account, the difference does not appear to be that great. The evidence on filicide in the present day is gleaned from the *Sunday Tribune*, 24 Apr. 2005.

[72] While still constituting a minority of suspects, women constituted a higher proportion of suspects in filicide cases than any other form of homicide. The relatively high proportion of female suspects in filicide cases is also evident in the present day. See C.M. Alder and Kenneth Polk, 'Masculinity and Child Homicide', *British Journal of Criminology*, 36.3 (1996), p. 400. The mother of the victim was suspected in six of the fifteen cases of filicide in Ireland between 2000 and April 2005 (*Sunday Tribune*, 24 Apr. 2005).

[73] There was only one case of a father killing his grown-up daughter. This occurred in Roscommon in July 1849 when Ellen Kelly, described as a spinster, was killed by her father because she 'had become a prostitute'. In the remaining cases, the victim was a child. See *Returns of outrages, 1847–49*.

[74] Even though the phenomenon of step-parenting was probably not wholly uncommon in pre-Famine and Famine Ireland, I have only come across one case where there is a possibility that the accused was a stepparent. This is the case of Anne Fox, 'an illegitimate child of 4 years old', who was killed by a kick to her head by her mother's husband. The fact that Anne was described as illegitimate and her mother was married would suggest that the accused was her stepfather. See *Returns of outrages, 1843–45*.

[75] For a discussion of these cases in the present day, see Alder and Polk, 'Child Homicide', pp. 403–5 and Ewing, *Fatal Families*, pp. 97–8.

[76] *Returns of outrages, 1843–45*.

factors in these cases.[77] At the Fermanagh summer assizes of 1827, Joseph Horsefield, the elder, was charged with the murder of his 'three or four year old' son, Joseph Horsefield, the younger, in May of the same year. During the trial, it was revealed that while in the British Army in Spain and Sicily during the Napoleonic wars he was reported to be suicidal and

> the commanding officer [of his regiment] had directed an eye be kept on [him] to prevent his injuring himself or others [...] he was also gagged repeatedly [and] on a long march into France [he] was deprived of his arms, and a drum stick put across his mouth to hinder him from hurting anyone; it was allowed his insanity sprung from hunger in the campaign.

As one witness put it, Horsefield was 'a peaceable, quiet man when he did not get liquor [but] conceived [he] was completely deranged when in drink'.[78]

Parallels can also be drawn with the present day in those cases where parents resorted to lethal violence out of a sense of 'hopelessness, helplessness and uselessness'. In such cases, parents can act from a sense of 'misguided altruism', feeling that 'the filicide [is] in the best interests of the children'.[79] There are cases in our sample where the parent's inability to care and/ or provide for the child probably led to feelings of such inadequacy that homicide came to be seen as the only way out. Such cases often reveal a high degree of premeditation. In Shanaglish, Co. Galway, in June 1844, Peter Larkin, a pensioner from the 87th foot, was charged with the murder of his two sons, Martin and Bernard Larkin, aged twelve and fifteen respectively. Larkin, who had fallen on hard times and been forced to give up some land, regarded the killing of his children as the only means of resolving the situation he found himself in. On the night of the incident, he entered the room where three of his children, two sons and one daughter, were sleeping in the same bed and with a razor cut the throats of his two sons and cut at the breast of his daughter who managed to escape and raise the alarm. When questioned by a neighbour as to why he committed these murders, he replied that 'he thought he was doing the finest work in the world – sending them to heaven.'[80]

A mixture of poverty and an inability to cope with caring for a child is

---

[77] Homicides committed by mentally-ill parents in the present day are briefly discussed in Ewing, *Fatal Families*, pp. 98–9.

[78] *Enniskillen Chronicle and Erne Packet*, 9 Aug. 1827.

[79] Alder and Polk, 'Child Homicide', pp. 405–6.

[80] *Galway Vindicator*, 7 Aug. 1844.

also evident in the case of John Blakely, who was charged at the Armagh summer assizes of 1840 with the murder of his son Felix Blakely, a 'child of 6 or 7 years' on 1 March of that year. Blakely, who was 'too poor to engage professional assistance' for his defence, was reported to have had 'four or five children' with a woman called Mary Turley, of which Felix was 'the youngest but one'. Turley had died giving birth to their last child and John was left to care for the remaining family members. Felix had suffered from small pox, as a consequence of which he lost his sight in one eye and the 'second toe' on his right foot had decayed, and he also suffered from a bowel complaint. Prior to the killing of his son, John had been living in the house of a Mrs Rainey, who ran a huckstery, and it was here that Felix had come to live with him after having been cared for by John's sister. Difficulties arose at this point, as Mrs Rainey was hostile towards the child and ultimately requested that Blakely find 'another lodging for it'.[81] This encouraged Blakely to take decisive action to rid himself of the burden of caring for the child. He took his son from the boarding house in which they were lodging and returned later saying that he had left the child 'in the country'. The child's dead body was discovered five weeks later when rain had washed away the ground in which it was buried. When the body was discovered Blakely was confronted by his sister, one of the main prosecution witnesses in the case, and asked if the body was that of Felix, after remaining silent for 'about five or ten minutes', he replied by asking 'What could he do with [the child]? Sure he was tormented with the trouble it gave to everybody – no one would take his week's earning to take care of it.'[82]

The onset of the Famine may have increased the likelihood of such cases. In May 1847 in Co. Galway, Mary Connelly, 'an illegitimate child aged 7 years, was thrown into Lough Beg [...] by her mother'.[83] The desperation of some parents was also reflected in a case, which, although not recorded as a homicide, certainly raised suspicions among the police. This was the case of a woman who was found drowned in a 'dike of water' with her three children in Co. Kilkenny. The coroner's jury returned a verdict of death by drowning but was uncertain as to whether it was by accident or design of the mother. According to the report, the family were starving and in a bad

---

[81] According to one witness at the trial, Mrs Rainey had reportedly 'advised the prisoner to take the head off the child, and throw it behind the fire'. This was because Rainey believed the child to be 'bewitched like', which, the witness explained, was 'the opinion of the country-people [...] that a bewitched child is a sickly one which has been left in place of a fine child taken away by the fairies'. Mrs Rainey denied that she thought the child a changeling. See *Belfast Newsletter*, 11 August 1840.

[82] *Belfast Newsletter*, 11 August 1840.

[83] Ibid.

way previous to the incident.[84] The conditions created by the Famine led, in some cases, to the serious neglect of children. At the Kilkenny summer assizes of 1850, Thady Moylan was tried for causing the death of his son John 'through neglect'.[85]

Sibling homicide

Within our samples there are a combined total of twenty-two homicides involving siblings.[86] These were, as in the present day, largely male affairs.[87] There are no recorded cases of a sister killing a sister, and there are only three cases involving a brother and sister. The remaining nineteen cases arose from disputes among brothers. All the cases involved adults. This again follows a pattern evident in the present day.[88]

What were the circumstances of these cases? Disputes over property were more likely to emerge among siblings than any other relationship within the immediate family. Of the twenty-two homicides, eight arose from disputes between brothers over property. These disputes were often over the division of land and will be discussed in greater detail in the next chapter. The majority of cases involving siblings in our samples, however, still arose from personal disputes. Cases involving sisters and brothers arose where one impeded or attempted to impede the other. In Galway in December 1848, Michael Holland 'died from the effects of injuries inflicted on his head by his sister and a man called John Holland'. The motive, in this case, was, according to the police, 'to remove an obstruction to an improper intercourse which existed between the accused parties'.[89] In cases between

---

84   NAI, outrage papers, Kilkenny, 1846/33587. How many such cases went unrecorded must remain a mystery, although it should be noted that I have not come across any other cases of even suspected familicide in any of my samples. The tendency of mothers to drown their children follows the pattern found in the present day. It was noted in an article on the murder of children by their parents in present-day Ireland that 'mothers [...] are more likely [than fathers] to drown or choke their victims.' In five of the six homicides of a child by its mother between 2000 and April 2005, the victim was drowned. See *Sunday Tribune*, 24 Apr. 2005.

85   NAI, Crown books for the Co. Kilkenny assizes, 1846–52, 1D/57/25

86   The rate of sibling homicide in Ireland between 1843 and 1845 was 0.01 per 100,000. In Armagh between 1835 and 1850 the rate was 0.02; in Fermanagh between 1811 and 1850, the rate was 0.03; in Kilkenny between 1835 and 1850 the rate was 0.14; in Queen's Co. during the same period the rate was 0.04. On a national level, the rate of sibling homicide rose during the Famine to 0.10 per 100,000.

87   Ewing, *Fatal Families*, p. 117.

88   Ewing, *Fatal Families*, p. 117. Those involved could be elderly. In Antrim in January 1843, Margaret McClarnon, 'who was 90 years old, received injuries from her brother, aged 64, which caused her death'. See *Returns of outrages, 1843–45*.

89   *Returns of outrages, 1847–49*.

brothers, some arose from jealousy and/or rivalry and were probably rooted in longstanding tensions. In Longford in October 1847, Hugh Quigley died from injuries inflicted by his elder brother, Michael. In this case, it was revealed that the accused resented the fact that Hugh was 'more highly thought of by the family'.[90] In Co. Fermanagh in 1848, Thomas Wilson was accused of the murder of his brother, John. The accused had recently returned to the local area from London, where he had worked as a policeman for the previous twelve years. He was not on good terms with his brother and was said to be jealous of his sibling's position as woodranger to Lord Enniskillen. The accused entered into a conspiracy with two other men, one an ex-employee and the other a current employee of his brother's, to carry out the murder.[91]

Such premeditation, however, seems rare. Most cases reveal that petty disputes sparked off these confrontations with little by way of premeditation on the part of those involved.[92] In Kerry in December 1844, John Murphy was stabbed by his brother with a knife he was using to cut tobacco. The dispute arose when Murphy had attempted to prevent his brother from entering a house to smoke on their way home from the market in Tralee.[93] Lethal intent was absent in many cases. In Co. Mayo in 1844, Michael Gaughan died as a result of a blow he received from his brother in a 'sudden quarrel'. The injury was 'inflicted in the heat of passion, and without any intention on the part of the offender to take life'. The victim in this case 'forgave his brother and apologized, on his deathbed, for having been responsible for a fatal flare-up between the two of them'.[94]

Other relatives

Within our samples there are a combined total of fifty-eight homicides involving relations from outside the immediate family. These were also predominantly male affairs. Of the fifty-eight cases gleaned from our national and county-based samples, forty-nine were exclusively male affairs, there were four cases where men were suspected of killing female relatives and there were a further four cases where a woman was co-accused with a man of killing a male relative.[95] There was only one reported homicide case

---

90   *Returns of outrages, 1847–49.*
91   *Armagh Guardian*, 23 Jul. 1849. This case also involved a robbery.
92   Modern-day studies of sibling homicides reveal similar circumstances surrounding such killings. See Ewing, *Fatal Families*, pp. 115–17.
93   *Returns of outrages, 1843–45.*
94   See *Returns of outrages, 1843–45* and McCabe, 'Law, Conflict and Social Order', p. 90. The case is reported in the *Mayo Constitution*, 25 Mar. 1845.
95   Even where women were accused along with men, their role in the actual act of violence was often minimal. This is evident, for instance, at the trial of John Johnston and his

in which a woman was accused of killing another woman. This was the case of Ann Bolger who was tried at the Kilkenny spring assizes of 1847 for the murder of Bridget Lynch, her niece (through marriage).[96]

In what circumstances did these cases arise? A sizeable proportion of these cases, over forty per cent, arose from conflicts among relatives over land, property and economic resources. Thirteen cases, for instance, arose from conflicts over land.[97] A further five cases arose from disputes over items of property. In Cork in June 1843, Catherine Buckley was killed by her brother-in-law in a 'dispute about fowl'. The cases drawn from the Famine years also reveal incidents of robbery involving relations from outside the immediate family. These reflect competition among relatives for scarce resources during the crisis years of the Famine. In Mayo in April 1847, Pat Dixon, aged fourteen, was killed when he tried to prevent his seventeen-year-old cousin from 'taking food belonging to [his] mother'.[98]

Yet, while disputes over land and other resources gave rise to a considerable proportion of the cases, the majority still arose from more personal disputes. Although, those involved were not members of the immediate family, the cause of the homicide could, on occasion, be rooted in difficulties arising from relationships within the immediate family, in particular, the marriage relationship.[99] In Mayo in November 1845, 'Pat Gibbons, while beating his wife, was struck on the head with a stone by his nephew, and died of the injury.'[100] Most incidents arose in circumstances similar to those identified heretofore – arising, in the main, from a petty dispute or disagreement. In Queen's Co. in January 1839, John Lark died after being hit on the head with a stone during an argument with relatives over a song. The accused and the deceased were said to be 'close neighbours and near relations and always on the best of terms'.[101] In May 1839, John Russell died as a consequence of injuries received in a confrontation between two families, the Fennys and the Russells. In this case, both sides in the dispute pointed out that 'they

mother, Jane Johnston, for the murder of an in-law, James McSorley, at the Fermanagh assizes of 1821. Bridget Kerr, the main prosecution witness in the trial, pointed out that during the attack 'Jane the mother was present all the time but did nothing except [move] her hand and say the deceased was dead' (*Enniskillen Chronicle and Erne Packet*, 22 Mar. 1821).

96   They both lived in the same house and Bolger was accused of poisoning Lynch with white arsenic. See *Kilkenny Journal*, 17 Mar. 1847.

97   These cases will be discussed in chapter four.

98   *Returns of outrages, 1847–49.*

99   There were four cases where a man was killed by his in-laws because they were unhappy with his actions towards or treatment of his wife.

100   Ibid.

101   NAI, outrage papers, Queen's Co., 1839/8.

were all relations, and that it was a drunken quarrel, which [was] the only cause assigned for it'.[102]

There is little evidence of premeditation. In Armagh in 1844, David White, an elderly publican, was killed in a drunken fight with his nephew George White. The uncle was the aggressor, attacking his nephew with a stick as he passed by his house, and the nephew responded by wresting the stick from his uncle and striking him with it. He was said to be unaware that the blow he administered to his uncle was fatal.[103] There is little evidence of lethal intent in many of the cases. In King's Co. in October 1843, Margaret Tracy died after being hit with a stone by 'a relative, whose motive, it is alleged, was merely to frighten the deceased'.[104] On the whole, while serious acts of violence could arise among relatives, there is little evidence that violence was central to such relationships or even that they were a common occurrence.

III

Rates of intra-family homicide in the first half of the nineteenth century were not much higher, and at certain times and in certain places, were lower, than in the present day. Intra-family conflict, as McCabe has pointed out, was clearly kept within limits, rarely reaching the level of homicide. There is, moreover, no reason to assume, based on a study of homicide at least, that violence was necessarily a much greater factor in familial relations in the first half of the nineteenth century than in the present day. The family was and remains an arena for considerable conflict, violence and aggression; it can, however, also be one of negotiation, accommodation and cohesion in which the extent of violent conflict is limited and controlled.

Similar to personal disputes among unrelated males, the underlying causes of violent conflict among family members identified in this study are by no means unique to pre-Famine or Famine Ireland. The circumstances in which many of the personal disputes arose, the profile of those involved and the characteristics of the acts themselves bear a striking resemblance to those found in modern-day studies of family homicide, in Ireland and elsewhere, and point to remarkable continuities in the extent and nature of lethal violence within the family unit across time and place. Indeed, the patterns of violence in personal disputes both inside and outside the family

---

[102] NAI, outrage papers, Queen's Co., 1839/3164.
[103] See *Returns of outrages, 1843–45*; *Armagh Guardian*, 26 Jul. 1844; *The Banner of Ulster*, 23 Jul. 1844.
[104] *Returns of outrages, 1843–45*.

identified in this book need to be understood in the light of circumstances beyond the relatively narrow confines of Irish social and cultural life.

How then might we explain the continuities across time and the similarities with other cultures? A number of historians of violence have grappled with the similarities in patterns of violence across cultures and have looked to biology and, in particular, evolutionary psychology for an explanatory model. Evolutionary psychology offers a framework for understanding violence by relating it to an underlying 'mental architecture' which is common to all human societies and, in doing so, seeks to identify 'recurrent regularities' in patterns of violent activity.[105] In this view, the utility of violence is deep-rooted in evolutionary processes and continues to be utilised by individuals, in a variety of different ways and forms, to assert their position in society. Such violence is underpinned, moreover, by a concern to promote 'fitness' (reproductive success). The extent to which violence is useful within certain contexts is, in turn, shaped to a considerable degree by broader economic, social, cultural and environmental forces. In this sense, evolutionary psychology allows for some variability and diversity across time and space while asserting that there are also deep biological roots which shape the nature of aggressive behaviour in all human societies.[106]

Evolutionary psychology is not, however, a 'theory of motivation'.[107] It does not claim, for instance, that each individual is necessarily bound to act in a particular way in pursuit of 'fitness', or that all behaviour is necessarily adaptive. In this sense, it does not predict individual behaviour, but rather seeks to explain broad patterns of behaviour in the light of evolutionary theory. It looks, in essence, at why men and women pursue particular goals, and argues that these goals are underpinned by or somehow related to the pursuit of fitness. This, in turn, leads to a number of expectations concerning patterns of violent behaviour: men are more likely than women to engage in violent competition for access to sexual partners and are more likely than women to engage in violent activity with other unrelated rivals of the same sex in order to maintain, assert or advance their status or position in society. In cases of domestic violence, husbands are most likely to use violence against their wives when they suspect infidelity (imagined

---

[105] Wood, 'The Limits of Culture?', p. 102. See also John Carter Wood, 'A Change of Perspective: Integrating Evolutionary Psychology into the Historiography of Violence' *British Journal of Criminology*, 51.3 (2011), pp. 479–98.

[106] As Wood points out, there is no inherent contradiction between the variability of male violence and the claim that it is shaped by 'universal, evolved predispositions. Innate aspects of the psyche create a framework within which variability occurs, generating a wide (though not limitless) variety of proximate causes of violence'. Wood, 'The Limits of Culture?', p. 104. See also Hanlon, 'The Decline of Violence in the West'.

[107] Daly and Wilson, *Homicide*, p. 7.

or real) or fear desertion, and parents are less likely to be violent towards their genetic children than towards stepchildren.[108]

Can we apply the insights of evolutionary psychology to the cases of personal and familial violence we have examined? In the case of family violence, there are definite difficulties in doing so. In our sample, there is little evidence that most cases of spousal homicide arose 'out of the husband's jealous, proprietary, violent response to his wife's (real or imagined) infidelity or desertion'.[109] Far more often, the impression emerges that these acts are the products of deep dissatisfaction with lives settled to the point of stagnation and are unconnected to jealousy, on the part of men, of a sexual rival (imagined or real). There is little sense also that those who, in a small number of cases, killed from jealousy were, or were seen to be, representative of a wider view that violence was an understandable or rational response to sexual jealousy, given that forty per cent of those who were motivated by jealousy in our sample were deemed insane.[110]

The evidence from cases involving children also does little to suggest that stepchildren were prominent amongst child victims of homicide. The overwhelming majority of such cases did not involve stepchildren in the pre-Famine and Famine period and this is confirmed in samples from later periods.[111] Evidence from elsewhere also indicates that the overrepresentation of child victims living with parents other than their genetic parents, is by no means inevitable or consistent.[112]

---

[108] See, generally, Daly and Wilson, *Homicide*.

[109] Daly and Wilson, *Homicide*, p. 202.

[110] In her study of the late nineteenth century, Conley also finds that the courts were generally unsympathetic in cases where jealousy was the motive for spousal homicide. The courts were, however, more lenient in cases of violence by husbands against their wives' lovers. See Conley, *Melancholy Accidents*, p. 65.

[111] This finding is based on three samples: (1) In a sample of forty-six cases of child homicide drawn from the 1840s, there were twelve cases in which parents were accused of killing their children and of these only one appears to have involved a stepchild; (2) In a sample of forty-two cases of child homicide drawn from the years 1879 to 1890, only nine cases involved children and their parents and of these only one involved a stepparent, who was the co-accused along with her husband. This case also did not involve an overt act of violence, but arose from 'neglect and ill-treatment'; (3) In a sample of fifteen cases of filicide between 2000 and 2005, there was none in which the accused was identified as a stepparent. These samples are admittedly small and it is not possible to calculate rates to compare the experiences of stepchildren to those of other children, but the fact that one sample includes no cases involving stepparents suggests it would be an error, at this stage, to assume a disproportionate level of violence against stepchildren in modern Ireland. The nineteenth-century samples are based on the *Returns of outrages, 1843–45*, *Returns of outrages, 1847–49* and the *Irish Crime Records*. The evidence on filicide in the present day is gleaned from the *Sunday Tribune*, 24 Apr. 2005.

[112] Hans Temrin, Susanne Buchmayer and Magnus Enquist, 'Step-Parents and Infanticide:

The fact that pregnant women were the subject of lethal violence in some cases in our sample, that close to one in six pregnant women experience domestic abuse, and nearly as many cases of abuse are triggered by pregnancy as jealousy in the present day also does little to support the view that a concern with 'fitness' is the driving force behind violence.[113] Why attack (and kill) the very person who is carrying your child if 'the bearing and rearing of children is the meaning of life and the point of all striving'[114]? It might be argued, of course, that the violence stems from a belief, on the part of the perpetrator, that the child is not his or other causes, such as inability to adequately provide for the child or a desire to control the actions of a sexual partner. To assume that suspicions of infidelity on the part of the perpetrator or fears over an inability to provide influenced behaviour, without any corroborating evidence, is, however, to make assumptions which simply serve to bend the facts to fit the theory. That violence might reflect an unwillingness to provide for the child or anger towards the woman for becoming pregnant raises further questions about the applicability of evolutionary psychology – why further diminish the future prospects of the child by inflicting an act of non-lethal violence on the mother? To argue that the violence stems from a desire to control the partner's behaviour (perhaps

The New Data Contradict Evolutionary Predictions', *Proceedings of the Royal Society: Biological Sciences*, 267 (2000), pp. 943–5. For a critique of the Swedish data, see Martin Daly and Margo Wilson, 'An Assessment of Some Proposed Exceptions to the Phenomenon of Nepotistic Discrimination against Stepchildren', *Annales Zoologici Fennici*, 38 (2001), pp. 287–96. Daly and Wilson demonstrate that although stepchildren are not overrepresented amongst all child victims, there was an overrepresentation in these cases of very young child victims in stepfamilies. For a response, see Johanna Nordlund and Hans Termin, 'Do Characteristics of Parental Child Homicide in Sweden Fit Evolutionary Predictions?', *Ethology*, 113 (2007), pp. 1029–37. Here, the authors concede that the Daly and Wilson model applies in some cases, but also argue that the situation is sufficiently complex to warrant not one model based on evolutionary theory but rather a variety of different approaches. There is also strong evidence that the overrepresentation of stepparents found in some contexts is not replicated in cases where children are adopted, which seems to undermine any invariable link between a non-biological relationship and increased risk of vulnerability to violence. See, for instance, Marinus H. van IJzendoorn, Eveline M. Euser, Peter Prinzie, Femmie Juffer and Marian J. Bakermans-Kranenburg, 'Elevated Risk of Child Maltreatment in Families with Stepparents but not with Adoptive Parents', *Child Maltreatment*, 14.4 (2009), pp. 369–75.

113 Such violence is also by no means unique to Ireland. In the United States in the present day, it is estimated that at least 150,000 pregnant women experience violence every year. See Julie A. Gazmararian, Ruth Petersen, Alison M. Spitz, Mary M. Goodwin, Linda E. Saltzman and James S. Marks, 'Violence and Reproductive Health: Current Knowledge and Future Research Directions', *Maternal and Child Health Journal*, 4.2 (2000), pp. 79–84.

114 Daly and Wilson, *Homicide*, p. 95.

the most plausible explanation) merely gives rise to the question of why the desire to control behaviour supersedes solicitude for the unborn child.

To reduce the broad range of motivations behind many of these cases to sexual jealousy, or to see violence as guided by a desire, rooted in evolutionary processes, to preserve and maintain 'fitness', is to offer too narrow a perspective on the nature of domestic violence. The violent actions of men and women seem to emerge far more from the frustrations and disenchantments of particular married lives and family circumstances which are rooted more in the realm of the social and cultural than in any broader evolutionary process. The continuities over time and the similarities with other countries might then be more often explained by the dull thud of continuing and pervasive ideas of male dominance and superiority rather than the evolved tendency towards sexual jealousy on the part of men or any greater likelihood, rooted in evolution, that step- or adopted children will be more often abused by step- or adoptive parents than genetic parents.

There is evidence, then, in cases of family violence, which contradicts the expectations of evolutionary psychology. It might be argued, of course, that this is to be expected as evolutionary psychology does not predict individual behaviour but rather seeks to identify recurrent regularities in general patterns of behaviour. It would be naïve to expect individual behaviour to be wholly determined by the pursuit of fitness. This, however, merely points to a key problem with evolutionary psychology, namely that it does not give adequate weight to contradictory evidence.

Evolutionary psychology asserts that men are inherently, although admittedly not inevitably, drawn to certain patterns of behaviour, which means that activity that does not fit within this model is seen as irrelevant to or deviant from those inherent characteristics or, alternatively, such behaviour must in some way be related to those inherent or underlying causes. Thus, men attack their pregnant wives because they suspect infidelity and/or doubt paternity or, if the evidence does not directly support this idea, then the behaviour is of a kind which does not necessarily contradict the theory as one cannot expect, in a complex world, that all behaviour will necessarily be adaptive. In this sense, the ostensibly reasonable argument that the pursuit of fitness profoundly influences but does not determine behaviour becomes a means by which all evidence, whether in support of or contradictory to an argument, can be integrated into a broad theoretical framework without impinging on the integrity of the theory. The theory becomes, in certain respects, unfalsifiable. This, of course, leaves us with a slightly trickier question: does this also mean it is wrong?

In the case of family violence, it certainly appears to fall down on the evidence. There is, however, stronger support for evolutionary psychology when it comes to the preponderance of men among the perpetrators of violence and, particularly, to the understanding of violence among unrelated males. The predominance of men as perpetrators of lethal violence across cultures is a profound and incontestable fact. The use of interpersonal violence by men against other men to protect, assert and advance status (however rare or common in a given society) is also a common feature found across many cultures. More broadly, the pursuit of status, however managed, is undoubtedly a key factor in any understanding of human history. Is this behaviour thus rooted in a particular biological orientation shaped by our deep history? Is it shaped by forces which lie beyond the limits of culture?[115] Again the answer to this question must lie in the realm of speculation. The fact that behaviour is found across cultures does not necessarily imply that the behaviour has its roots outside culture. It is unlikely also that historians, at least, can identify or adequately discuss causes which lie beyond the realm of culture – common patterns, moreover, do not necessarily imply common causes. The evidence from the cases of family violence raises sufficient doubts and should also make us wary of asserting that we have found guiding principles for behaviour rooted in a universal mental architecture. In particular, to view the goal of sexual reproduction as the central guiding force underpinning and influencing motives is to offer too narrow a view of human behaviour. It does a disservice to the complexity of that behaviour and, more importantly, is, in some cases at least, not sustained by the available evidence.

It is also highly problematic and, indeed, logically flawed, to argue that theories (such as evolutionary psychology) that are the product of culture and which need to be interpreted within a cultural framework can offer an insight into a realm 'beyond culture' which, in turn, provides the fundamental basis for both exploring and even defining cultural life. Ultimately, evolutionary psychology is a product of culture based on a study of social and cultural practice, claiming access to knowledge beyond culture, to explain culture.

What cannot be doubted, however, is that the roots of male predominance in violence lie not in the recent past, but have their origins deep in human history. It would also be naïve in the extreme to expect such predominance to easily or quietly cease to form a part of social and cultural life in the near future. Its persistence over several centuries in Ireland is but a fragment of a much wider picture, but if there is a biological dimension to this it is one which is not invariably guided by the pursuit of fitness but one which is open to a myriad of different and often complex motivations.

---

[115] Wood, 'The Limits of Culture?'. See also Hanlon, 'The Decline of Violence in the West'.

4

'The tranquillity of a barrel of gun powder': Homicide and land

Disputes over the use, control and occupation of land have been central to explanations of violent conflict in Ireland in the first half of the nineteenth century. The focus of study has very much been on conflicts between and among the various social groups in rural society and the degree to which these were rooted in and accentuated by the demographic pressures and prevailing economic conditions of the period. Cornewall Lewis argues, for instance, that rural unrest in Ireland was primarily rooted in pre-existing tensions in the relationship between landlord and tenant, which were accentuated by the demographic and economic circumstances of the late eighteenth and early nineteenth century with the 'increase of the agricultural population, the want of employment and the consequent desire to get possession of land'.[1] The conflict of interests between landlord and tenant found its clearest expression in the often violent activities of agrarian secret societies which were, in Lewis's view, 'a vast trades' union for the protection of the Irish peasantry' whose chief object was to keep the occupier 'in possession of his land, and in general to regulate the relation of landlord and tenant for the benefit of the latter'.[2]

Landlord/tenant relationships also feature prominently in the historiography. For Beames, the main source of rural conflict in pre-Famine and Famine Ireland was conflict between tenant farmers and landlords over 'the occupation and control of land'.[3] Beames regards such conflicts as arising not so much from pre-existing divisions within the land system, but rather from attempts to change that system.[4] It was, he claims, the activities of 'a particular type of enterprising landlord' and the incursion of the 'pressures of the market' into local society which gave rise to

[1] Lewis, *On Local Disturbances*, p. 48.
[2] Ibid., p. 80.
[3] Beames, 'Rural Conflict', p. 280.
[4] Ibid., p. 269.

violent conflict. The activities of agrarian secret societies were, for Beames, primarily a reaction to the incursion of such market forces.[5] For Joel Mokyr too, the primary cause of economic conflict was the 'difference of interests between landowners and tenants'.[6] He also identifies the roots of this conflict in broader economic changes. In particular, he cites the desire on the part of landowners, post-1815, to consolidate small farms into larger ones in order to reap the greater benefits of pasture farming over the more labour intensive tillage farming which had dominated the rural economy from the late eighteenth century. This shift 'away from tillage' was, according to Mokyr, 'a primary [...] cause of violence and lawlessness' in the thirty years before the Famine.[7] Moreover, 'the depth and persistence' of such conflict was 'uniquely Irish in nineteenth-century Europe'.[8]

Others have offered alternative and more diverse explanations for violent conflict. While acknowledging that conflict could arise between landlord and tenant, some historians have emphasised the extent to which the demographic pressures and economic conditions of the late eighteenth and early nineteenth centuries gave rise primarily to violent conflicts between labourers and tenants. Samuel Clark and J.J. Lee have both claimed that much of the violence in early nineteenth-century Ireland was the product of disputes between labourers and tenant farmers, particularly over access to conacre land.[9] Others have sought to stress the importance of family alignments and individual interests over communal or class consciousness. David Fitzpatrick has emphasised the extent to which rural unrest was a product of conflicts arising from struggles within and between families over land. He stresses the extent to which violence was used to assert both individual and familial interests in opposition both to rival families and rival family members.[10] Andres Eiriksson too has emphasised the often

---

[5] Ibid., p. 280.
[6] Joel Mokyr, *Why Ireland Starved: A Quantitative and Analytical History of Ireland 1800–50* (London: Allen & Unwin, 1983), p. 144.
[7] Ibid., p. 145.
[8] Ibid., p. 144.
[9] See Samuel Clark, *Social Origins of the Irish Land War* and *idem*, 'The Importance of Agrarian Classes: Agrarian Class Structure and Collective Action in Nineteenth-Century Ireland' in *British Journal of Sociology*, 29.1 (1978), pp. 22–40. See also J.J. Lee 'Patterns of Rural Unrest in Nineteenth-Century Ireland: A Preliminary Survey' in L.M. Cullen and François Furet (eds), *Ireland and France, 17th–20th Centuries: Towards a Comparative Study of Rural History* (Paris: Éditions de l'École des Hautes Études en Sciences Sociales, 1980), p. 234. According to Lee, while landlord/tenant conflict was the mainstay of agrarian unrest in the mid to late eighteenth century and in the late nineteenth century, 'the growth of population and the increase in the number of labourers from the late eighteenth century led to increasing farmer/labourer conflict until the Famine.'
[10] Fitzpatrick, 'Class, Family and Rural Unrest'.

self-interested and individual nature of much of the conflict that arose over land in Ireland at this time. For Eiriksson, the struggle for land was not characterised by 'communalism and solidarity' but rather 'individualism and competition'.[11] Thus, rather than reflecting communal norms or class interests relating to land, violence was primarily an expression of individual and familial interests.

The emphasis on violence as an expression of various forms of communal, class, familial or individual conflict has meant that the prevalence and the part that violence actually played in such conflicts has been a secondary consideration. In particular, commentators have not reflected to any great extent on whether interpersonal violence was the primary or dominant means of resolving conflicts over land within and between the various social groups in Irish society at this time. The dominant position and certainly the underlying assumption in much of the historiography is, however, that the use of violence (and the rejection of the law which it seemed to imply) was often central to the regulation and control of land.

For Lewis, when conflict arose, violence was used by agrarian secret societies to assert and impose communal norms of behaviour relating to land and other economic issues. He identified a series of secret society-inspired disturbances in various counties in Ireland in the first thirty-five years of the century. These included the unrest instigated by the Trashers (or Treshers) in areas of the west of the country in 1806–7, disturbances in Tipperary, Waterford, Kilkenny, Limerick, Westmeath, Roscommon and King's Co. in 1811–12, unrest again in Tipperary, King's Co., Westmeath, Limerick and Louth between 1815 and 1818, disturbances in Galway in 1820 and again in Limerick in 1821, as well as the Terry Alt disturbances which emerged in Clare and Limerick in 1830–1 and the unrest in Queen's Co., King's Co. and Co. Kilkenny in the early to mid-1830s.[12] Moreover, when there was an absence of violence it was a consequence of the ubiquity and effectiveness of the threat of violence. Thus, even when these areas of the country were tranquil, it was, Lewis claims, merely 'the *tranquillity of a barrel of gun powder*'.[13] In this sense, violence was an expression of conflict and a means of regulating it and was essential to enforcing communal norms in opposition to the aims of landlords and their agents.

Lewis's perspective on agrarian violence has had a significant influence on the historiography. A number of historians have stressed the degree to

---

[11] Andres Eiriksson, 'Crime and Popular Protest in Co. Clare 1815–52' (PhD thesis, Trinity College Dublin, 1992), p. 360.

[12] Lewis, *On Local Disturbances*, pp. 32–5. For a good overview of these episodes of unrest, see Eiriksson, 'Crime and Popular Protest', pp. 17–21.

[13] Lewis, *On Local Disturbances*, p. 226.

which the mass of the people had to resort to violence to impose their own norms and regulations for the operation of the rural economy. As Gearóid Ó Tuathaigh has argued, 'the social tensions of the economic system could not always be contained and the governing code of regulation was often a violent one'. He points out that the landlord and his employees may have 'enjoyed the backing of the law of the land, but in the violent methods of the secret societies the land-hungry peasantry had a remedy that was more summary and often no less effective'.[14] MacDonagh has claimed that the 'gun and knife, the instruments of maiming, killing and intimidation, were the means of enforcing a particular form of order upon the countryside'. The effectiveness of secret societies, he argues, 'depended on threat and terror, [which] were ruthlessly employed as needed'.[15] According to Beames, lethal violence was used against those who had broken 'the norms of the local peasant community'. It was, he claims, those landlords who evicted tenants and those who took land from evicted tenants who were the most likely victims of rural conflict.[16] Mokyr agrees with Beames that 'most outrages were aimed against landlords, landlord agents, or the incoming tenants replacing those ejected' from their farms.[17] He claims that violence played a prominent part in slowing down and in some cases preventing the consolidation of small farms into larger ones.[18] Charles Townshend, following Lewis, has emphasised the psychological impact of such violence rather than its extent. He points out that while the incidence of violence may not have been high compared to other jurisdictions, violence was used in an exemplary fashion to uphold communal norms relating to land and to enforce an order alternative to that of the state.[19]

Thus, whether the incidence of violence was high or not, it was the threat of violence which was central to economic relationships. In this sense, violence and the threat of violence constituted powerful weapons in the armoury of ordinary people in their attempts to assert their own interests and to exert some control over the rural economy in a time of economic uncertainty. This position has dominated the historiography and has, in many respects, gone unquestioned.[20]

---

[14] M.A.G. Ó Tuathaigh, *Ireland Before the Famine, 1798–1848* (2nd ed., Dublin: Gill & Macmillan, 1990), pp. 134–5.

[15] MacDonagh, *States of Mind*, p. 71.

[16] Beames, 'Rural Conflict', p. 280.

[17] Mokyr, *Why Ireland Starved*, p. 139.

[18] Ibid., p. 132.

[19] Charles Townshend, *Political Violence in Ireland: Government and Resistance since 1848* (Oxford: Clarendon Press, 1983), p. 9.

[20] For a more sceptical view, however, see Ó Gráda, *New Economic History*, pp. 336–7.

Even those who have queried the cohesion and communal nature of violent activity have regarded the use of violence as a significant element in the operation of the rural economy in the pre-Famine period. Clark, for instance, points out that 'for generations rural people in Ireland had used violence to defend their customary rights' and that during the 'pre-famine social and economic crisis, this tradition of popular violence became a desperate struggle to preserve the very means of existence'.[21]

Did violence and the threat of violence, whether in pursuit of individual, familial, class or communal interests, play a central or marginal role in the regulation of the use and occupation of land? This chapter addresses this question by examining the extent, nature and role of lethal violence in land-related disputes. It will be argued that, while significant in certain conditions and locations, violence or the threat of violence was not a central element in the regulation of the use and occupation of land. On the contrary, rural relationships were characterised as much by the avoidance of, than the resort to, interpersonal violence and the threat of violence, while certainly present, played only a marginal role.

I

To what extent did conflict over land give rise to violent activity in Ireland in the first half of the nineteenth century? The periodic outbursts of rural unrest in Ireland in the first half of the nineteenth century have been used to demonstrate the frequency and extent of violent conflict in that period. This approach is evident in Lewis's study where he catalogues the different episodes of rural unrest from the latter half of the eighteenth century to the early decades of the nineteenth. A number of historians have adopted a similar approach. Clark and Donnelly noted that 'every decade between 1760 and 1840 was punctuated by at least one major outbreak of rural discontent' and that during this period 'Irish peasants compiled a record of collective protest probably unequalled anywhere else in Europe'.[22]

Others have queried this approach and warned against exaggerating the extent and prevalence of violent activity arising from rural unrest.[23] The evidence offered in this chapter supports the latter perspective and seeks to demonstrate that disputes over land were by no means a primary or dominant cause of violent conflict in this period and that land-related

---

[21]   Clark, *Social Origins*, p. 70.
[22]   Clark and Donnelly, *Irish Peasants*, pp. 25–6.
[23]   See Ó Gráda, *New Economic History*, p. 332; Fitzpatrick, 'Unrest in Rural Ireland', p. 100; Hoppen, *Elections, Politics and Society*, p. 342; and chapter one of this book.

violence was, outside of certain areas and periods, relatively rare. This will
be based primarily on a study of land-related homicides, but it will also
make use of data on land-related non-lethal violence collected by Eiriksson
in his study of Co. Clare in the pre-Famine period.

How common were land-related homicides?

Table 4.1   The incidence of land-related homicides in pre-Famine and Famine Ireland

	Ireland 1843–5	Ireland 1847–9	Armagh 1835–50	Fermanagh 1811–50	Kilkenny 1835–50	Queen's Co. 1835–50
All reported homicides arising from disputes over land	65	33	10	3	17	8
Percentage of all homicide cases	15.58	12.64	10.98	4	14.91	10.25
Rate per 100,000	0.25	0.37	0.27	0.05	0.6	0.34

Despite the centrality of conflicts over land in many explanations of
violent conflict in Ireland, homicides arising directly from such disputes
constituted a minority of the reported cases in all our samples. It is clear
from Table 4.1 that land was by no means the dominant cause of lethal
violent conflict in Ireland at this time. Disputes over land accounted for
15.58 per cent of all homicides reported, on a national level, between
1843 and 1845 and the rate at which such cases arose was lower than
that for homicides arising from both personal and family disputes.[24]
The proportion of cases fell further during the Famine – accounting
for only 12.64 per cent of cases. The rate at which such cases occurred
did, however, rise somewhat (along with an overall rise in the rate of
homicide), but it was still a good deal lower than the rate for personal
and family disputes.[25]

There was also a high degree of regional variation in the occurrence of
these homicides.

[24]   For a breakdown of the motives surrounding homicides in Ireland at this time, see
Appendix two, Table 7.1.
[25]   For rates of homicide arising from personal and family disputes, see chapters two and
three, above.

Table 4.2 Regional distribution of land-related homicides in pre-Famine and
Famine Ireland (%)

	Connacht	*Leinster*	*Munster*	*Ulster*
Ireland, 1843–5	11	23	55	11
Ireland, 1847–9	12	12	64	12

In the sample of reported homicides in Ireland between 1843 and 1845,
well over half of those related to land occurred in the southern province
of Munster.[26] This regional pattern was very much reinforced during the
Famine, with Munster accounting for close to two-thirds of land-related
cases in our sample.

We must be careful, however, not to exaggerate too much the difference
between Munster, or at least most of it, and the rest of the country. As in
our quantitative analysis in chapter one, much, although admittedly not all,
of the disparity between Munster and the rest of the country is due to the
relatively high number of cases in Co. Tipperary. Discussing the prevalence
of 'agrarian outrages', which were, in the main, offences relating to land,
the Devon Commission reported in 1845 that 'in Tipperary for a long time
past, and in some other counties more recently, there has prevailed a system
of lawless violence, which has led in numerous instances to the perpetration
of cold-blooded murders'.[27] Tipperary was exceptional for the level of
incidents relating to land which occurred within its borders (such cases
accounted for 31.5 per cent of all cases in the county over this three-year
period). The number of land-related cases in Tipperary was also over four
times that of any other county in the country at the time. It accounted for
63.88 per cent of land-related homicides in Munster and 35.38 per cent of
such homicides in the country as a whole.[28] During the Famine, the county
with the highest number of homicide cases relating to land was, once again,
Tipperary – which accounted for 27.27 per cent of all such cases in our

---

[26] In 1841, Munster would have accounted for 29.31 per cent of the population, Leinster
24.14 per cent, Ulster 29.19 per cent and Connacht 17.35 per cent. This clearly indicates
that Munster was overrepresented in our sample while Ulster and, to a lesser extent,
Connacht were underrepresented. The findings from Leinster suggest that the number
of cases in that province was broadly consistent with its share of the population before
the Famine.

[27] *Report from Her Majesty's commissioners of inquiry into the state of the law and practice in
respect to the occupation of land in Ireland*, p. 42, [605], HC 1845, xix, I.

[28] In 1841 Tipperary accounted for 18.17 of the population of Munster and just over five
per cent of the country as a whole. To say that it was overrepresented when it came to
land-related homicides would be somewhat of an understatement.

sample and just over forty per cent of land-related cases in Munster (42.85 per cent). Thus, the extent of land-related homicides in the country as a whole is somewhat distorted and exaggerated by their prevalence in certain areas, in particular Co. Tipperary. In most of the country, land disputes were a relatively minor cause of lethal violence at this time.

This is also reflected in our county-based samples. Disputes over land accounted for just over one in eight cases in Co. Kilkenny, just over one in ten cases in Armagh and Queen's Co. and a little below one in twenty in Fermanagh. The relative rarity of violent disputes over land at this time is also supported, to a large degree, by the evidence given by witnesses from the four counties to the Devon Commission.[29] Eleven witnesses from Co. Kilkenny gave evidence before the Devon Commission on the incidence of agrarian outrages in their localities. Of these, nine claimed that there were very few or none at all.[30] Indeed, one witness, land agent Richard Eaton esq., claimed that his locality was 'in a state of perfect quietness'.[31] The five witnesses from Queen's Co. also attested to the relative rarity of agrarian outrages in their county at the time.[32] The one example cited by the witnesses also focused on a single attack on property rather than acts of violence against the person.[33] Only one witness gave evidence from Co.

[29] These witnesses generally gave evidence relating to their own localities or to localities of which they had some knowledge, rather than the county as a whole.

[30] Of the eleven witnesses from Co. Kilkenny who gave evidence, five were agents, three were farmers, one was a landlord, one was a merchant and the mayor of Kilkenny city and one was the assistant barrister for the county. The other two witnesses did not comment directly on their localities, but one, a landlord, detailed a case of conspiracy to murder him and the other referred to some outrages in a neighbouring area. See *Report from Her Majesty's commissioners of inquiry into the state of the law and practice in respect to the occupation of land in Ireland, minutes of evidence, part i* pp. 98–9, [606], HC 1845, xix, 57 (hereafter cited as Devon Commission, *Minutes of evidence, part i*), and *Report from Her Majesty's commissioners of inquiry into the state of the law and practice in respect to the occupation of land in Ireland, minutes of evidence, part iii*, pp. 377, 379, 384, 388, 391, 394, 408, 415, 445, 732–4, [657], HC 1845, xxi, I, (hereafter cited as Devon Commission, *Minutes of evidence, part iii*).

[31] Devon Commission, *Minutes of evidence, part iii*, p. 379.

[32] Of the five witnesses who gave evidence, two were farmers, two were land agents and one was a Roman Catholic curate. Four of the five witnesses pointed out that there were either 'very few' agrarian outrages or none at all in their localities. The other witness did not comment on the prevalence of agrarian outrages in his locality, but did cite one example of damage to livestock. See Devon Commission, *Minutes of evidence, part iii*, pp. 324–6, 332, 346–50, 588, 621–2.

[33] Of the five witnesses, only two gave an example of a recent outrage. Both referred to the same incident where twenty-nine head of cattle belonging to a land agent, William Hamilton esq., were destroyed. The chief suspect was a disgruntled tenant. See Devon Commission, *Minutes of evidence, part iii*, pp. 349–50.

Fermanagh, and he could only cite one example of an agrarian outrage. This had actually occurred in Co. Tyrone and did not involve an act of interpersonal violence, but rather the burning of a house.[34] The only exception to these generally positive assessments was Co. Armagh, where a number of witnesses referred to individual incidents which had taken place in the county, in particular, the murders of George McFarland, Brian McCresh and Thomas Powell, which all occurred in a particular area in the south of the county in the late 1830s and early 1840s.[35] The extent to which these cases were isolated incidents or reflected wider unrest in the county is, however, unclear. A number of witnesses, in referring to these cases, did not offer any coherent or general assessment of levels of land-related disturbances in their areas. Of the six witnesses who did offer such an assessment, however, four reported that there were few or no cases in their localities.[36] On the whole, the available evidence from our samples suggests that land-related homicides and disturbances were in general relatively rare and were by no means the primary source of violent conflict at this time.

The relative rarity of violent conflict arising from land-related disputes is further emphasised by Eiriksson's data from pre-Famine Co. Clare on crimes arising from disputes over land. Eiriksson's study of Co. Clare reveals that 366 land-related crimes were reported by the police in the county between 1836 and 1845.[37] Thus, in a county with a population of circa 286,000 people in 1841, there was an average of only 36.6 land-related crimes reported every year. This implies that it would have been quite unusual for someone to be the victim of a land-related offence. Indeed, even if this figure were twenty-five times the reported rate and allowing for a generous estimate of three victims per crime, this would still have meant that less than one per cent of the population would have been victims of land-related crimes every year. The number of people who perpetrated crimes relating to land was also low. Eiriksson estimates that an average of 100 people a year participated in crimes arising from disputes over the occupation of

---

34 *Report from Her Majesty's commissioners of inquiry into the state of the law and practice in respect to the occupation of land in Ireland, part ii*, p. 144, [616], HC 1845, xx, I.

35 Each of these cases will be discussed in greater detail below.

36 Of the nine witnesses from Co. Armagh who gave evidence, two were landlords, two were agents, three were clergymen and two were farmers. Three witnesses made no general comment, but referred to particular incidents of a serious nature within their localities. One witness, a Roman Catholic priest, claimed that there had been 'several' outrages in his locality. Another witness claimed that there had been 'some' outrages and, as noted above, four claimed that there had been few or none. Devon Commission, *Minutes of evidence, part i*, pp. 412, 152, 487, 833, 368, 406, 436, 341–4, Devon Commission, *Minutes of evidence, part iii*, pp. 715–17, 855–9, 866–7.

37 Eiriksson, 'Crime and Popular Protest', Tables 4.8 and 4.9, p. 175.

land between 1836 and 1845.[38] This is, to say the least, a tiny proportion
of the population. Even if this figure were again twenty-five times higher
with 2,500 perpetrators every year, it would still amount to less than one
per cent of the total population. This hardly suggests a county that was
ravaged by frequent conflicts over land or a population which was quick to
resort to criminal activity to resolve conflicts over land. This, moreover, was
in a county which Eiriksson describes as 'one of the most disturbed Irish
counties' in this period.[39]

It is also striking that violence against the person played a minimal role.
From a total of 219 cases where the nature of the offence is given, only
thirty-seven cases over a ten-year period involved acts of violence against
the person –16.89 per cent of all cases. The remaining cases consisted of
threatening letters and attacks on property.[40] If this percentage was applied
to the overall total of cases it would mean that there were 61.81 cases of
violent crime relating to land over a ten-year period or an average of 6.18
cases per year (2.16 per 100,000 of the population). By this reckoning, the
overwhelming majority, or 99.99 per cent of the population, would not have
been victims of a land-related violent crime. It is, of course, possible that
these figures underestimate the extent of violent land-related disputes in the
county.[41] Yet, even if the figure were twenty-five times higher it would still
only amount to around 150 cases of land-related violent crime per annum
and assuming three victims per crime, more than 99.95 per cent of the
population would still have remained unscathed by the ravages of violent
land-related crimes every year.

We need to be careful, of course, as much of our data is drawn from the
period after 1835. It may be that land-related violence was more common
before 1835. Certain areas of the country were disturbed by violent conflicts
over land before 1835. Lewis, as noted earlier, identified a number of areas,
mainly in the south and midlands of the country, which were subject to
periods of considerable unrest before this date and there can be little doubt
that there were relatively high levels of violence during, for instance, the
Rockite disturbances of the early 1820s or the Terry Alt unrest of the early
1830s.[42] Such high levels of unrest can also be found before 1835 in two of

38   Ibid., p. 157.
39   Ibid., ii.
40   Ibid., Tables 4.11, 4.13, 4.15, pp. 178, 182, 185.
41   It should be noted that Eiriksson does *not* believe that a high proportion of land-related
     crimes went unreported, claiming that the 'dark figure' for land-related crimes was
     relatively low and that there was no real reluctance to co-operate with the police when
     it came to land-related crime. See Eiriksson, 'Crime and Popular Protest', p. 155.
42   See J.S. Donnelly, Jr, 'Pastorini and Captain Rock: Millenarianism and Sectarianism in
     the Rockite Movement of 1821–4' in Clark and Donnelly, *Irish Peasants*, pp. 102–39; *idem*,

the counties in our sample. A number of the witnesses from Queen's Co. and Co. Kilkenny before the Devon Commission were keen, for instance, to stress that agrarian outrages had been far more common in their localities in the early to mid-1830s.[43]

Yet, the prevalence of such disturbances in Ireland as a whole at this time should not be exaggerated. The extent of unrest in both counties was, as noted in chapter one, quite exceptional at this time. The evidence from the Poor Law Commission also suggests that the majority of counties in Ireland did not experience such levels of disturbance or unrest with most areas reporting that they were not affected by serious unrest in the period between 1815 and 1835.[44] Moreover, the unrest in counties such as Kilkenny and Queen's Co. was by no means a constant or ubiquitous phenomenon, but rather was restricted to certain periods and to certain locations within the counties.[45]

In many areas of the country, there was probably little difference between the period before and after 1835 and, in some areas, the rate of land-related violence may have actually increased post-1835. The evidence from Fermanagh, the one county for which we have reasonably reliable data for the early decades of the century, indicates that the incidence of land-related homicide was not much higher before 1835 than afterwards – of the three reported cases between 1811 and 1850, two occurred before 1835 and one after. There is insufficient evidence from the other northern county, Armagh, to reach firm conclusions about the extent of land-related homicides before 1835. Given, however, that rates of homicide were generally low in the county, that witnesses before the Poor Law Commission reported

'The Terry Alt Movement, 1829–31' in *History Ireland*, 2.4 (Winter, 1994), pp. 30–5; *idem, Captain Rock: The Irish Agrarian Rebellion of 1821–1824* (Madison, WI: The University of Wisconsin Press, 2009). See also David Ryan, '"Ribbonism" and Agrarian Violence in County Galway, 1819–20', *Journal of the Galway Archaeological and Historical Society*, 52 (2000), pp. 120–34. For an example of unrest in the north east, see Terence Dooley, *The Murders at Wildgoose Lodge: Agrarian Crime and Punishment in Pre-Famine Ireland* (Dublin: Four Courts Press, 2007).

43 For Queen's Co., see Devon Commission, *Minutes of evidence, part iii*, pp. 332, 346–7, 588; for Co. Kilkenny, see Devon Commission, *Minutes of evidence, part i*, p. 98; Devon Commission, *Minutes of evidence, part iii*, pp. 379, 394, 408. See also generally the *Select committee on the state of Ireland, minutes of evidence 1831–32* and Gibbons, 'Captain Rock'.

44 See Ó Gráda, *New Economic History*, p. 332 and chapter one, above.

45 See Poor Law Commission, *appendix e* and *Poor inquiry (Ireland): appendix (F.) containing baronial examinations relative to con acre, quarter or score ground, small tenantry, consolidation of farms and dislodged tenantry, emigration, landlord and tenant, nature and state of agriculture, taxation, roads, observations on the nature and state of agriculture and supplement containing answers to questions 23 to 35 circulated by the commissioners*, H.C. 1836 (38), xxiii, 1 (hereafter cited as Poor Law Commission, *appendix f*).

that the county was not much disturbed between 1815 and 1835, and that the county was praised by the judiciary at this time for its peaceful state, there is little to suggest that the county experienced higher rates of land-related homicides or disturbances before 1835 than after. If anything, land-related disputes actually increased in the county after 1835.[46]

There were also other areas of the country where levels of land-related violence increased after 1835. According to Eiriksson, land-related crimes occurred with 'increasing frequency' in Clare from the early 1830s to the mid-1840s, and reached their height in the early to mid-1840s. This, he points out, was 'caused by falling agricultural prices after 1839 and by a population pressure which intensified the competition for land'.[47] It is unlikely, therefore, that the data in our study, although drawn primarily from the period after 1835, underestimates the extent of land-related homicides in the first half of the nineteenth century – it may even exaggerate it!

Overall, outside of certain areas, in particular Co. Tipperary and in other areas at certain times throughout the first half of the century, the extent of lethal violence and non-lethal violence arising from disputes over land was kept within definite limits and was by no means the primary or dominant cause of violent conflict in the country.

II

Who was involved in these cases? It is often difficult to identify precisely the social standing of those involved in homicide cases arising from disputes over land. It does appear, however, that landlords, their employees and officials were very much in the minority. It was certainly unusual for the gentry to be suspected of a homicide arising from a land dispute. There were only two land-related cases in which someone drawn from the ranks of the landed gentry was suspected of homicide in our county-based sample.[48] There were also no cases in our county-based sample in which the employees of a landlord (agents, stewards, drivers, herds etc.) or officials such as bailiffs and process servers were accused of homicide arising from land-related disputes. Although the national samples provide very little information on

---

[46] The impression is that land-related offences increased in Co. Armagh in the late 1830s and in the 1840s. See generally, Select committee on outrages, *Minutes of evidence 1852*.
[47] Eiriksson, 'Crime and Popular Protest', p. 354.
[48] In Kilkenny in December 1849, John Walker Watson, a twenty-year-old who acted as the land agent to his father, Captain Watson, shot Michael Butler following a dispute over the non-payment of rent. Watson was later convicted of manslaughter at the Kilkenny summer assizes of 1850 (*Kilkenny Journal*, 24 and 27 Jul. 1850). The other case involved the killing of Mr John Woolsey in Co. Armagh in 1850 by members of his own family.

the accused, there is also little to suggest that landlords, their employees or officials were often held responsible for acts of lethal violence.[49]

Table 4.3   The victims of land-related homicides in pre-Famine and Famine Ireland

Victims	Ireland 1843–5	Ireland 1847–9	Armagh 1835–50	Fermanagh 1811–50	Kilkenny 1835–50	Queen's Co. 1835–50
Landlords and gentlemen	8	3	1	0	2	1
Agents and other employees	7	3	3	0	2	0
Officials	1	4	0	0	1	0
Other victims	49	23	6	3	12	7
Totals	65	33	10	3	17	8

The gentry, their servants and officials were more likely to be on the receiving end of violent activity, but even here they still constituted but a minority of victims. In our national sample from before the Famine, 1843–5, there were eight land-related homicides in which landlords were victims – accounting for 12.30 per cent of such homicides. Those directly employed by landlords also appear to have constituted a minority of victims – accounting for only seven cases in our sample or 10.76 per cent of victims. This means that landlords and their employees accounted for over one in five victims in land-related homicide cases (23.07 per cent).

According to our sample from the Famine years the vulnerability of landlords declined somewhat. There were three cases accounting for 9.09 per cent of victims in land-related cases. There were also three cases where the employee of a landlord was killed. If these cases are added to those involving landlords then the proportion of cases during the Famine in which landlords and their employees were victims is just under one in five (18.18 per cent) of all land-related cases. Similar findings are evident from our county-based samples. From a total of thirty-eight cases recorded in the four counties there were nine in which the gentry or their employees were victims – accounting for under one in every four cases (23.68 per cent of

[49]   There is only one case in the sample in which a landlord seems to have been held responsible for a homicide. In Cork in February 1848, Owen Sullivan 'died of injuries he received while his house, (in which he lay ill) was being levelled by his landlord' who was attempting to evict both the deceased and his family. See Returns of outrages, 1847–49.

victims).[50] Lethal attacks on officials were also relatively rare: only one case was reported between 1843 and 1845. The vulnerability of this group seems, however, to have increased during the Famine when there were four cases in which officials were killed. There was also one case, during the Famine, in our county-based sample in which a bailiff was killed.

In total, cases involving landlords, their employees and officials accounted for just under one in four victims in land-related cases on a national level, between 1843 and 1845, and less than one in three land-related cases in the sample from the Famine years. Our county-based samples also reveal that these three groups accounted for just over one in four victims. When viewed in the context of the overall number of homicides, the relative rarity of the use of lethal violence against landlords, their employees and officials arising from land disputes becomes even more apparent. Such cases accounted for just over two per cent of all reported cases in the four counties and between three and four per cent of cases on a national level both between 1843 and 1845 and in our sample from the Famine years – confirming that disputes over the use and occupation of land between landlord and tenant were by no means a major cause and were very far from being the dominant cause of lethal violence in Ireland at this time.[51] It should be borne in mind, of course, that landlords accounted for a fraction of the male population of Ireland at this time.[52] It would seem, therefore, that while land-related homicides were

---

[50] These findings are similar to those from later in the century, suggesting that when homicides relating to land did occur, landlords and their employees were no more likely to be victims in land-related homicides than they were later in the century. According to Vaughan, 'if all homicides of landlords and their servants are combined they accounted for only 24 per cent of agrarian homicides' (W.E. Vaughan, *Landlords and Tenants in Mid-Victorian Ireland* (Oxford: Clarendon Press, 1994), p. 143).

[51] There was also considerable regional variation in the susceptibility of the gentry and their employees in these cases. They seem, for instance, to have been particularly vulnerable in Co. Tipperary, which was the epicentre of agrarian unrest at this time. Of the eight land-related homicides involving the gentry in our national sample between 1843 and 1845, five occurred in Co. Tipperary while the other three cases arose in neighbouring King's Co., Queen's Co. and Co. Clare. A similar pattern is evident in our sample from the Famine years, where of the three recorded cases in which landlords were killed, one occurred in Co. Tipperary, one in King's Co. and one in Co. Clare. Such regional variations are also evident, although less clear-cut, in cases involving landlords' employees. Before the Famine, two of the seven cases involving employees of a landlord occurred in Tipperary while the other five cases arose in Kilkenny, Cork, Leitrim, Roscommon and Cavan. In our Famine sample, a driver was killed in Co. Mayo and two agents were killed in Co. Clare.

[52] It has been estimated by Clark that there were circa 10,000 landlords in Ireland at this time in a country with a population of just over eight million in the early 1840s. They constituted, therefore, a tiny but highly significant element of the population. See Clark, *Social Origins*, pp. 33–4.

relatively rare, when they did occur members of the gentry were particularly vulnerable. This probably reflects, as W.E. Vaughan has pointed out in the context of the post-Famine period, the fact that 'landlords formed the pivot for a large number of transactions' relating to land and, therefore, had the potential to come into conflict with a larger number of people than those lower down the social scale.[53] While this is certainly a valid point, it also, to some extent, serves to emphasise the potential problems with a system which placed one individual at the heart of so many transactions and allowed him considerable scope and power over the lives of large numbers of ordinary people without being accountable to them in any direct or clearly defined way. In such circumstances, it is hardly surprising that in our sample, aside from one case from Co. Armagh where it was suspected that a gentleman was shot by members of his family, those accused of carrying out or sponsoring such killings were generally from lower down the social scale – being tenants, dispossessed tenants or, on occasion, those who supported tenants in their disputes with the landlord or his agent. Of course, whether an alternative system would have produced more or even less violence must remain a matter of (counter-factual) speculation.

Although landlords and their employees may have been disproportionately vulnerable to lethal attacks in land disputes, the majority of protagonists in our samples were still drawn from the mass of the people. It is difficult, however, to ascertain the precise social origin of those involved. The national samples provide little information on the status of the victims or perpetrators outside of the three groups already discussed. The information in our county-based samples is somewhat more reliable. This indicates that there were no cases in our county-based samples involving disputes between labourers and farmers and, contrary to Clark and Lee's position, there is little evidence that conflict between tenants and labourers over conacre land was a leading cause of violent activity in this period.[54] Rather, the majority

---

53   Vaughan, *Landlords and Tenants*, p. 161.
54   This view is certainly consistent with the evidence given before the Poor Law Commission in 1835 on the operation of the conacre system in the preceding decades. Of the twenty-seven areas visited by the commissioners, only four reported conflict arising from conacre. Two of these were in Co. Limerick and one was in Co. Clare and referred to disturbances in both counties in the early 1830s which had since ceased. The other area was in Co. Waterford, where there was some reported disturbance in 1810 but since then the system had operated without giving rise to disturbances. The remaining twenty-three areas (or eight-five per cent) reported that the conacre system was not a cause of conflict in their areas and that the threat of violence was not a factor in the regulation of conacre land. A number of witnesses, indeed, referred to the mutual confidence which existed between tenants and labourers in the operation of the system and that it was generally mutually beneficial to both groups. See Poor Law Commission, *appendix f*, pp. 1–34.

of cases in our county-based samples involved disputes between farmers[55] or, in some cases, among farming families.[56]

III

In what circumstances did people resort to lethal violence to deal with land-related disputes?

Table 4.4   The circumstances of land-related homicides in pre-Famine and Famine Ireland

	Ireland 1843–5	Ireland 1847–9	Armagh 1835–50	Fermanagh 1811–50	Kilkenny 1835–50	Queen's Co. 1835–50
Eviction	30	15	6	2	9	5
Possession of disputed of land	15	6	3	1	2	1
Access to land	7	0	0	0	1	1
Rent	5	11	0	0	4	0
Other disputes	8	1	1	0	1	1
Totals	65	33	10	3	17	8

The single most common cause of these land-related homicides in both of the national samples as well as the four counties was eviction.[57] The

---

55   In Armagh, the protagonists in five of the ten cases of land-related homicide between 1835 and 1850 were drawn exclusively from the farming class. In seven of the eight cases arising from land in Queen's Co. the protagonists were farmers, while in nine of the seventeen cases in Co. Kilkenny the protagonists were drawn exclusively from the farming class. Finally, in all three cases of land-related homicide in Fermanagh the protagonists were members of the farming class. The lower proportion of cases involving disputes among farmers in Armagh and Kilkenny is due to the somewhat higher proportion of cases in those counties involving the gentry and officials. The term 'farmer' is, of course, a very general description, encompassing those with relatively small properties and those with substantial tracts of land. Unfortunately, it is difficult, aside from occasional hints, to ascertain the extent of the property held by the protagonists in our cases.

56   There were three cases of intra-family homicide in both Kilkenny and Armagh and one case in both Queen's Co. and Fermanagh. On a national level, there were also ten cases between 1843 and 1845 in which homicides over land arose within the family, while our sample from the Famine shows six homicides over land involving members of the same family.

57   A similar situation is evident in Co. Clare, where 'evictions seem to have been at the root of almost 70% of land-motivated crimes' between 1836 and 1845 (Eiriksson, 'Crime and Popular Protest', p. 175). Evictions, although constituting a lower proportion of cases,

prospects for dispossessed tenants in pre-Famine and Famine Ireland were, to say the least, bleak. Many faced the often less than appealing prospect of emigration while dispossessed tenants who stayed in their localities often had to contend with a definite lowering of economic and social status within their communities and, at a more basic level, a threat to their actual survival. Mokyr has shown that a sizeable proportion of evicted tenants in pre-Famine Ireland probably faced very difficult circumstances indeed. Many were reduced to poverty, became landless labourers or, in some instances, received other holdings in bogs.[58] In these circumstances, violence may have been seen by the perpetrators as a useful and perhaps even a necessary means of protecting and defending their economic and social position as well as a means of punishing those who either caused or tried to benefit from their dispossession.

In some cases the act of violence was directed against landlords and their employees. Between 1843 and 1845, six of the eight cases in which a landlord was the victim of a land-related homicide arose from the eviction of a tenant or tenants. In Co. Clare in November 1844, Mr Arthur Gloster, a landlord, was waylaid and shot as he was travelling along a road. He had recently served some tenants with notices to quit and was reputed to be a 'harsh and severe landlord'.[59] There was also one case where a landlord's employee was killed. This was in Co. Tipperary in October 1844 when Thomas Shanahan, acting in his capacity as a land agent, took over an acre of land from which a tenant had been evicted.[60] Two of the three cases in which a landlord was killed in our sample from the Famine years also arose from the eviction of tenants. William Roe esq. J.P. was 'shot dead on the high road near his residence' in Co. Tipperary in October 1847 after evicting a tenant from his holding.[61] One of the two cases involving a landlord's agent also arose from an eviction. In Co. Clare in October 1847, the 'under-agent' Patrick Frawley, who had served an ejectment process, died of injuries inflicted by a party of men.[62]

Six of the nine cases involving landlords or their employees in our county-based samples also arose from an attempt to evict a tenant or tenants. Three such cases arose in Co. Kilkenny. In 1835, Lundy Foote esq., a

also seem to have been the leading cause of agrarian outrages in the post-Famine period. According to Vaughan, they were the single largest cause of 'agrarian outrages' between 1848 and 1880 – accounting for thirty per cent of such cases. See Vaughan, *Landlords and Tenants*, p. 158.

58 Mokyr, *Why Ireland Starved*, p. 134.
59 *Returns of outrages, 1843–45*. See also Eiriksson, 'Crime and Popular Protest', p. 177.
60 *Returns of outrages, 1843–45*. See also Beames 'Rural Conflict', p. 273.
61 *Returns of outrages, 1847–49*. See also Beames 'Rural Conflict', pp. 271–2.
62 *Returns of outrages, 1847–49*.

seventy-one-year-old gentleman and landowner, was murdered following the eviction of a tenant, James Murphy, from a farm of seven or eight acres.[63] In November 1842, Mr John Mortimer, described as a gentleman, died from the effects of a beating which he received for planning to 'dispossess some persons of land'.[64] One month later in December 1842, Mr Richard Murphy, a land steward on the estate of a General Kearney, was shot. He had come into conflict with a number of people from whom he had 'threatened to take land' and had also had a disagreement with a number of workmen on the estate.[65]

The other three cases in our county samples occurred in Co. Armagh. In April 1850, Mr John Woolsey, a gentleman 'of rather opulent circumstances', was shot in his own home. He had served ejectment notices on some members of his family and both his brother and his brother-in-law were suspected of carrying out the deed.[66] In the other two cases, prominent employees of landlords were killed following an attempt or at least a perceived attempt to remove a large number of tenants from their properties. In January 1841, a Mr Thomas Powell, who was employed as an 'agriculturalist' on the estate of William Charles Quinn esq., was shot dead. In this case, Quinn had served notices to quit on a number of his tenants on land he wished to take under his own control and promised to move them to other lands on the estate.[67] He had also charged Powell with making a number of changes or 'improvements' to the estate. It soon became clear, however, that there was resistance to any planned moves. This was because other tenants had been removed from these lands and they clearly felt that there would be inherent dangers and difficulties involved in taking over such property.[68] Nor were the changes undertaken by Powell well received on the estate. The cumulative effect of these factors seems to have led to the attack on Powell. Following

---

63   *Kilkenny Journal*, 21 Mar. 1835. It should be noted that Foote was not the head landlord, but rather was leasing the land from which he evicted Murphy.

64   NAI, outrage papers, Kilkenny, 1843/7341.

65   See Devon Commission, *Minutes of evidence, part iii*, p. 388; *Returns of outrages, 1843–45*.

66   *Armagh Guardian*, 25 Mar. 1850.

67   In doing so, he was determined that 'none were to be left without a residence and some land' and thought that the 'the majority of [tenants] would be infinitely more comfortable on reduced farms, with constant employment on the land' (Devon Commission, *Minutes of evidence, part i*, p. 343).

68   Devon Commission, *Minutes of evidence, part i*, p. 368. Rev. Michael Lennon, parish priest of Upper Creggan, had heard that Quinn had 'offered to give some places to some of the tenants in another neighbourhood, a good distance off but at the place he was sending them to, the people there thought they had a claim upon [Quinn] for being put away; and the people therefore, did not like to go, thinking they would not be well received'.

the murder, 'all the improvements [the landlord] was making' on the estate were halted.[69]

The threat of mass eviction also seems to have led to the killing in May 1850 of Robert Lindsey Mauleverer. This incident was, according to the *Newry Examiner*, 'as atrocious a murder as ever was committed in blood-stained Tipperary itself'.[70] Mauleverer, a magistrate in Co. Londonderry, was acting as a land agent for 'many properties', including some in Co. Armagh at the time.[71] There were tensions between Mauleverer and the tenantry on an estate in Crossmaglen.[72] Matters seem to have come to a head upon the death of a middleman on the estate who held a lease on some property, which, according to the coroner, 'extended over a townland'.[73] His death allowed Mauleverer the opportunity to serve ejectments on an estimated 200 tenants on the estate. The exact reason for serving these eviction notices is somewhat obscure however. According to the deceased's brother, Billing Mauleverer, the '200 ejectments and notices were almost all a mere legal form, essentially necessary on the death of a middleman, so as to bring the occupying tenants under their new and then immediate landlord, but without the least idea of proceeding to eviction'.[74] If this was the case it certainly does not seem to have been made clear either to the tenants or indeed the county coroner who conducted the inquest into the death. The coroner believed that those tenants against whom the ejectments were issued faced the dilemma as to 'whether one life should be sacrificed, or hundreds should be exposed to slow but certain death by starvation'.[75] The ejectments clearly generated a good deal of fear and ill-feeling towards Mauleverer among the tenantry and, soon after, he was beaten to death with a stone on a public road between Crossmaglen and

---

[69] Select committee on outrages, *Minutes of evidence 1852*, p. 160.

[70] Cited in *Times*, 27 May 1850. A brief account of this murder is also to be found in W.S. Trench, *Realities of Irish Life* (London: Longmans, Green, and Co., 1868), p. 187.

[71] Two years previous to his murder he was appointed as a 'receiver, under the Court of Chancery, for his brother-in-law, the Rev. Mr. Hamilton, who owned one third of an estate near Crossmaglen'. Over the course of the ensuing two-year period leading up to his murder he also became an agent for the remaining two-thirds of the estate, which were owned by a Mr Stanus Tipping and a Mr Jones, respectively. See *Times*, 29 May 1850.

[72] The manner in which Mauleverer conducted himself on the estate was, the *Newry Telegraph* noted, 'not altogether calculated to make him a favourite with the peasantry' (cited in *Times*, 29 May 1850). He was said to be active in seizing property for rent and rent arrears from tenants on the estate.

[73] *Times*, 30 May 1850.

[74] *Times*, 5 Jun. 1850.

[75] *Times*, 30 May 1850.

Culloville.[76] Following this killing, 'a large arrear of rent was struck off the property' and an 'acreable reduction was made to the tenants'.[77]

However, neither the landlord nor his agent was the target in the majority of cases; more usually, it was those who took over land from which a tenant had been evicted. Thomas Bowers esq., who described himself as a 'private country gentleman', claimed before the Devon Commission in 1844 that agrarian outrages occurred 'principally where tenants were ejected from their holdings for non-payment of rent, and replaced by new tenants. That seldom or never failed to produce agrarian disturbances, bloodshed, and battering, and everything that was bad'.[78] In a number of cases the victims were caretakers who took temporary control of the property on behalf of the landowner. In Queen's Co., in 1846, Joseph Cantrell was shot because he acted as a caretaker on some lands 'which defaulting tenants had been dispossessed of and for so doing he made himself objectionable'.[79] In Co. Kilkenny in 1850, a caretaker named Richard Kineally and his son were also killed in a dispute with an evicted tenant.[80] In other cases, the parties involved were related. In Monaghan in April 1847, James Henry died from wounds inflicted by his son, also James, in 'revenge for having served [James the younger] and his brother with ejectment processes'.[81]

In the majority of cases, however, the victim was another (unrelated) farmer who came to take over the land on a permanent basis. In Queen's Co. in April 1841, Edward Byrne was shot dead while working in a field on the family farm. Byrne's family 'had lately got possession of the lands from which a family [...] had been recently evicted'.[82] In Fermanagh in April 1845, William Craig, a young boy, 'was shot through the body in his father's house, when preparing for bed'. In this case, 'the deceased's father, the intended victim, had taken land from which a tenant had been ejected'.[83] In Kilkenny in 1844, Mathew Brennan, a 'young man under 30 years of age' was killed after he 'got possession of a farm from Lord Frankfort's agents [... which was] previously held by two brothers, Thomas and Patrick Purcil'. According to the police reports, the brothers who were evicted 'were greatly

---

76   *Times*, 30 May 1850.

77   Select committee on outrages, *Minutes of evidence 1852*, p. 36. For another example of a case involving the murder of a land agent in south Ulster around this time, see Michael McMahon, *The Murder of Thomas Douglas Bateson, Co. Monaghan, 1851* (Dublin: Four Courts Press, 2006).

78   Devon Commission, *Minutes of evidence, part i*, p. 408.

79   NAI, outrage papers, Queen's Co., 1846/2941.

80   *Kilkenny Journal*, 19 Mar. 1851.

81   *Returns of outrages, 1847–49*.

82   NAI, outrage papers, Queen's Co., 1841/5455.

83   *Returns of outrages, 1843–45*.

incensed at the time, for being dispossessed, and swore that they would have revenge'.[84] In such cases, the act of violence was clearly used to punish those who tried to benefit from evictions.

Such acts were also a means of discouraging others from taking land. In Armagh in 1837, George McFarland was murdered in an attack on the house of his son-in-law. The authorities believed that the murder was 'one of those connected with a system which has been unfortunately acted on in this county for many years back, with the view of deterring persons from taking lands'.[85] It was reported that John Johnston, the victim's son-in-law, had

> become an object of particular dislike in the neighbourhood first because he had become tenant to land out of which a family named Garvey had been ejected three years ago and second because as bailiff of his landlord (Mr Armstrong) he had in such capacity taken up possession of other farms.[86]

There could also be some local support for the perpetrators of such acts. In the abovementioned Brennan case, it was reported that

> there [was] a strong feeling amongst the Tenantry on Lord Frankfort's property to screen the perpetrators of this Murder there being many of them who expect to be dispossessed for non-payment of Rent, and who think that this murder may be the means of deterring the agent from ejecting them.[87]

Lethal violence could also be effective in these cases. Before the trial for the murder of McFarland, the crown solicitor remarked that the properties from which Armstrong, the landlord, had ejected tenants remained 'unlet [sic]; and [that] in the present state of the country [were] likely to be so, unless [let] to their original holders'.[88] Johnston himself gave up the land immediately after his father-in-law had been murdered or as John Garvey, the original tenant who had been evicted from the land, put it, he 'never

---

[84] NAI, outrage papers, Kilkenny, 1844/17419.
[85] NAI, outrage papers, Armagh, 1838/5717. This case arose from a series of disagreements over a ten-year period between the landlord of the property, Mr William Armstrong esq., and a family called Garvey who had been evicted from the land that Johnston held. See the Devon Commission, *Minutes of evidence, part iii*, pp. 854–9 and Devon Commission, *Minutes of evidence, part i*, p. 369 and pp. 407–8.
[86] NAI, outrage papers, Armagh, 1837/141.
[87] NAI, outrage papers, Kilkenny, 1844/17419.
[88] NAI, outrage papers, Armagh, 1837/141.

cropped [the land] afterwards'.[89] The landlord, Armstrong, also admitted that after this incident he was 'obliged to keep [the land] in [his] own hands'.[90]

The use of violence as a means of defending property and position as well as punishing those who tried to benefit from the difficulties of others is also evident in those cases arising from the payment or, more accurately, the non-payment of rent. These cases almost invariably arose from the attempt to distrain goods for the non-payment of rent and in the overwhelming majority of cases it was the person who attempted to distrain the goods who was the victim.[91] Landowners, to whom such rent was due, could be among the targets. There is one such case in our samples. In Co. Tipperary in November 1845, Patrick Clarke esq. was 'shot through the head in his demesne at South-hill'. He had 'distrained the corn of some of his tenants for rent'.[92]

It was the employees of landlords, however, who were more likely to be victims.[93] In Co. Kilkenny in November 1845, James Costello was shot dead after his father, a 'rent warner', had seized two cows belonging to a herd named Martin Broderick. The cows were seized for rent due to the landlord and, shortly after, an auction was held in which 'the deceased was the auctioneer, & his father bid for the cattle'.[94] Punishment could also be meted out to ordinary people who tried to benefit from or participated in the distraint of goods.[95] In Antrim in November 1848, John Fletcher was killed by an assailant who was endeavouring 'to prevent the removal of corn purchased by the deceased, and which had been seized for rent'.[96]

The use of violence to defend or assert the position of the perpetrators is also evident in disputes over rights of access to land. These cases could

[89]   Devon Commission, *Minutes of evidence, part i*, p. 408. Indeed, by 1844 it seems there were little or no tenants on the estate. See Devon Commission, *Minutes of evidence, part i*, p. 833.

[90]   Devon Commission, *Minutes of evidence, part iii*, p. 858.

[91]   In seventeen of the nineteen cases arising from the distraint of goods for non-payment of rent in our samples the perpetrator was trying to resist the distraint of his goods. There were, therefore, only two cases where the person resisting the distraint was killed.

[92]   *Returns of outrages, 1843–45*. See also the case in Co. Kilkenny in 1833 when Joseph Leonard esq. was waylaid and killed by a tenant whose cattle had been distrained for the non-payment for rent. This killing took place on the day before the cattle was due to be put up for sale by Leonard (*Strabane Morning Post*, 26 Mar. 1833).

[93]   There are ten such cases in our samples.

[94]   Costello had also reported Broderick to the landlord for having too much livestock on the land, which led to the seizure of the cattle for rent. NAI, outrage papers, Kilkenny, 1845/23977.

[95]   There were six such cases in our samples.

[96]   *Returns of outrages, 1847–49*.

be the product of long-standing tensions within certain localities. In Queen's Co. in April 1835, William Carter, a Protestant farmer who had held around eighty acres of mountainous farmland under Lord Maryborough near Mountrath for nearly thirty years, was killed in a dispute over the enclosure of land. According to counsel for the crown in this case, the enclosure 'created an animosity towards Carter among his poorer neighbours, who had been in the habit of trespassing and feeding their cattle on this land'.[97]

Other cases were rooted in disagreements over the possession of disputed land. These could emerge among neighbours who had competing claims to areas of land. In Armagh in 1839, Brian McCresh was 'attacked by a party, and stabbed to the heart', as he made his way home from a fair in Crossmaglen. This case arose from a disputed division of land made by the landlord between the farm of McCresh's family and that of his neighbour.[98] Some were the product of longer-term differences over land. In Mayo in June 1845, Hugh Caffrey died from wounds he received in a fight over 'disputed land held by [his] father for 20 years'.[99]

A number of cases over disputed land also arose within families. Christopher James, a barrister and landholder from Co. Kilkenny, claimed before the Devon Commission in 1844 that agrarian outrages arose not only in cases of ejectment and distress but also 'generally from family disputes among the farmers themselves'. He pointed out that when one member of the family seized family land it could sometimes 'set the others at defiance'.[100] Some cases arose within the immediate family.[101] There was one case between a father and a son. In Monaghan in October 1848, Pat Conley was found murdered in his home. His son was suspected of carrying out the murder following a disagreement with his father over 'the possession of disputed land'.[102] The majority of these disputes within the immediate

---

[97] *Leinster Express*, 18 Jul. 1835.

[98] In this case, according to a local Presbyterian minister, the victim's landlord 'wished to make straight mearings upon his farm, and, in doing so, it appeared that a piece of land was cut off from the land of a neighbour of McCresh's and given to him'. Those who originally held the land were angry at this development and threatened McCresh, but he refused to give up the land as he did not 'like to refuse the offer of his landlord'. Devon Commission, *Minutes of evidence, part i*, p. 406. See also the case of Patrick Marmion, a surveyor who was apparently killed in Co. Armagh in May 1838 (NAI, outrage papers, Armagh, 1838/52). An account of this incident is also available in Kevin McMahon and Thomas McKeown, 'Agrarian Disturbances around Crossmaglen, 1835–1855, Part II' in *Seanchas Ard Mhaca*, 10.1 (1980–81), pp. 149–75.

[99] *Returns of outrages, 1843–45*.

[100] Devon Commission, *Minutes of evidence, part iii*, p. 392.

[101] Of the combined total of fifteen cases of homicide arising from disputed claims to land that arose within families, five arose within the immediate family.

[102] *Returns of outrages, 1847–49*.

family occurred among brothers.[103] In such circumstances, violence could be used to defend or uphold a claim to family land. In 1835 in Co. Kilkenny, farmer Thomas Hanrahan was attacked by a man with a 'two-handed wattle' while riding his horse from his stable to a field. Hanrahan was going to 'surrender' some land to a local landlord, Robert St George esq. J.P., but his brothers objected to this, claiming 'a partnership in the land'. The police believed that the brothers, 'fellows of bad character, caused the beating which ended in his death' in order to prevent him surrendering the land.[104] In November 1837, James Cody, a 'wealthy and respectable farmer', was shot by his own brother. The police reported that 'any cause of feeling between them originated in a disputed division of property'.[105]

Homicides arising among relations from outside the immediate family over disputed land were somewhat more common, many involving disputes among in-laws.[106] In Tyrone in 1845, Peter Kelly died after being severely beaten by his son-in-law in a dispute over land.[107] Women whose husbands had passed away were also vulnerable to attacks from in-laws. In 1840, Fanny Fox, a widow with three children, was found with wounds to her head in a well close to her house in Armagh. She died three days later. John McElinden, the deceased's brother, claimed that when Fanny's husband, Bernard Fox, died, in September of the previous year, he 'left her a house and [a] small piece of land <u>rent free</u> which [Bernard's] brothers wanted to make her pay rent for, and threatened if she did not they would make her be sorry for it'.[108] Disputes of this kind were accentuated by fear that an in-law might re-marry and thereby remove the land from family control. In January 1836, the *Enniskillen Chronicle and Erne Packet* reported the killing of 'a poor widow named Quirke, who resided on a small farm near Kilmoyler', Co. Tipperary. The widow was 'about to be married for the third time, contrary to the wishes of the relatives of her former husband, to one of whom, in the event of her remaining single at her demise, the farm would revert'.[109]

Violence could also be used to gain possession of property which had not been held previously by the perpetrators or to which they had no direct claim. There were two such cases within our sample and both arose within

[103] Four of the five cases within the immediate family involved disputes between brothers.
[104] NAI, outrage papers, Kilkenny, 1835/57.
[105] Ibid., 1837/169.
[106] Of the combined total of fifteen cases of intra-family homicide arising from land-related disputes in our samples, ten involved relations from outside the immediate family.
[107] *Returns of outrages, 1843–45*.
[108] NAI, outrage papers, Armagh, 1840/10249.
[109] *Enniskillen Chronicle and Erne Packet*, 28 Jan. 1836.

the family. In Armagh in October 1845, James Patten, who was clearly somewhat unpopular with his family, 'was poisoned either by his wife, father or brother'. The police believed that this incident stemmed from a desire on the part of the accused 'to possess themselves of deceased's property'.[110]

Some incidents also reveal that violence could be used in an effort to advance the position of the perpetrators by altering, in a very definite way, the management of a particular estate. For instance, George White, the last life in a lease, was shot in Queen's Co. in 1842 and died three months later in 1843. White, described in the police report as a 'reduced gentleman', was the victim of a conspiracy among the tenants on the Moate estate who were 'anxious to become directly connected with the head landlord who is represented as an indulgent kind man'.[111]

But the use of lethal violence to gain possession of land to which the perpetrator had no previous claim or to regulate the management of an estate was relatively rare, and in the majority of cases it was the use of violence to defend, and to punish those who threatened position, rather than to necessarily advance position which underpinned the actions of the perpetrators. There are, for instance, very few cases in our sample where lethal violence was employed to gain control over land for which the perpetrator had no previous claim. Nor does it seem that there was any attempt to regulate the occupation of land in a more positive manner by, for instance, using violence or even the threat of violence to keep rents at a low level.[112] In sum, lethal violence arising from land disputes was, in the main, reactive rather than acquisitive.

IV

What were the characteristics of these acts? A striking difference between land-related homicides and those examined in previous chapters is the often high level of premeditation and lethal intent involved in many of the cases. Premeditation is most obvious in those cases where specific threats were made to the intended target. Patrick Donovan was ejected from his land in June 1840 for non-payment of rent, and for alienating two of the acres by sale. The land was taken over by a Thomas Rigby, who held the land for eight months before his murder. In the spring of 1841, Donovan went into a field where Rigby and his family were planting potatoes and picked up

---

[110] *Returns of outrages, 1843–45.*

[111] NAI, outrage papers, Queen's Co., 1842/18665.

[112] This is consistent with Mokyr's findings and with evidence given before the Poor Law Commission in 1835. See Mokyr, *Why Ireland Starved*, pp. 125–8; Poor Law Commission, *appendix f.*

some earth from the ground and declared 'I know that I will be burning in hell, where brimstone will be going through my nose and my belly, and I don't care as much for my soul as for this piece of clay, and the first of you I catch on my ground I will settle him.' In May of the same year he carried out his threat. On the morning of the incident, Donovan passed by where Rigby was working and shook his head at him. This was interpreted by Rigby's son as a clear threat. Later that day, Donovan and another man called John Walsh (who later turned approver) returned to the farm and followed Rigby to the field where he was working and beat him to death. Rigby's family found him later badly beaten and, before passing away, he identified Donovan as his assailant.[113]

The issuing of a threat in the form of a letter was not uncommon.[114] Before he was killed in Co. Armagh in 1841, Mr Thomas Powell received a threatening letter that informed him that both he and the landlord, Quinn, were 'to be shot [at] the first opportunity' and that a 'collection' had been made and that 'the man that will kill [him would] go to America'.[115] The threat could be well known in the locality. In the case of the murder of Robert Lindsay Mauleverer in 1850, the *Newry Telegraph* believed that it was 'perfectly well known throughout the country about Crossmaglen, that a conspiracy had been formed to shoot him' and pointed out that another gentleman residing in the neighbourhood had written to Mauleverer 'about two months [beforehand], informing him of the intention to murder him'.[116]

In some cases, the homicide could be the culmination of previous acts of intimidation and lesser forms of violence against the eventual victim and his family. While discussing the prosecution of violent crimes perpetrated by secret societies, Maxwell Hamilton esq., crown solicitor for the north-east circuit, claimed before the 1852 select committee on outrages that such cases 'generally commence in a beating of the party whom they want to deter from doing some particular thing, and if he does not mind that warning, he is generally murdered'.[117] A clear, although probably extreme, example of such intimidation can be found in the case of William Carter, who was murdered in Queen's Co. in April 1835. Fifteen years earlier Carter's eldest son was so severely beaten that he was reduced to a 'state of idiocy [...] from the effects of a fracture on his skull, inflicted by a party who attacked him, and

---

[113] *Kilkenny Moderator*, 11 Aug. 1841. See also NAI, CRF/1841/Donovan/53.

[114] For a discussion of the role of threatening letters in pre-Famine Ireland, see S.R. Gibbons, *Captain Rock, Night Errant: The Threatening Letters of Pre-Famine Ireland, 1801–45* (Dublin: Four Courts Press, 2004), esp. pp. 9–44.

[115] Devon Commission, *Minutes of evidence, part i*, p. 342.

[116] Cited in *Times*, 29 May 1850.

[117] Select committee on outrages, *Minutes of evidence 1852*, p. 145.

left him for dead in the fields'. He was subsequently committed to a lunatic asylum. Twelve months previous to his father's murder, another son, James Carter, was beaten on his father's land and 'was insensible for some time after'. Of the remaining six children, four (two sons and two daughters) emigrated to America a few years before the murder 'in consequence of the disturbed state of the country, and their lives having been several times threatened'. Indeed, the *Leinster Express* claimed that there was 'scarcely a member of the family that [did] not exhibit the marks of wounds received in the various attacks made on them from time to time'.[118]

In a number of cases groups of men ganged together to carry out the act of violence. This again would imply a degree of planning and organisation. This is evident in the case of Thomas Powell, when a group of seven or eight men called to his house on the evening of 2 January 1841 and forced their way in. They confronted Powell in his parlour and then dragged him outside before shooting him through the heart.[119] In the case of the murder of George McFarland, on the night of 27 December in Co. Armagh, a party of between twenty and thirty men came to the house of McFarland's son-in-law who had taken over the land of evicted tenants. McFarland was, according to the report, 'battered in a most frightful manner with a hatchet the perpetrator found on the premises'.[120]

The use of assassins in some cases also indicates a high degree of premeditation and planning. Maxwell Hamilton, the crown solicitor for the north-east circuit, claimed that there was a system in place whereby assassins could be hired through a secret society, known as the Ribbonmen. He believed that

> if a man thinks he is aggrieved, and wishes to have a person either murdered or beaten, he goes to the parish master of the Ribbon society, and he says he wishes to have a particular thing done; he names the sum of money which is to be given for it; and the business of the parish master is to appoint the persons who are to perpetrate the outrage.[121]

There is little evidence of such a high level of organisation in the cases in our sample, but there is some evidence for the use of assassins. In Co. Kilkenny in 1846, James Fennell was shot while returning from a fair at 10.30 at night while travelling on a car with his son and a servant woman.

[118] *Leinster Express*, 11 Apr. and 18 Jul. 1835.
[119] See *Belfast Newsletter*, 18 Mar. 1841.
[120] NAI, outrage papers, Armagh, 1837/144.
[121] Select committee on outrages, *Minutes of evidence 1852*, p. 145.

The officer reporting the case believed that an assassin had been hired by Fennell's brother-in-law and remarked, rather ruefully, that 'when strangers can be hired to commit murder no man's life is secure.'[122] The police later identified this stranger as a man called Michael Nolan, who was described as a 'man steeped in crime, and known better in the Queen's Co. as Mick the devil, than by his name of Nolan'.[123]

Table 4.5   Means employed in land-related homicides in pre-Famine and Famine Ireland[124]

	Shot	*Blunt instrument*	*Sharp instrument*	*Beating*	*Other*
Ireland, 1843–5	21	12	3	14	2
Ireland, 1847–9	12	1	1	10	2
County-based samples	11	12	5	3	3

There can be little doubt either of the lethal intent in many of these cases. The gun, as the table above indicates, was often the favoured weapon. In Queen's Co. in March 1846,

> three man came to the house of the Widow Cantrill [...] and on the widow's son Joseph Cantrill hearing their dog bark and opening the door, one of said party of three men discharged a loaded pistol and lodged the contents in the body of the said Joseph Cantrill upon which said three men then ran away.[125]

There can also be little doubt of lethal intent in those cases where the victim was attacked by a group. At the trial for the murder of William Carter, Doctor Smith testified that he 'counted *nineteen* distinct puncture wounds on the body [of the deceased], such as a bayonet might give'. He also identified an 'extensive fracture on the back of his head, and four transverse wounds close and parallel to each other, on the side and lower part of the neck, apparently inflicted by a blunt hatchet'.[126]

---

[122] NAI, outrage papers, Kilkenny, 1846/18559 and 18655.

[123] NAI, outrage papers, Kilkenny, 1850/372.

[124] This table is based on those cases where the weapon employed could be clearly identified.

[125] NAI, outrage papers, Queen's Co., 1846/2941.

[126] *Leinster Express*, 18 Jul. 1835. See also the account of the murder of Thomas Douglas Bateson in Co. Monaghan in 1851 in McMahon, *The Murder of Thomas Douglas Bateson*, pp. 13–17.

V

What part did violence play in disputes over land? There is some evidence to support the dominant view within the historiography that violence and the threat of violence was central to the regulation of the occupation of land. This is most obvious in the use of violence as a means of preventing evictions and punishing those who attempted to benefit from evictions. Lethal violence was clearly resorted to by dispossessed farmers as both a punishment for those who took over their land and as a warning to others who may have been tempted to do so. It could also be utilised where a sizeable number of people were threatened with eviction by a landlord. In such circumstances, lethal violence could clearly be used to protect and defend the economic and social position of the perpetrators and those in their communities. Such violence could also be carried out, at times, with the support or at least acquiescence of a sizeable proportion of the local community. The clear premeditation and often obvious lethal intent, which was certainly a good deal more clear-cut in land-related cases than in other cases examined in this study, also seems to reflect a wider view that such violence could, in certain circumstances, be legitimate. In the baronies of Maryborough East and West, the Poor Law Commissioners reported in 1835 that

> *John Barker*, occupier of seven acres, and all the small farmers and labourers, stated that the committal of outrages [arising from eviction] was certainly sanctioned by the mass of the agricultural working people, and that it was adopted as the only means of protecting themselves from the tyranny of their landlords.[127]

These cases may, therefore, reflect and be an expression of a widespread and deeply ingrained view that a tenant should not be removed from his or her land and replaced by another without consent and/or due compensation and, more importantly, that violence was a legitimate way of dealing with such issues. We have also seen in a number of cases that lethal violence could also be very effective in discouraging people from taking over land from which others had been evicted and in inhibiting landlords from making changes in the administration of their estates that were seen as inimical to the interests of the tenants.

It may be, therefore, that the relatively low incidence of land-related homicides can be attributed to the effectiveness of the threat of violence as

---

[127] Poor Law Commission, *appendix f*, p. 56.

landlords, afraid to evict, and farmers, afraid to take over land, bowed to the threat of popular retribution. In this view, the low incidence of lethal violence arising from disputes over land can be largely explained with reference to the periodic resort to violence and also to the effectiveness of the threat of violence as a means of imposing communal norms relating to land. It may indeed have been, as Lewis has argued, the 'tranquillity of a barrel of gun powder'.

This is by no means an implausible theory, but is ultimately an unconvincing one. To begin, not all these cases had communal support or sanction or were related to wider communal or even class struggles. It is clear, as Eiriksson and Fitzpatrick have argued, that some disputes over land were rooted more in the immediate interests and desires of the individual or the family concerned rather than stemming from any clear or direct sense of communal or even class solidarity. Some cases in our sample were certainly isolated incidents arising from disputes among and between individual families which neither garnered widespread popular support nor reflected widespread agrarian unrest. Following the murder of Edward Byrne in Queen's Co. in April 1841, the resident magistrate investigating the incident reported that 'the neighbourhood in which this unfortunate event has taken place is altogether free of any general agrarian crime' and it was felt the case was restricted to a dispute between two families.[128] Those cases that arose within families also reflect the desires and preoccupations of individuals more than any clear sense of communal solidarity.[129]

Moreover, not all victims of land-related homicide were necessarily objects of popular hostility. At the funeral of Lundy Foote esq. in Co. Kilkenny in 1835, 'the tenantry upon the estate attended the funeral in a body and insisted upon bearing their lamented landlord's remains to the grave – a distance of some miles from where he resided'.[130] The burial of Joseph Leonard esq., killed in Co. Kilkenny in 1833, was 'attended to the grave by a numerous assemblage of all classes' in Waterford city. It was also noted that

the vessels in the river had their colours half-mast high, the windows

---

[128] NAI, outrage papers, Queen's Co., 1841/5457. Edmond Smithwick esq., a merchant from Co. Kilkenny, also informed the Devon Commission that there were 'only two outrages connected with land in twelve months, but they were private outrages, and not connected with any mass of the people'. He also pointed out that no prisoner was awaiting trial from his locality and that 'under all circumstances the Kilkenny people are extremely well conducted' (Devon Commission, *Minutes of evidence, part iii*, p. 377).

[129] Huggins reaches similar conclusions relating to family disputes over land in his study of pre-Famine Co. Roscommon, See Huggins, *Social Conflict in Pre-Famine Ireland*, p. 119.

[130] *Strabane Morning Post*, 13 Jan. 1835.

of the greater part of the shops were closed and every desire was evinced by the citizens to pay respect to the memory of the deceased, and mark their deep detestation of the sanguinary act by which society has been deprived of a valuable member.[131]

This would suggest real limits to both communal support and sympathy for land-related homicides and that communal sanction and support was by no means a necessary pre-condition for violent activity.

Another and, perhaps, more compelling critique of the above position is the fact that violence or the threat of violence was simply not wholly effective. This is evident even in cases of eviction where there could clearly be a fundamental threat to the livelihood of those who were or were about to be dispossessed. The evidence from the Famine years indicates, for instance, that, despite widespread and large-scale evictions, it was exceedingly rare for landlords or their agents to fall victim to acts of violence, let alone acts of lethal violence. Considering that there were, even by a conservative estimate, tens of thousands of evictions and hundreds of thousands people evicted in this period, there were only a relatively small number of acts of lethal violence against landlords or those who took over land.[132] As Donnelly has noted, there was 'remarkably little resistance and still less shooting' in response to evictions during the Famine.[133] Eiriksson also points out that 'no serious unrest occurred as a consequence of the large scale evictions executed [from] 1847 onwards' in Co. Clare, a county which suffered more than most from the impact of evictions at this time.[134] In such circumstances,

---

[131] Ibid., 26 Mar. 1833.

[132] There is a considerable degree of uncertainty surrounding the number of evictions carried out during the Famine. As O'Neill has pointed out, the 'number of Famine evictions will remain a matter of approximation rather than accurate recording' (T.P. O'Neill, 'Famine Evictions' in Carla King (ed.), *Famine, Land and Culture in Ireland* (Dublin: University College Dublin Press, 2000), p. 51). Vaughan estimates that there were around 70,000 evictions of families in Ireland between 1846 and 1853 – assuming an average of five people per family, this would imply that circa 350,000 people were evicted between 1846 and 1853. See Vaughan, *Landlords and Tenants*, p. 24. Donnelly has argued that this figure probably underestimates the actual level of evictions as it 'deals only with formal evictions and makes no allowance for the extraordinary number of informal evictions and involuntary surrenders which [...] also marked these years, and it probably underestimates even the formal evictions of 1846–48' (J.S. Donnelly, Jr, *The Great Irish Potato Famine* (paperback ed., Stroud: Sutton Publishing, 2002), p. 27). O'Neill has also suggested that Vaughan's figures underestimate the extent of evictions at this time – arguing, instead, that the number of those evicted was probably closer to 600,000 between 1846 and 1854. See O'Neill, 'Famine Evictions', p. 48.

[133] Donnelly, *The Great Irish Potato Famine*, p. 139.

[134] Eiriksson, 'Crime and Popular Protest', p. 355. See also Tom Yager, 'Mass Eviction in the

the threat of violence was clearly not very effective in discouraging some landlords from attempting evictions, and in some cases on a large scale.

There is also evidence to indicate that this situation was not simply due to the extraordinary conditions created during the Famine, but rather was an extenuation of the patterns which existed beforehand. There were certainly large-scale clearances of tenants on individual estates in the years preceding the Famine.[135] Ó Gráda has also claimed that 'evictions were frequent before the Famine' with 'tens of thousands of people evicted annually in the late 1830s and early 1840s'.[136] Between 1839 and 1843, there were over 25,000 civil bill ejectment cases with over 71,000 defendants brought before the Assistant Barrister's court alone. Decrees were issued in 16,864 or just over sixty-five per cent of these cases – an average of 3,371 per annum.[137] Assuming an average of 2.84 defendants per decree,[138] this would mean that there were 9,574 families or, assuming an average of five people per family, 47,870 people evicted annually between 1839 and 1843.

We need, of course, to be careful as there are considerable difficulties with these figures. In a number of cases, landowners and their agents may simply have used the threat of eviction as a tactic in managing their estates. For example, an ejectment could be resorted to in order to encourage a defaulting tenant to pay his rent. If the rent was paid, the tenant could maintain his position on the land and the decree would not be carried through to eviction. Even where an eviction was carried out, the tenants could later be readmitted to their holdings – this occurred in an estimated twenty per cent of cases.[139] It may be, then, that the figures above exaggerate the real level of eviction. Yet, even if only fifty per cent of the 16,864 decrees issued actually led to permanent evictions of families it would still indicate a considerable number of evictions. There would still have been an average of 1,686

Mullet Peninsula during and after the Great Famine', *Irish Economic and Social History*, 23 (1996), pp. 24–44. Yager, while offering a compelling account of mass eviction on the peninsula, does not cite evidence of violent resistance to the process.

[135] For a number of examples, see O'Neill, 'Famine Evictions', p. 29.

[136] Ó Gráda *New Economic History*, p. 122 n. 27.

[137] *Appendix to minutes of evidence taken before Her Majesty's commissioners of inquiry into the state of the law and practice in respect to the occupation of land in Ireland, part iv*, appendix 104, pp. 303–19, [672], H.C. 1845, xxii, I.

[138] This figure is based on the average number of defendants per case as indicated in the available figures for the period 1839–43. Large numbers of tenants, however, could be affected by a small number of decrees. O'Neill, for instance, cites an example from Co. Kerry where 715 families were evicted on the basis of thirty-nine decrees between March 1847 and February 1848. See O'Neill, 'Famine Evictions', p. 41.

[139] For an analysis of the use of eviction as a means of estate management, see Vaughan, *Landlords and Tenants*, pp. 29–34. The estimate of the rate of readmission to holdings is based on the figures provided in Vaughan, *Landlords and Tenants*, appendix one.

decrees executed per annum and, assuming an average of 2.84 defendants per decree, this would mean that over 4,700 families or 23,500 people were evicted annually between 1839 and 1843, or nearly 120,000 people over a five-year period.[140] This, of course, is a relatively small proportion of the population and may or may not have been near the total which landlords may have wished to evict, but it certainly suggests that landowners were not wholly inhibited from carrying out their intentions by violence or the threat of violence.[141] This, moreover, does not include those cases brought before the higher courts or where a landlord managed to remove tenants without resorting to the courts.[142] The above figures indicate, therefore, that the effectiveness of the threat of violence was, at the very least, limited in preventing the removal of tenants from their holdings.

The lack of violent resistance to eviction is also largely confirmed by the evidence given to the Poor Law Commission. Of the twenty-seven areas visited by the Commission in 1835, in eighteen or two-thirds of the areas it was reported that there was no violent resistance to evictions.[143] In the barony of Omagh in Co. Tyrone, it was reported that although there were 'plenty of ejectments every sessions', there were very few reported cases of violent resistance and the people of the area, as far as the commissioners could ascertain, did 'not generally resist ejection'.[144] The commissioners also reported that in the barony of Lower Fews, Co. Armagh, there was 'no connexion direct or indirect in this neighbourhood, between crime and the taking of land [...] or other charges affecting land' and that there was 'no such thing as Whiteboyism, or intimidation, or combination among

[140] The estimate of fifty per cent may reflect actual practice. Barnaby Scott, esq., a solicitor based in Kilkenny, informed the Devon Commission in 1844 that he had brought 'a great number of ejectments [before the Assistant Barrister's court] for different landlords', but he did not think that 'one-half of the ejectements' were 'ever executed' (Devon Commission, *Minutes of evidence, part iii*, p. 361).

[141] It should be noted also that, as Vaughan has demonstrated in the context of the post-Famine era, a low eviction rate does not necessarily imply that landlords were discouraged by the threat of violence from carrying out evictions. There could be more 'prosaic obstacles' to carrying out evictions. See Vaughan, *Landlords and Tenants*, pp. 34–9. These might include the protection afforded by the law to tenants, the bad publicity which might be attached to larger-scale evictions and the fact that evictions could prove costly for landlords in terms of legal fees and costs.

[142] As one witness from Kilkenny before the 1835 Poor Law Commission pointed out, 'it would not be easy, perhaps not possible, to learn the number of persons ejected within a given time, as it has not always been necessary to resort to legal means to procure a surrender of the lands' (Poor Law Commission, *appendix f*, p. 90).

[143] Ibid., pp. 80–132.

[144] Ibid., p. 132. For a similar pattern of non-resistance to eviction in the county during the years of the Famine, see O'Neill, *Famine Evictions*, p. 41.

the peasantry'.[145] In Co. Cavan, according to a local parish priest, 'ejected tenants entertain no active animosity against those who take their farms.'[146]

Moreover, even in counties with reputations for unrest, the threat of violence was by no means ever present. In 1835, it was agreed by a number of the witnesses before the Poor Law Commission in Queen's Co. that the ejectment of tenants in order to consolidate farms in the baronies of Maryborough East and West was, in previous years, prevented by 'the fear of outrage', but that this was no longer the case. They also pointed out that 'the peasantry sometimes resist ejection by legal process, but never by violence' and while 'two or three years' beforehand those who took over land were 'frequently threatened' this 'practice [had] now ceased'.[147] Even at times of high disturbance in a county, by no means all areas felt the full impact of agrarian unrest. While admitting that threats and violence had been resorted to by ejected tenants in other parts of county, the witnesses from the barony of Portnahinch in Queen's Co. stated that 'the ejected tenantry have never in this barony resorted to threats or violence' against those who took over consolidated farms.[148] In the barony of Coshlea in Co. Limerick, it was reported that tenants resisted eviction by legal means as they have a 'very great dislike to leave their holding, but they have not here in any case resisted by violence'.[149] In the parish of Corcomroe, Co. Clare, it was also reported that 'the peasantry [did] not generally resist ejection'.[150] We must, of course, always be careful when dealing with such evidence as witnesses may have been keen to present a good impression of their local area for the commissioners (in itself, perhaps, a significant act) and may, therefore, have downplayed the extent of resistance in their areas. Yet, there can also be little doubt but that much of this evidence is consistent with the available statistical data.

This does not mean, of course, that violence was wholly negligible or that the threat of violence had no effect at all. It is evident from our study that violence could emerge in particular circumstances. It could arise where existing practices and positions on an estate were threatened by innovation on the part of a landlord or his agent. Indeed, what is most striking about the cases in our sample is that the landlord or his agent had recently come to take control of the estate and attempted to make changes in its organisation.[151]

[145] Poor Law Commission, *appendix f*, p. 72.
[146] Ibid., p. 126.
[147] Ibid., p. 102.
[148] Ibid., p. 104.
[149] Ibid., p. 117.
[150] Ibid., p. 109. See also Eiriksson, 'Crime and Popular Protest', p. 179.
[151] Beames has, as noted earlier, identified a similar pattern in Co. Tipperary at this time.

This indicates that it was primarily where traditional or customary patterns on an estate were broken by someone who had come from outside that lethal violence against landlords and their employees was resorted to. This was rare, however, and it is probable that tenants did not invariably respond to such changes by resorting to violence. It is probable also that most landlords operated within the bounds of expected, if not always accepted, behaviour when dealing with their tenants.

Donnelly has demonstrated that, in pre-Famine Cork, care was taken by landlords when evicting tenants. This could involve assisting evicted tenants to emigrate, the provision of compensation for those who were dispossessed and the demonstration of a degree of sensitivity, on the part of the landlord, in the use and occupation of the land after eviction.[152] Similar care was taken by some in the counties in our sample. Mr John Roberts, a farmer holding land in Queen's Co. under Sir Charles Coote, explained to the Devon Commission how he had carried out the consolidation of a farm upon which sixteen or seventeen tenants had held land. He pointed out that he had 'got rid of them by degrees' and that he 'did not get rid of them for ten years altogether'. In order to remove the tenants he had to forgive them their rent and let them keep 'their crops and their houses'. In the case of one man, he had to pay 'upwards of £40 to get rid of him, and *any feeling there might be against me*'.[153] According to William Hamilton esq., a land agent in Queen's Co., the removal of tenants from an estate had to be done 'with much care and tenderness, and with every possible attention to the feelings of the persons to be removed'. Moreover, while there might be a threat of violence from a minority of tenants, if evictions were handled with a degree of care the 'majority of the persons affected acquiesce in their necessity and are often benefited by them'.[154] The threat of violence, where it existed at all, was not so much successful in imposing communal norms in opposition to the aims of the landowner, but may have been useful in tempering the aims of those who had control over land. In this sense, the threat of violence may have reduced the severity of the impact of a landowner's intentions rather than thwarting their achievement.

It is hard to see this as the triumph of the threat of violence or the victory of communal norms over the interests of landlords. This is especially so if we consider the prospects of those who were dispossessed (even with compensation). A permanent eviction from land generally involved a drop

---

See Beames, 'Rural Conflict', p. 280.

[152] J.S. Donnelly, *The Land and People of Nineteenth-Century Cork* (London: Routledge, 1975), pp. 54–9.

[153] Devon Commission, *Minutes of evidence, part iii*, pp. 325–6 [my italics].

[154] Ibid., p. 344.

not only in living standards but also in social position and status. In such circumstances, it hardly seems surprising that some would resort to violence or even lethal violence to assert or defend their position. What is striking, however, is that in many and probably the overwhelming majority of cases they did not do so, often deciding to accept limited compensation and a lowering of economic and social position instead. In such circumstances, it seems that the actions of tenants were characterised more by the avoidance of, rather than the resort to or threat of, violence.

Of course, not all acts of land-related homicide were rooted in disputes arising from evictions or were directly related to wider disputes arising from the relationship of landlord and tenant. Violence could emerge, as we have seen, where individuals and/or families came into conflict over a wide variety of land-related issues. Such activity, however, was exceptional and there is little to suggest that serious acts of violence were a central or primary means of defending, asserting or advancing claims over land on the part of individuals or families. As we saw earlier in the chapter, both lethal *and* non-lethal violence arising from disputes over land were, outside of certain areas and periods, rare and atypical, the overwhelming majority of the population neither participating in nor being the victims of such violence. Moreover, even when violence, or at least lethal violence, was resorted to, it was largely defensive and was rarely used to simply advance or improve the position of the perpetrators beyond the economic and social position they already held.

On the whole, violence in pursuit of individual, familial, class or communal interests, played a limited and, indeed, marginal role in the regulation of the use and occupation of land in pre-Famine and Famine Ireland. The rarity of land-related lethal and non-lethal violence was not a reflection of the effectiveness of the threat of violence in imposing communal norms or, as Lewis puts it, 'the tranquillity of the barrel of gun powder', or, indeed, due to an absence of conflict between the various social groups in Irish society. Rather, it was rooted in the ability of ordinary people to deal with conflicts which arose among themselves and with their landlords without resorting to serious acts of violence. Thus, although violence could, at times and in certain places, come to play a prominent role, there was also considerable effort made, on all sides, to ensure that it did not do so.

A more wide-ranging study of the role of land-related violence and the regulation of land occupation is needed. In particular, a more in-depth study of dispute or conflict resolution over land, on a local level, is required as well as a more sustained and comprehensive examination of non-lethal violence arising from land disputes. This chapter has, however, demonstrated that while particular incidents or episodes of rural unrest should not be ignored or lightly dismissed, nor should they be seen as wholly representative of rural relationships and, in particular, the role of violence within such relationships. The cataloguing of violent conflicts over land, whether communal, familial or individual, can do much to highlight the sources of conflict and fissures in Irish society. It can also serve, however, to obscure or draw attention away from the willingness and ability of all groups in Irish society to keep conflicts within certain bounds and limits, to the benefit of some and the detriment of others. This does not mean that conflict between and among these groups did not exist, but rather that the resort to violence to deal with conflicts over land was generally limited and controlled within communities.

5

'The madness of party':
Homicide and sectarianism

*Such is [...] the madness of party that Mohammedans
and Jews are not more adverse to each other, nor actuated
by a more persecuting spirit than the opposing parties in
this country.*[1]

The first half of the nineteenth century, following the Act of Union,[2] is
often seen as a time of increased and increasing sectarian tensions in
Ireland.[3] This rise in sectarian feeling was both reflected in and extenuated
by a variety of different developments. To begin with, there was the legacy
of the political upheavals of the 1790s, culminating in the 1798 Rebellion.
Despite the avowed anti-sectarianism of many of those involved, the 1790s
witnessed an upsurge in sectarian animosity and violence which left Irish
society 'more bitterly polarized than before'. It also contributed, in the
longer term, to a 'legacy of militant Catholic nationalism and Protestant
loyalism' in the country.[4] The latter being most clearly expressed in the form

---

[1] Mr McCartney, K.C., in stating the case at a trial for murder at the Armagh spring
   assizes of 1824. See *Belfast Newsletter*, 16 Mar. 1824.

[2] See *An act for the union of Great Britain and Ireland* (39 & 40 Geo. III c. 67); *An act for
   the union of Great Britain and Ireland* (40 Geo. 3 c. 38 [Ire.]).

[3] According to Thomas Bartlett, 'sectarian feeling in Ireland remained at a high level,
   indeed, almost certainly increased in the post-Union period' (Thomas Bartlett, *The
   Fall and Rise of the Irish Nation: The Catholic Question, 1690–1830* (Dublin: Gill and
   Macmillan, 1992), p. 273).

[4] Marianne Elliott, 'Religious Polarization and Sectarianism in the Ulster Rebellion'
   in Thomas Bartlett, David Dickson, Dáire Keogh and Kevin Whelan (eds), *1798: A
   Bicentenary Perspective* (Dublin: Four Courts Press, 2003), p. 279. There are a number
   of different perspectives and considerable debate on the role and nature of sectarianism

of the Orange Order, an oath-bound society dedicated to the maintenance of Protestant ascendancy in Ireland, and the former finding expression through organisations such as the Defenders and, later, the Ribbonmen.[5]

The issue of Catholic emancipation also came increasingly to dominate the political agenda. Although the distinct possibility or even expectation of Catholic emancipation had been raised before the Act of Union, it was thwarted in the early decades of the nineteenth century and was only granted under a considerable degree of popular and political pressure in 1829.[6] In the intervening period there was an often acrimonious campaign for emancipation. In particular, the highlighting of Catholic grievances by the Catholic Committee during the first two decades of the century and, perhaps more importantly, the emergence in the 1820s of popular Catholic nationalism as a significant organised force in Irish political life, in the shape of the Catholic Association, served to emphasise sectarian divisions.[7]

---

in the 1798 rebellion. See, among others, Tom Dunne, 'Popular Ballads, Revolutionary Rhetoric and Politicization' in David Dickson and Hugh Gough (eds), *Ireland and the French Revolution* (Dublin: Irish Academic Press, 1990), pp. 139–55; Tom Dunne, *Rebellions: Memoir, Memory and 1798* (Dublin: Lilliput Press, 2004); Kevin Whelan, *The Tree of Liberty: Radicalism, Catholicism and the Construction of Irish Identity, 1760–1830* (Cork: Cork University Press, 1996); J.S. Donnelly, Jr, 'Sectarianism in 1798 and in Catholic Nationalist Memory' in Laurence Geary (ed.), *Rebellion and Remembrance in Modern Ireland* (Dublin: Four Courts Press, 2001), pp. 15–37.

5   For an account of the role of the Orange Order in the 1790s, see Hereward Senior, *Orangeism in Ireland and Britain, 1790–1836* (London: Routledge and Kegan Paul, 1966); D.W. Miller, 'The Origins of the Orange Order in Co. Armagh' in A.J. Hughes and William Nolan (eds), *Armagh: History and Society: Interdisciplinary Essays on the History of an Irish County* (Dublin: Geography Publications, 2001), pp. 583–605; James Wilson, 'Orangeism in 1798' in Bartlett et al., *1798*, pp. 345–62. For the first half of the nineteenth century, see Senior, *Orangeism in Ireland*. For a more general account of the Orange Order, see Kevin Haddick-Flynn, *Orangeism: The Making of a Tradition* (Dublin: Wolfhound Press, 1999). On the Defenders see, among others, Thomas Bartlett, 'Select Documents 38: Defenders and Defenderism in 1795' in *Irish Historical Studies*, 24.95 (May 1985), pp. 373–94; L.M. Cullen, 'The Political Structure of the Defenders' in Dickson and Gough (eds), *Ireland and the French Revolution*, pp. 117–38. On the Ribbonmen, see J.J. Lee, 'Ribbonmen' in T.D. Williams, (ed.), *Secret Societies in Ireland* (Dublin: Gill & Macmillan, 1973), pp. 26–35; Tom Garvin, 'Defenders, Ribbonmen and Others: Underground Political Networks in Pre-Famine Ireland' in *Past & Present*, 96 (1982), pp. 133–55, and Jennifer Kelly, 'A Study of Ribbonism in Co. Leitrim in 1841' in Joost Augusteijn, Mary Ann Lyons and Deirdre McMahon (eds), *Irish History: A Research Yearbook No. 2* (Dublin: Four Courts Press, 2003), pp. 32–42.

6   *An act for the relief of His Majesty's Roman Catholic subjects* (10 Geo. 4, c. 7).

7   For an account of the background to the introduction of the act, see, among others, Brian Jenkins, *Era of Emancipation: British Government of Ireland 1812–1830* (Kingston and Montreal: McGill-Queen's University Press, 1988); S.J. Connolly, 'Mass Politics and Sectarian Conflict' in W.E. Vaughan (ed.), *Ireland under the Union, I. 1801–70* (Oxford:

The 1820s, therefore, witnessed, as Connolly puts it, a 'sharp resurgence of sectarian hostility, affecting all levels of Irish society'.[8]

Some of the activities undertaken at this time by the major church bodies in Ireland, Anglican, Catholic and Presbyterian, also seem to have increased tensions between the Catholic and Protestant communions. The renewed vigour, enthusiasm and organisational discipline of both the Catholic Church and the Church of Ireland served to heighten the tension between them. The proselytising activities of some members of the Church of Ireland and the consequent reaction of the Catholic Church also seem to have been a significant contributory factor in the rise of sectarian animosity.[9] The turn away by sizeable sections of the Presbyterian community in these decades from the more radical politics of the 1790s, which had incorporated a demand for Catholic emancipation, also served to put a strain on relationships with the majority Catholic population.[10] The payment of tithe by all denominations to support the minority Anglican Church, which led to disturbances in the early 1830s, particularly in areas of the south of the country, probably also contributed to Catholic resentment towards the Anglican Church and, more specifically, its clergy.[11]

The authorities, both local and central, contributed, at times, to the heightening of sectarian feeling. The Dublin administration certainly could, particularly in the early decades of the century, display a sectarian bias. Individuals within the administration were seen as acting, and at times

---

Oxford University Press), pp. 74–107; Bartlett, *The Irish Nation*; Suzanne T. Kingon, 'Ulster Opposition to Catholic Emancipation, 1828–9', *Irish Historical Studies*, 34.134 (November 2004), pp. 137–55. The impact of sectarian animosity on a popular level can also be seen in the appearance of Pastorini's prophecies in southern areas of the country in the early 1820s, which predicted the destruction of Protestantism in 1825. For an account of the impact of these prophecies, see Donnelly, 'Pastorini and Captain Rock', pp. 102–39.

8   Connolly, 'Mass Politics and Sectarian Conflict', p. 74.

9   For an overview, see Connolly, 'Mass Politics and Sectarian Conflict'; Bartlett, *The Irish Nation*. See also D.H. Akenson, *The Church of Ireland: Ecclesiastical Reform and Revolution, 1800–1885* (New Haven, CT and London: Yale University Press, 1971), chapter two; Irene Whelan, *The Bible War in Ireland: The 'Second Reformation' and the Polarization of Protestant-Catholic Relations, 1800–40* (Madison, WI: University of Wisconsin Press, 2005).

10   Jonathan Bardon, *A History of Ulster* (Belfast: Blackstaff Press, 1992), pp. 250–2.

11   For an account of the impact of tithe agitation on a county level, see T.G. McGrath, 'Interdenominational Relations in Pre-Famine Tipperary' in William Nolan, (ed.), *Tipperary: History and Society: Interdisciplinary Essays on the History of an Irish County* (Dublin, Geography Publications, 1985), pp. 256–87; Michael O'Hanrahan, 'The Tithe War in Co. Kilkenny, 1830–1834' in William Nolan and Kevin Whelan, (eds), *Kilkenny: History and Society: Interdisciplinary Essays on the History of an Irish County* (Dublin: Geography Publications, 1990), pp. 481–505.

certainly did act, favourably towards the Protestant side.[12] The forces of law and order did not escape accusations of sectarian bias either. The magistracy was predominantly Protestant in composition and many individual magistrates were seen in the early decades of the century as being more than sympathetic to the Protestant cause. The yeomanry[13] was also seen as having a pronounced sectarian dimension. According to Bartlett, the yeomanry at this time was often 'on the Protestant side, for the force was almost entirely a Protestant – and indeed, an Orange – one'.[14]

Efforts were made at reform, particularly in the later decades of the period under review, with the establishment of a countrywide police force as the primary means of law enforcement, the introduction of professional or stipendiary magistrates, and a number of attempts to reform and revise the magistracy itself.[15] There were attempts to appoint more Catholics to the magistracy and the new police force included a considerable number of Catholics within its rank and file.[16] There were also attempts to control and limit the expression of party allegiance through a ban on party processions.[17] By the late 1830s, the administration in Dublin,

---

[12] For examples, see Bartlett, *The Irish Nation*, p. 321.

[13] The Irish yeomanry was raised in 1796 and established by statute in 1797. *An act for encouraging and disciplining such corps of men as shall voluntarily enroll themselves under officers to be commissioned by His Majesty, for the defence of this kingdom during the present war* (37 Geo. III, c. 2 [Ire.]). This body was 'a voluntary, part-time military force [...] for local law and order duties with the potential for military service during invasion or insurrection' (A.F. Blackstock, "A Dangerous Species of Ally': Orangeism and the Irish Yeomanry', *Irish Historical Studies*, 30.119 (May 1997), p. 393). The yeomanry was disbanded in 1834. See also A.F. Blackstock, *An Ascendancy Army: The Irish Yeomanry, 1796–1834* (Dublin: Four Courts Press, 1998).

[14] Bartlett, *The Irish Nation*, p. 322.

[15] For an account of law and order policy in this period, see Crossman, *Politics, Law and Order in Nineteenth-Century Ireland*. See also Broeker, *Rural Disorder* and Palmer, *Police and Protest*.

[16] By 1833 Catholics accounted for thirty-six per cent of the rank and file of the Irish constabulary. See Palmer, *Police and Protest*, p. 348. It should be noted, however, that although not as obviously dominated by Protestants as the yeomanry, the police force still encountered accusations of sectarian bias. This is particularly the case in Ulster and in the early years of its operation. See Palmer, *Police and Protest*, p. 346.

[17] In August 1832 parliament passed *An act to restrain for five years, in certain cases, party processions in Ireland* (2 & 3 Will. 4, c. 118). This was renewed in 1838 by *An act to continue for five years, and from thence until the end of the then next session of parliament, an act of the second and third years of the reign of His late Majesty, to restrain for five years, in certain cases, party processions in Ireland* (1 & 2 Vict., c. 34). In August 1844 parliament passed *An act to continue until the first day of June one thousand eight hundred and forty-five an act of the second and third years of His late Majesty, for restraining for five years in certain cases, party processions in Ireland* (7 & 8 Vict., c. 63). This act lifted the ban on party processions, but an act of 1850 re-imposed the ban (See *An act to restrain*

under a Whig/Liberal government, was also more clearly sympathetic to Catholic claims.[18] Yet, despite these efforts at reform in later decades, the developments outlined above almost certainly served to at least maintain and probably increase sectarian tensions in Irish society in the first half of the nineteenth century.

The dominant view in the existing historiography is that such sectarian animosity was a significant and direct cause of violent conflict. According to Kerby Miller, 'in the last quarter of the eighteenth century and the first half of the nineteenth, sectarian outrages frequently occurred throughout the island.'[19] Sean Connolly has also claimed that 'sectarian animosities were a source of recurrent fighting throughout this period principally though not exclusively in Ulster'.[20] Others, while acknowledging the prevalence of sectarian animosity, have, challenged the notion of sectarian tension as a major source of violent conflict. Donald Harman Akenson, for instance, has pointed out, in a study of nineteenth- and early twentieth-century Ireland, that the 'differences between Irish Catholics and Irish Protestants, though strongly held, were for the most part not violent. In many local and in myriad social situations, the two groups got on peaceably together, the surface amity being like the thin ice on a newly frozen pond.'[21] Indeed, Akenson goes further, suggesting that it was *because* of – not in spite of – the character of the two Irish belief systems, Protestant and Catholic, that the two tribal groups managed to coexist'. In his view, both sides emphasised and, indeed, luxuriated in the 'small differences' between them. This, in turn, provided a clear and uncomplicated world view that offered both comfort and stability to each community, thereby lessening the need for violent conflict between them.[22]

What was the relationship between sectarian animosity and violent activity in Ireland in the first half of the nineteenth century? While agreeing with Akenson that sectarian animosity was not a major cause of violent conflict, a somewhat different interpretation of the relationship between sectarianism

party processions in Ireland (13 Vict., c. 2)). See also N.P. Maddox, 'A Melancholy Record: The Story of the Nineteenth-Century Irish Party Procession Acts', *The Irish Jurist*, 39 new series (2004), pp. 243–74.

18 See M.A.G. Ó Tuathaigh, *Thomas Drummond and the Government of Ireland, 1835–41* (Dublin: National University of Ireland, 1978).

19 K.A. Miller, 'The Lost World of Andrew Johnston: Sectarianism, Social Conflict and Cultural Change in Southern Ireland during the Pre-Famine Era' in J.S. Donnelly, Jr, and K.A. Miller, (eds), *Irish Popular Culture, 1650–1850* (Dublin: Irish Academic Press, 1999), p. 223.

20 S.J. Connolly, *Priests and People*, p. 208.

21 D.H. Akenson, *Small Differences: Irish Catholics and Irish Protestants 1815–1922: An International Perspective* (Dublin: Gill and Macmillan, 1991), p. 4.

22 Ibid., pp. 147–9.

and violence will be offered here. It will be argued that the relatively low rate of sectarian homicide evident in Ireland at this time was rooted less in the extenuation or exaggeration of religious difference, but rather was a product of the complex interplay of wider forces and controls operating on and, more particularly, within both the Catholic and Protestant communities.

I

To what extent did sectarian animosity give rise to acts of lethal violence? The data gleaned from the national samples suggests that sectarian animosity was not a major cause of lethal violence in this period. On a national level, there were only seven reported cases of sectarian homicide between 1843 and 1845 – a rate of 0.02 per 100,000, which is the same as the rate of parricide in Ireland at this time.[23] Sectarian homicides accounted for a mere 1.67 per cent of all reported homicides. Indeed, three times as many reported homicides arose from sporting contests (twenty-one cases, accounting for 5.03 per cent) than from sectarian conflict.[24] The rate increased in the sample from the Famine years to 0.10 per 100,000. The proportion of such homicides also rose – accounting for 3.44 per cent of homicides reported. The higher rate and percentage of incidents for these years is due to the inclusion in the figures of the somewhat exceptional Dolly's Brae incident in Co. Down on 12 July 1849. On this day, six people were fatally injured as a consequence of a confrontation between Orangemen and Ribbonmen.[25] This incident, however, was due more to local tensions which pre-dated 1845 and the wider political climate created after the failed rebellion of 1848 than with the immediate conditions of the Famine.[26] Indeed, during those years when

---

[23] See chapter three, n. 62.

[24] This finding is also consistent with that for late nineteenth-century Ireland, where sectarian homicide only accounted for 2.6 per cent of reported homicides in the period 1866–92. See Conley, *Melancholy Accidents*, pp. 173–4.

[25] For a thorough and comprehensive account of this incident, see John Moulden, 'The Printed Ballad in Ireland: A Guide to the Popular Printing of Songs in Ireland, 1760–1920' (PhD thesis, National University of Ireland, Galway, 2006), chapter fourteen, esp. pp. 432–8. Moulden expertly undermines claims that up to thirty Ribbonmen may have been killed in this encounter and confirms that the death toll was in single figures. See also Christine Kinealy, 'A Right to March? The Conflict at Dolly's Brae' in D. G. Boyce and Roger Swift, (eds), *Problems and Perspectives in Irish History since 1800: Essays in Honour of Patrick Buckland* (Dublin: Four Courts Press, 2004), pp. 54–79.

[26] Neither Moulden's nor Kinealy's account sees the Famine as a significant influence on the events of that day.

the impact of the Famine was at its height, 1847 and 1848, the incidence of sectarian homicide in the country was remarkably low.[27]

There was some regional disparity in the incidence of these cases. The highest number of cases occurred, perhaps unsurprisingly, in the north of the country where the population was more evenly divided between Catholic and Protestant groupings. This is reflected in the national data for 1843–5 where three of the seven cases arose in the province of Ulster (north), two in Munster (south) and one each in Connacht (west) and Leinster (east). It is further emphasised in the sample drawn from the years 1847–9, where eight of the nine cases occurred in Ulster and of these six were related to the incident at Dolly's Brae.

This regional difference is also evident in the figures from the more long-term study of the four counties, Co. Armagh and Co. Fermanagh in the north, Co. Kilkenny and Queen's Co. in the south. These counties had somewhat different religious make-ups and varying reputations for sectarian violence. Armagh had a high proportion of Anglicans, mainly living in the north of the county, and Catholics primarily but not exclusively in the south. There was also a small but not insubstantial Presbyterian population in the central areas of Armagh.[28] The county was the birth place of the Orange Order and that organisation had a substantial presence in the county in the first half of the nineteenth century.[29] It was also generally regarded as the most sectarian and deeply divided county in Ireland at this time. Garnham, in his study of violence in eighteenth-century Ireland, describes Armagh as the 'nursery of sectarian conflict' in Ireland.[30] There was a considerable upsurge in sectarian conflict in the county in the late eighteenth century.[31]

---

[27]   In the sampled months for 1847 and 1848 sectarian homicides accounted for only 0.94 per cent of reported homicides.

[28]   For an account of the denominational make-up of Co. Armagh, see Miller, 'The Origins of the Orange Order', pp. 583–9.

[29]   According to evidence given before the Select committee on Orange lodges in 1835 there were over two hundred Orange lodges in Armagh at that time. See *Report from the select committee appointed to inquire into the nature, character, extent and tendency of Orange lodges, associations, or societies in Ireland, with the minutes of evidence, and appendix*, p. 113, H.C. 1835 (377), xv, 1 (hereafter cited as Select committee on Orange lodges, 1835).

[30]   See Neal Garnham, 'How Violent was Eighteenth-Century Ireland?', *Irish Historical Studies*, 30.119 (May 1997), p. 392.

[31]   For a discussion of the development of sectarian conflict in late eighteenth-century Armagh see, among others, Peter Gibbon, *The Origins of Ulster Unionism: The Formation of Popular Protestant Politics and Ideology in Nineteenth-Century Ireland* (Manchester: Manchester University Press, 1975); D.W. Miller, 'The Armagh Troubles, 1784–95' in Clark and Donnelly (eds), *Irish Peasants*, pp. 155–91; Cullen, 'The Political Structure of the Defenders'; Whelan, *The Tree of Liberty*; Frank Wright, *Two Lands on One Soil: Ulster Politics before Home Rule* (Dublin: Gill and Macmillan, 1996); Miller, 'The Origins of the Orange Order'; Sean Farrell, *Rituals and Riots: Sectarian Violence and Political*

Co. Fermanagh also had a high proportion of both Anglicans and Catholics within its borders, with the former again mainly in the north of the county and the latter in the south.[32] The Orange Order was also quite prominent in Fermanagh and the county had a reputation, although not as pronounced as Co. Armagh, for sectarian conflict.[33] The presence of Protestants was less obvious in the southern counties. Of the two southern counties, Queen's Co. had the more substantial Protestant presence within its borders and a greater reputation for sectarian animosity.[34] The Orange Order was also more prominent in the county, especially in the mid-1830s.[35] Kilkenny had a relatively small Protestant population and the Orange Order was almost non-existent in the county.[36] As Table 5.1 indicates, there was a marked contrast in the number of sectarian homicides between the north and south of the country in this period.

Table 5.1 Sectarian homicides in four Irish counties

	Co. Armagh 1835–50	Co. Fermanagh 1811–50	Co. Kilkenny 1835–50	Queen's Co. 1835–50
No. of sectarian homicides	9	11	0	1
Percentage of all homicides	9.89	14.66	0	1.28
Rate per 100,000	0.24	0.19	0	0.04

Culture in Ulster, 1784–1886 (Lexington, KY: University Press of Kentucky, 2000), chapter one. For disturbances which had a sectarian dimension to them in other areas of the country, particularly Co. Meath, in the late eighteenth century, see M.J. Powell, 'Popular Disturbances in Late Eighteenth-Century Ireland: The Origins of the Peep of Day Boys', *Irish Historical Studies*, 34.135 (May 2005), pp. 249–65.

[32] Fermanagh and Armagh were quite distinctive in that they were, as Whelan points out, 'the only counties where Anglicans were not heavily outnumbered by Catholics and Presbyterians'. According to Whelan, this created the 'social base for a hegemonic landed class and a populist loyalism that was not possible elsewhere'. See Kevin Whelan, 'Introduction to Section III' in Bartlett et al., *1798*, pp. 192–3.

[33] It was claimed that there were also over two hundred Orange lodges in Co. Fermanagh in the mid-1830s. See Select committee on Orange lodges, 1835, p. 113.

[34] According to Gibbons, the county had a 'larger than usual proportion of Protestants' for a county in the south of the country. Actual estimates of the proportion of Protestants in the county, however, varied widely from one-in-four to one-in-twelve. Gibbons also points out that there was a 'deepening of sectarian animosities [in the county] in the eighteen-twenties'. See Gibbons, 'Captain Rock', p. 491.

[35] It was reported before the select committee in 1835 that there was an increase in the number of Orange lodges in the county in the mid-1830s. See Select committee on Orange lodges, 1835, pp. 198–200.

[36] According to the evidence before the select committee in 1835, there were no Orange lodges in Co. Kilkenny at that time. See Select committee on Orange lodges, 1835, p. 113.

In Armagh there were nine times as many homicides arising from sectarian conflict between 1835 and 1850 as in Queen's Co. In Fermanagh the incidence of such cases was also higher than those counties in the south. We must, however, be aware that our sample does not include data from before 1835 for three of the four counties. In the one county where data is available, Co. Fermanagh, the evidence suggests that sectarian homicides were more common before 1835. Of the eleven homicides reported, eight occurred in the period before 1835, most of them in the 1820s. The extent of the difference between pre- and post-1835 should not, however, be exaggerated. Four of the eight homicides in Co. Fermanagh before 1835 arose from a single confrontation in 1829 and were related to particular tensions surrounding the passing of the Catholic Emancipation Act (1829).[37] This year was probably the highpoint for sectarian violence in Ireland in the first half of the nineteenth century.[38] Outside of this contentious period, however, the extent of sectarian violence was probably quite limited. According to Farrell, in the years between 1800 and 1820 'outbreaks of sectarian violence were sporadic and small in scale', only emerging, to any great extent, between 1811 and 1814.[39] We have also seen in previous chapters that there was a low rate of homicide in both Fermanagh and Armagh in the decades before 1835 and, in the evidence given before the Poor Law Commission, that there was a low level of social unrest generally in both counties. Both also won considerable praise from the judiciary for their generally peaceful state during this period.[40] Thus, while rates of sectarian homicide may have been higher before 1835, there is little to suggest that, outside a particularly contentious period in the late 1820s, sectarian killings were markedly more prevalent before 1835 in the two northern counties.

The lack of sustained statistical evidence from before 1835 may be more significant in Queen's Co. and Co. Kilkenny as both suffered from severe rural unrest in the late 1820s and early 1830s and had a far greater reputation for violence than their northern counterparts at that time. Moreover, a significant element of this unrest stemmed from the issue of the tithes to be paid to the Anglican Church. The period of tithe agitation in the early 1830s did produce a number of violent attacks on Protestants.[41]

---

37 This case will be discussed in detail below.

38 Farrell, *Rituals and Riots*, pp. 96–9.

39 Ibid., p. 99. Michael Huggins has also drawn attention to the relative rarity of sectarian conflict in Roscommon. He points out that in the first three decades of the nineteenth century, 'the sum of sectarian feeling in Co. Roscommon was a month-long call for a boycott of Protestant shops in Strokestown and some other isolated instances of sectarian sentiment' (Huggins, *Social Conflict in Pre-Famine Ireland*, p. 79).

40 See chapter one.

41 For examples, see McGrath, 'Interdenominational Relations'.

Yet, even in the context of Co. Kilkenny where the tithe war originated in the early 1830s, a place where and a time when one might expect to find violent sectarian activity, violence, when it did occur, was directed more at the forces of law and order who enforced tithe collection rather than towards local Protestants in sectarian hostility. Kilkenny was the location for one of the most infamous violent incidents of the tithe war when, at Carrickshock, on 14 December 1831, the process server Edmund Butler and thirteen policemen were killed attempting to serve processes (latitats) for tithes.[42] Attacks arising directly from sectarian animosity, however, remained relatively rare.[43] Tithe did not invariably divide people along sectarian lines but could actually bridge the gap. In Queen's Co., Catholic and Protestant farmers seem to have been as one in their refusal to pay tithe in the early 1830s.[44] In Armagh, too, there was a degree of Protestant involvement in anti-tithe agitation and most violent action and intimidation lacked a clear sectarian dimension, occurring, for the most part, within rather than between communities.[45] Thus, the tithe agitation did not lead to any considerable upsurge in lethal sectarian violence. This finding is also consistent with McGrath's study of interdenominational relations in pre-Famine Tipperary, a county generally regarded as the most disturbed in Ireland in the pre-Famine period. He argues that it is 'doubtful if many murders can be attributed to intrinsic sectarianism' at this time.[46] On the whole, it is likely that, even before 1835, sectarian homicide was rare in both Queen's Co. and Co. Kilkenny, which suggests, at the very least, that violent activity arising from sectarian animosity was clearly controlled within these areas.

It should, of course, be acknowledged that there is perhaps nothing unusual in the rare occurrence of homicide. Acts of lethal violence are usually rare and generally exceptional responses to wider social, economic

---

[42] For an account, see Gary Owens, 'The Carrickshock Incident, 1831: Social Memory and an Irish Cause Célèbre', *Cultural and Social History*, 1 (2004), pp. 36–64. See also James Mongan, *A Report of the Trials of John Kennedy, John Ryan, and William Voss, for the Murder of Edmund Butler, at Carrickshock, on the 14th December, 1831. Tried before the Hon. Baron Foster, at the Spring and Summer Assizes of Kilkenny, 1832* (Dublin: Richard Milliken and son, 1832).

[43] See O'Hanrahan, 'Tithe War'.

[44] Gibbons, 'Captain Rock', p. 499.

[45] In Armagh, Catholics and Protestants came together to oppose the payment of tithe in an organisation called the Tommy Downshire's boys. See Blackstock, *An Ascendancy Army*, p. 255. This coming together of Protestants and Catholics in the one movement was, Blackstock argues, 'perhaps the exception that proved the rule'. On Protestant involvement in anti-tithe agitation in Forkhill, Co. Armagh, in the 1830s, see Kyla Madden, *Forkhill Protestants and Forkhill Catholics, 1787–1858* (Liverpool: Liverpool University Press, 2006), p. 99.

[46] McGrath, 'Interdenominational Relations', p. 273.

and/or personal problems, tensions and grievances. Yet, and perhaps of more significance, sectarian homicides constituted but a small proportion of all acts of lethal violence in these areas. Sectarian homicides were, in this sense, a rare manifestation of an already rare phenomenon.[47] In Queen's Co., for instance, sectarian homicides accounted for only 1.28 per cent of cases. In the north, the proportion of sectarian cases was somewhat higher. In Fermanagh between 1811 and 1850, homicide cases arising from sectarian strife accounted for 14.66 per cent of reported homicides in the county and in Armagh the nine homicides arising from sectarian strife accounted for close to ten per cent of all reported homicides. Yet even in the northern counties the proportion of sectarian homicides was still relatively low. In Armagh over four times, and in Fermanagh over three times, as many cases arose from personal and family disputes as from sectarian animosity. This would suggest that when violence did arise, sectarian animosity was not a particularly prominent cause or motivation for the protagonists. Thus, outside of particular periods such as 1829, sectarian animosity was not a major cause of lethal violence or wider social unrest. This was the case both for the country generally and in the northern counties such as Fermanagh and, particularly, Armagh, which were most affected by sectarian strife.

It should be noted, however, that my figures do not include 'political' homicides (which in the Irish context may have had sectarian overtones). There can be little doubt but that, as Hoppen has demonstrated, serious acts of lethal violence could arise from political contests and rivalries. For instance, in Carlow alone, in 1832, fourteen people were killed in a riot arising from the election of that year. Such incidents underline the considerable potential for violent political conflict in Ireland at this time.[48]

Yet, lethal violence arising from political conflict must be seen in context.

47 Assuming that around five per cent of homicides between 1841 and 1850 arose from sectarian animosity (this would in itself be a generous estimate) the rate of sectarian homicide in the country as whole would be 0.098 per 100,000 or less than 1 per 1,000,000 inhabitants per annum.
48 For a discussion of electoral violence, see K.T. Hoppen, 'Grammars of Electoral Violence in Nineteenth-Century England and Ireland', *English Historical Review*, 109.432 (1994), pp. 597–620 and *idem, Elections, Politics and Society*, pp. 388–408.

Table 5.2   The incidence of homicides arising from political disputes in pre-Famine and Famine Ireland

Cause	Ireland 1843–5	Ireland 1847–9	Armagh 1835–50	Fermanagh 1811–50	Kilkenny 1835–50	Queen's Co. 1835–50
Homicides arising from political disputes	2	1	0	0	1	1
Percentage of all homicide cases	0.47	0.38	0	0	0.8	1.28
Rate per 100,000	0.007	0.01	0	0	0.03	0.04

The evidence from our samples certainly suggests that political rivalries were not, for the most part, a major cause of lethal violence. The figures are also consistent with Desmond McCabe's findings. McCabe has shown that only 0.5 per cent of homicides in Co. Mayo between 1823 and 1845 were rooted in political causes.[49] This suggests that, although political tensions and contests could, at certain times, give rise to serious acts of violence, they were not a major cause of lethal violence – particularly when compared to more personal or familial conflicts. Moreover, the addition of these political homicides to those arising more directly from sectarian animosity would not alter in any significant way the finding that lethal violence arising directly or indirectly from sectarian feeling was a relatively rare occurrence.

II

In what circumstances did sectarian animosity give rise to violent conflict and what forms did such violence take? The following study is based primarily on a number of sectarian homicides that took place in Co. Fermanagh between 1811 and 1850 and Co. Armagh between 1835 and 1850. In Armagh between 1835 and 1850 there were, as noted above, nine homicides that arose from seven different incidents, while in Fermanagh, over a forty-year period between 1811–50, our sample includes eleven homicides arising from eight separate incidents.

Such incidents generally took three main forms: large-scale communal confrontations, smaller-scale disputes between groups and disputes between individuals. Of the seven incidents recorded in Armagh between 1835 and 1850, one can be seen as a communal confrontation, two arose from disputes between rival groups, while the other four incidents were the product of arguments between individuals. In the Fermanagh sample, one case arose

---

[49]   McCabe, 'Law, Conflict and Social Order', p. 82.

from a dispute between individuals, six incidents involved conflicts between groups and there was one large-scale communal confrontation.

There were generally three key aspects to these cases. First, they almost invariably and perhaps quite predictably involve an attempt by one side to assert itself over the other and over a particular area or territory. Second, they reveal a willingness to respond to threats from the opposing side by resorting to acts of violence. Third, they show that violence or at least lethal violence was rarely premeditated, but rather tended to emerge in the context of the specific situation in which the parties found themselves.

Communal violence

Large-scale confrontations usually coincided with the annual commemorations that took place on the twelfth of July to mark the success of William III over James II at the Battle of the Boyne in July 1690. Such commemorations, and the Orange processions which often accompanied them, had, as Christine Kinealy points out, 'acquired a reputation for sectarian violence' in this period.[50] The clearest example of such a confrontation in our sample occurred in Macken, Co. Fermanagh, on Monday 13 July 1829[51] when four Protestant men, Edward Scarlet, Robert Mealey, George Price, and James Robinson were killed in the so-called 'Macken fight'.

The following account of that incident is primarily based on the evidence given by a total of fifty witnesses (twenty-four for the prosecution and twenty-six for the defence) over the course of three trials at the spring assizes of Co. Fermanagh in 1830.[52] There are obviously conflicting accounts of what occurred at Macken between the case put forward by the prosecution

---

[50] Kinealy 'A Right to March?', p. 57. For an account of the Battle of the Boyne itself, see Pádraig Lenihan, *1690: Battle of the Boyne* (Stroud: Tempus Publishing, 2003).

[51] The traditional Orange commemorations were held on 13 July this year because the twelfth fell on a Sunday.

[52] The main sources employed in my account are the reports of the trials in the *Enniskillen Chronicle and Erne Packet*, 25 Mar., 1 Apr., 8 Apr. and 15 Apr. 1830. This paper is described by the *Waterloo Directory of Irish Newspapers and Periodicals* as being both Protestant and conservative. Although it was undoubtedly very sympathetic towards the Protestant position in its reporting, at the time of these trials the paper was, in fact, owned by a Catholic. Randall Kernan, a barrister from Enniskillen, also referred to the paper as a 'milk and water paper; it is neither the one thing nor the other [... the] articles are as frequently Orange as they are Catholic'. See *The third report of the select committee appointed to inquire into the nature, character, extent and tendency of Orange lodges, associations or societies in Ireland*, p. 72, H.C. 1835 (476), xvi, 1 (hereafter cited as Third report on Orange lodges, *Minutes of evidence 1835*). My account of the incident also draws on information given to magistrates by witnesses, the report of the crown solicitor on the incident and the reports of the trials included in the third report of the select committee on Orange lodges in 1835.

and that put forward by the defence. There are also inconsistencies within both the prosecution and defence cases as to the precise timing of the events. Yet the accounts given are by no means mutually exclusive and it is possible to give an outline of the main events of the day even if their nature and sequence are somewhat unclear or disputed.

The Macken fight occurred just three months after the passing of the Catholic Emancipation Act in April of that year. This significant national political change also provided an opportunity for greater Catholic assertiveness on a local level. As Marianne Elliott has pointed out, while 'Catholic emancipation brought little immediate benefit to the average Catholic […] it did wonders for him psychologically and from 1829 onwards Orange parades were challenged at every level'.[53]

Some members of the Catholic community in Co. Fermanagh certainly saw July 1829 as an opportune moment to express their objections to Orange marches taking place and did so successfully. On the day in question, 'about 1500 men', a number of whom had weapons,[54] gathered in the county to prevent, and if necessary actively resist, the occurrence of an Orange march. The police and a number of magistrates, including Lord Enniskillen, who at this time was Deputy Grand Master of the Orangemen of Ireland, arrived on the scene. Enniskillen attempted to get the men to disperse.[55]

The Catholic grouping, however, pointed to a number of Orangemen who had assembled at a nearby house and declared that they would not move until they were satisfied the Orangemen would not march. Enniskillen then went to the house where the Orangemen said they were afraid they would be murdered, but agreed to disperse if Lord Enniskillen wished them to. At this stage, another larger Orange party was seen marching from the direction of Belturbet. Enniskillen rode out and met this group who said they had 'heard the country was rising and were afraid of all being murdered'. He managed to convince them to turn around and return the way they came by telling them that the Catholics would disperse if the Orangemen did not

---

53 Marianne Elliott, *The Catholics of Ulster: A History* (London: Allen Lane, 2000), p. 348. There were, as noted earlier, a number of violent confrontations throughout Ulster in the summer of 1829. See Bardon, *Ulster*, p. 247; Farrell, *Rituals and Riots*, pp. 96–9.

54 According to one witness, Montgomery Armstrong esq., they were armed 'with long pitchforks, pikes newly fabricated, loys, bayonets and scythes on sticks'. Another witness, Lord Enniskillen, claimed that they had 'bayonets on poles, pikes, pistols, fleshforks, & c., there were a few muskets'. See *Enniskillen Chronicle and Erne Packet*, 25 Mar. 1830.

55 Ibid. Lord Enniskillen addressed the crowd, declaring: 'Good God, boys! What are you about, what brought you here, for God's sake go away'. In reply, he was told that the group 'would not allow the Orangemen to walk'. Enniskillen then gave assurances to the crowd that 'he would not allow them to walk, and begged the people to go home.'

march.[56] At this point, Lord Enniskillen returned to the Catholic group and again asked them to disperse. They eventually did so and a section of the crowd went in the direction of Macken with 'great shouting and cheering'.[57]

This combination of a significant national political change and greater Catholic assertiveness on a local level served to heighten fears and insecurities among members of the Protestant community in the area. It also probably strengthened resolve, among some Protestants at least, to rise to the challenge laid down by the Catholics on this day. Both of these factors were evident that evening when a group of about thirty Orangemen and members of their families dined at the house of Edward Scarlet, a Protestant farmer and Orangeman. It was here that the decision to walk through Macken, a predominately Catholic area, was taken and a party consisting of around thirty men, six of whom were 'armed with guns and bayonets' and a number of women and children left Scarlet's house and proceeded in the direction of Macken.[58]

The precise reasons for this decision are somewhat unclear. According to most of the prosecution witnesses at the trial, fears among the Orangemen were heightened when a report reached them that a 'number of Protestants had been waylaid and beaten on the highway at Macken by a number of riotous and disorderly persons'.[59] It was then decided that two of the men dining in Scarlet's house, Thomas and George Thompson, would need an escort home and the others present would accompany them along the road.

This version of events was certainly accepted at the trial by judge and jury and is by no means implausible. There are some doubts surrounding it however. According to the crown solicitor for the north-west circuit, it was not clear whether the report that Protestants had been beaten 'was well founded or not'.[60] At least one witness, James Armstrong, also admitted under cross-examination that 'it was not settled in the lodge at Scarlet's before the party left it to convey the Thompsons home.'[61] The group that left Scarlet's house was also soon augmented by 'a second party of Orangemen, consisting of about 16' along the road, who joined them on the way to Macken and of which a further 'five or six were armed with guns and bayonets'.[62] The fact that there was already an armed Orange party on

56 Ibid.
57 Ibid.
58 Third report on Orange lodges, *Minutes of evidence 1835*, appendix g, p. 216.
59 Ibid.
60 Ibid.
61 *Enniskillen Chronicle and Erne Packet*, 15 Apr. 1830.
62 Third report on Orange lodges, *minutes of evidence 1835*, appendix g, p. 216.

the road going in the direction of Macken would suggest that the escorting home of the Thompsons was not the sole motivation of those involved.

Just as Protestant fears had been raised by the Catholic gathering earlier in the day, the approach of a group of around fifty Protestants certainly raised fears among the Catholic community of Macken. Patrick McHugh, a defence witness, claimed that he was drinking in Widow Carron's public house when 'Mrs. Carron came to where witness was, and said there was a party coming to murder the people.'[63] Michael McManus, seeing an armed Orange party approaching his house and hearing them 'cheering each other to go on' left his house along with his wife and family 'for fear of being killed'.[64] A number of defence witnesses also indicated that the Orangemen acted in a provocative manner as they approached Macken. One witness, Philip Flanagan, claimed that he heard shouts of 'No Pope – No Surrender'. The above mentioned Mrs Carron also heard shouts of 'No Pope', 'No Surrender', and, somewhat incongruously, 'No King' coming from the Orangemen.[65]

As the Protestant party approached Macken they were met by Francis McBrien, a Catholic, who attempted to negotiate with Edward Scarlet and Robert Mealey, both Protestants.[66] A large group of Catholics had also assembled on the hill at Macken at this time. According to Christopher Carson, a prosecution witness, Francis McBrien, 'desired witness's party to go home peacably'.[67] Some agreement may have been reached at this stage as the Orange party began to retreat down the hill.

It was at this point, however, that conflict broke out. According to the prosecution case, the Protestant party made its way peacefully down the hill. George Thompson, a prosecution witness, claimed that the Orangemen 'did not say a word, nor do any thing' as they made their retreat. A number of defence witnesses, however, claimed that at least some of the Orangemen taunted the Catholics from the foot of the hill. Philip Flanagan gave evidence that he saw the Orange party take off their hats, and call on the party on the hill 'to come down for cowardly dogs'.[68] Whether provoked or not, a small group of Catholics (between fifteen and twenty people) did go

---

63 *Enniskillen Chronicle and Erne Packet*, 25 Mar. 1830.
64 Ibid.
65 Ibid., 1 Apr. 1830. The shouting of 'No King' may have reflected a certain disenchantment with the monarch, George IV, for signing the Catholic Emancipation Act in April 1829.
66 Ibid. McBrien was well placed to carry out this negotiation as he had been born and bred in Ballymenone, where many of the Orangemen had come from. He had only moved to Macken seven weeks before this incident and both he and his family were also said to have been 'always on good terms with the Orangemen'.
67 *Enniskillen Chronicle and Erne Packet*, 25 Mar. 1830.
68 Ibid.

down the hill in the direction of the Protestant party.[69] Before they reached them, however, two or three shots were fired from the Orange party as they continued their retreat from the hill.

A number of prosecution witnesses noted that these shots were fired into the air. John Quigley, for instance, claimed that 'the first two shots were fired in the air, when the Orange party had their faces towards Scarlet's'.[70] One of the shots, however, hit a Catholic, William Rooney, who was on the hill at the time. Rooney himself claimed that John Glass, a miller and member of the Protestant party, fired the shot at him deliberately 'without any provocation'.[71] Whatever the intention, the firing of these shots was clearly a provocative gesture[72] and it seems to have sparked off the general confrontation between the groups. At this point, a large group of Catholics came down the hill and attacked the Orangemen. A number of the Orangemen continued their retreat but others stayed and fought. The Orangemen were outnumbered and it was during this confrontation that Robert Mealey was killed after being stabbed with a pitchfork by one of the Catholic party and Edward Scarlet, James Robinson and George Price received the wounds that caused their deaths.

Similar circumstances surrounded the killing of John Boyle, a young Catholic man, by a gun-shot received in the course of a riot involving Orangemen and Catholics in Armagh in 1845.[73] This confrontation arose from an Orange procession on 12 July and it also followed a relatively significant national political development. The summer of 1845 was the first occasion on which Orange marches could legally take place in Ireland since 1832, following parliament's decision not to renew the Party Procession Act (1832) when it expired on 1 June 1845. This effectively allowed Orange marches to take place again after a thirteen-year prohibition.

It also provided the Orangemen with an opportunity to assert or re-assert

---

[69] They may or may not have been responding to Francis McBrien, who waved his hat in the air at this point. There was some confusion as to whether this was to stop the group or to encourage them to come down the hill. The jury seems to have accepted the former explanation as McBrien was acquitted at his subsequent trial.

[70] *Enniskillen Chronicle and Erne Packet*, 15 Apr. 1830.

[71] Third report on Orange lodges, *Minutes of evidence 1835*, appendix g, p. 246.

[72] James Armstrong, a prosecution witness, was clearly angry at those who fired the shots. According to his evidence at the trial, 'he was beside the men that fired, and asked were they mad to do so and they attacked as they were' (*Enniskillen Chronicle and Erne Packet*, 1 Apr. 1830).

[73] The following account is based on the evidence given by seventeen witnesses at the coroner's inquest into the case as reported in the *Armagh Guardian*, 22 Jul. 1845. An account of the incident and transcriptions of the inquest and subsequent trials may also be found in Réamonn Ó Muirí, 'The Orangemen, Repealers and the Shooting of John Boyle in Armagh, 12 July 1845', *Seanchas Ard Mhaca*, 11. 2 (1985), pp. 435–529.

their local strength. A procession consisting of around three hundred Orangemen left Armagh on the morning of 12 July 1845 for nearby Loughgall. A number of flags were on display, some of the men wore orange lilies and a number of party tunes such as 'Croppies lie down' were played.[74] The procession marched in 'good order' to nearby Loughgall, returning to Armagh city at around half-past five that evening. As they did so they fired a number of shots. According to Anthony Coyle, who was employed to drive one of the cars at the front of the procession, there might have been 'beyond thirty or [...] more [shots] fired by persons in the procession on coming back to Armagh'.[75]

Like Macken, there was an attempt, or at the very least a perceived attempt, by Orangemen to proceed towards a predominantly Catholic area. In this case, there were fears that the Orangemen would attempt to march towards Irish Street, which was in a Catholic area of the city.[76] Similar to Macken, the homicide in Armagh was by no means planned, but rather was triggered by events on the ground. Indeed, a relatively minor incident actually sparked off the confrontation. A young man on horseback called William Montgomery was leading the Orange procession up Thomas Street

---

[74] This tune came to prominence in the late eighteenth century, particularly after the 1798 rebellion, when it was adopted by the Orangemen as an accompaniment for marching. There are many texts accompanying this tune, which generally celebrate the suppression of the rebellion in 1798. For examples, see G.D. Zimmermann, *Songs of Irish Rebellion: Political Street Ballads and Rebel Songs, 1780–1900* (Dublin: Allen Figgis, 1967), pp. 307–10.

[75] *Armagh Guardian*, 22 Jul. 1845.

[76] William Barnes, the clerk of the petty sessions, approached John Kitson, who rode in one of four horse-drawn jaunting cars at the front of the procession, and said to him 'Johnny, I hope you don't intend going through Irish street [...] the town is in peace and quietness at present, and by going there it will cause disturbance.' Kitson denied that he would march to Irish Street, claiming that he would march along Thomas Street in the direction of Irish Street but would turn down Dobbin Street before he reached the Catholic area of the town. It is not clear, and, indeed, Barnes himself was unsure, whether or not Kitson would turn down Dobbin Street as he had indicated or continue through Thomas Street and Ogle Street to Irish Street. It is evident, however, that at least some of the Orangemen had resolved to march to Irish Street. Patrick Duffy, a car-driver who had been employed for the day by an Orangeman called Stoops, claimed that the latter instructed him to drive to Irish Street on their return to the city. Duffy claimed, however, that he objected, stating that he 'would not wish to go to Irish street'. He was reluctant to go there because 'during the day two or three young chaps, who were dressed, and with the procession, cried "To hell with the Pope" and [he] knew from that, if they went to Irish-street there would be a disturbance.' According to Duffy, Stoops replied to his objection by stating 'Go on – don't be afraid – we will gain the day.' Whatever the precise intentions of the Orangemen, the decision to march in the direction of Irish Street brought matters to a head.

when a number of small boys called out to him to play 'Garryowen'.[77] He replied 'Go to h_l; no "Garryowen" will be played here' and he then rode up the street in pursuit of the children. One of the boys then threw a stone at the horse and Montgomery was reported to have said 'by heavens he would *slay them like Philistines*'. As he pursued the children, however, his horse was 'caught hold of by a hostler called Tierney' who turned the horse around and forced the man to return in the direction of the Orange procession while the children continued to throw stones at him.[78]

When Montgomery went back into the Orange crowd a shot was fired from the Orange party in the direction of Ogle Street, which runs perpendicular to Irish Street. By this time, a group of '40 or 50' Catholics had assembled at the head of Ogle Street. Stone throwing then began on both sides and shots continued to be fired. Barnes, the petty sessions clerk, claimed that there 'were 50 shots, at least, fired in the course of the riot'. The firing came initially from the Orange party but after a time the Catholic group returned fire.[79]

The police did attempt to intervene. Sub-inspector Kelly met the Orangemen as they moved up Ogle Street. He stood in their way extending his 'sword in one direction, and [his] arm in the other, and said: 'Oh, my God, boys, surely you're not coming in this direction. Go back – go back.' The Orangemen, however, 'presented two or three pistols and fired one quite close to [Kelly ...] in the direction of Ogle St.', and the stone throwing and shooting continued on both sides. The extent of the stone throwing from Ogle Street forced the Orangemen to move back along the street. As they did so, however, they broke the windows of local businesses and continued to fire shots.[80] It was one of these shots that hit John Boyle, who had been throwing stones at the Orangemen from Ogle Street. He died the next day. The riot itself was not brought under control until the local magistracy[81] and, more particularly, the army arrived on the scene. The military marched

---

77 This song has a less explicitly sectarian dimension to it than 'Croppies lie down' although, as the above incident indicates, it was, to some extent at least, identified with the Catholic side. The text of the song celebrates the joys of drinking and fighting. It was also adopted by Irish regiments within the British Army and, later in the nineteenth century, by Irishmen serving in the United States Army.

78 *Armagh Guardian*, 22 Jul. 1845.

79 Ibid. Barnes declared that 'there were about 20 shots fired before he heard any shots from the direction of the Ogle-street party [the Catholics].'

80 Sub-inspector Kelly estimated that there 'were from 416 to 420 panes of glass broken' by the Orangemen along the street.

81 The response of the magistracy seems to have been quite tardy. The confrontation was in process for three-quarters of an hour before they arrived on the scene. This was apparently due to the fact that they were serving on the county grand jury at the time.

up Dobbin Street and eventually brought the situation under control, but by then the damage had been done.

Group violence

Incidents of group violence also involved attempts by one side to challenge, or assert itself over, the other. This is particularly evident in the attempts to achieve dominance over a particular occasion such as a fair. Bartlett has pointed out that the 'classic occasions for demonstrations of Catholic strength in numbers were the fairs and markets which were springing up or being revived around the country in the early nineteenth century'.[82] There were also, as Bartlett notes, considerable fears among Protestants about such demonstrations of strength and also a willingness among some to respond to such Catholic assertiveness with violence.[83] This is evident in Fermanagh in March 1824 when a Protestant, Robert Ingram, was killed at the fair of Ederney. This incident was the culmination of a number of violent clashes at the fair between Catholics and Protestants in which the latter had come out the worse for wear.[84] On the day in question, a number of Protestants decided that they needed to resist this Catholic aggression. As one of them put it, 'from the treatment the Protestants received, he thought it right to put [the Catholics] down [... and] he thought some measure should be resorted to prevent them rioting in Ederney' as the fair had become 'more a mart for assassination than for commerce'.[85]

Other occasions for group violence included race meetings. In Fermanagh in 1835, a William Lang was killed in a riot that followed the victory of a horse called 'Protestant Boy' at the Enniskillen races. This was, in fact, somewhat of an empty victory as the horse ran the course unopposed after another horse (presumably representing the Catholic interest) was withdrawn from the race.[86] Group conflicts also took place in or around pubs and could, similar in many respects to the personal disputes examined in chapter one, involve assertions of strength or superiority over seemingly minor matters. In Fermanagh in February 1841, George Latimer, a Protestant, died from injuries he received in a dispute in a pub between a group of Protestant men and a number of Catholics over a pipe.[87] In such circumstances, sectarian feeling could probably add to the animosity between the parties.

---

[82] Bartlett, *The Irish Nation*, p. 315.

[83] Ibid., p. 316. See also Farrell, *Rituals and Riots*, p. 76.

[84] According to one witness, Protestants 'found it dangerous to go to [the fairs in Ederney]' (*Enniskillen Chronicle and Erne Packet*, 12 Aug. 1824).

[85] Ibid.

[86] *Enniskillen Chronicle and Erne Packet*, 30 Jul. 1835 and 10 Mar. 1836.

[87] Disputes over items such as pipes and tobacco seem to have been a common enough

Often times no particular issue was at stake in these encounters, but rather a more general challenge was issued. In Armagh in April 1835, Hugh Donnelly was killed in a fight at a fair at Drumcree near Portadown. This incident was sparked off when Donnelly's son, Hugh junior, 'cursed' a number of Protestant men, calling one 'an Orange rascal' and another a 'turncoat rascal' and daring them to fight him. When a fight broke out, Hugh's father and a number of men came to his aid and Hugh senior was heard to declare that 'there was not a twelve stone Orangeman in the fair he could not beat.'[88]

In certain circumstances, those involved in these confrontations were often prepared for, or even expected to engage in, violent activity. For instance, in Fermanagh in 1824, a pre-arranged boxing match or challenge fight between two men, Lunny, a Catholic, and Kenny, a Protestant, was due to take place on the island of Inishmore. The challenge fight, according to one witness, was 'about the party quarrels'. Supporters of both men and curious onlookers gathered from about six o'clock in the morning on the day. Some came 'to see the fight, and shew [sic] fair play' others, however, brought weapons with them. One defence witness, in fact, revealed that he 'heard the challenge spoken of the evening before, the boys were to go there [and] every one of them had cudgels'.[89]

More sophisticated preparations could also be resorted to. Randall Kernan esq., a Catholic barrister on the north-west circuit, claimed in 1835 that it was

> constant practice in the morning of the fair, for the yeomen to lodge their arms in a particular place or depot; then if a row took place in the evening, or a riot, they fought for some time with sticks, and after this the yeomen generally went for their arms and fired upon the people assembled at the fair.[90]

feature of violent confrontations in Ireland in the nineteenth century, see Conley, *Melancholy Accidents*, p. 26. In this case, Latimer had borrowed a pipe from the owner of the pub and had given it to another Protestant man called Morton, who refused to give it up. Morton, in fact, 'put [the pipe] in his pocket, and said there was no puppy in the house would take it from him'. A Catholic called James Alwell made repeated efforts to retrieve the pipe but to no avail. He eventually confronted Morton with a stick and demanded the pipe from Morton three times but on each occasion the latter refused to give it to him. Alwell then hit him over the head with the stick and a number of people entered the room in his support. This, in turn, led to a general affray in which Latimer was killed. See *Enniskillen Chronicle and Erne Packet*, 10 Mar. 1842.

88 *Belfast Newsletter*, 31 Jul. 1835.
89 *Enniskillen Chronicle and Erne Packet*, 19 Aug. 1824.
90 Third report on Orange lodges, *Minutes of evidence 1835*, pp. 75–6.

He also recounted an incident which occurred in Co. Fermanagh in 1811 where a Catholic man was killed in a party fight between Orangemen and a group of Catholics. According to Kernan, 'they commenced fighting with sticks at an early hour; the Catholics had the best of the battle; the Orange yeomen retreated and got their arms, and then fired upon the people, which was the common way of concluding the fights in those days'.[91]

Events of a similar character are evident at the fair of Ederney in Co. Fermanagh in 1824 at which Robert Ingram was killed. On the fair day, a number of riots took place in the late morning and early afternoon during which 'several Protestants' were beaten. In response to these beatings, a number of Protestants formed a 'guard' made up of about '12 or 14' men that included the deceased, Robert Ingram. This guard was formed at about three or four o'clock at a place called Drumkeen where the men armed themselves. From Drumkeen the guard marched back to Ederney with 'guns and bayonets screwed on, over their shoulders' ready to confront the opposing side.[92]

Yet, while violence may have been expected, there is little evidence of premeditated killings in these incidents. In the case in Ederney, a number of Catholics took offence at the actions of the Protestant party and gathered together and began to throw stones at the guard. The guard then took up a position at the house of an innkeeper called Henry Tiernan and the group of Catholics gathered around them and threw stones at the house one of which hit Ingram on the head and fractured his skull.[93] These homicides generally emerged in the context of a general group fight. This is clearly evident in the above mentioned killing in 1842 of George Latimer, who was hit on the head with a pair of tongs in the course of a general affray and died six or seven weeks later. In the incident on Inishmore, William McCreery, a Protestant, was killed during a riot that broke out before the pre-arranged challenge fight could take place.[94] This pattern is also consistent with that found in riots that occurred in Belfast in the 1830s and 40s. Catherine Hirst, in her study of sectarianism in nineteenth-century Belfast, reveals how 'riots in the early to mid-nineteenth century were [...] remarkable for the low number of fatalities'. It would also confirm her suggestion that this may have been due to the fact that 'rioters in Belfast may also have followed an

---

[91] Ibid., p. 75. See also *Belfast Newsletter*, 20 Mar. 1812 and Farrell, *Rituals and Riots*, pp. 60–1.
[92] *Enniskillen Chronicle and Erne Packet*, 12 Aug. 1824.
[93] Ibid.
[94] Ibid., 19 Aug. 1824.

unwritten code of conduct' which, in turn, had its roots in earlier sectarian conflicts in rural Ulster.[95]

Parallels can also obviously be drawn with the practice of faction fighting, particularly in the south and west of the country, at this time. In such cases, large groups of men could meet at appointed times to vent factional animosity. Such fights also had a ritual dimension to them which allowed for conflict to be played out in set forms and within certain rules of engagement. Ritualised group fighting may, indeed, have channelled aggression, restricting it to particular occasions and events and thereby lessening the likelihood of serious interpersonal conflict at other times. In this sense, ritualised sectarian group violence and faction fighting may have been as much about the control of violent conflict as about its expression. This does not mean, of course, that they were not dangerous activities – in areas such as Tipperary and some surrounding counties, faction fights could give rise to serious acts of lethal violence and, as we have seen in our sample, fatalities also occurred in sectarian confrontations. It is probable, however, that the resort to lethal violence was generally not accepted as legitimate in these confrontations.[96]

Violence between individuals

Some cases were confined to individuals who attempted to assert themselves over others. In some cases no particular issue was at stake, but rather the incident revolved around a challenge stemming from a more general sectarian animosity. This is clearly evident in the killing of the two brothers, John and Michael Henderson, by Philip Fitzpatrick at Lurgan, Co. Armagh, on 20 May 1848.[97] This was, in relation to numbers killed, the most serious sectarian incident in Co. Armagh over the entire sixteen-year period of our sample. It was probably also, relative to the other cases at least, the most premeditated of all the homicides in our entire sample. On the night in question, both Michael and John Henderson had been drinking with four other men in a public house called McGeown's in Lurgan. When they left the pub that evening, having drunk 'a pint of whiskey, a quart of beer and two glasses of cordial' they walked out onto Back Lane. It was here that they

95 Catherine Hirst, *Religion, Politics and Violence in Nineteenth-Century Belfast: The Pound and Sandy Row* (Dublin: Four Courts Press, 2002), pp. 80–1. Farrell has also noted that 'contrary to their reputation as primal and spontaneous affairs, nineteenth-century riots between Orange and Green were almost universally set-piece confrontations' (Farrell, *Rituals and Riots*, p. 63).

96 See Appendix two for the incidence of homicide arising from factional disputes. For a discussion of the incidence of faction fighting in Ireland at this time, see chapter two.

97 *Armagh Guardian*, 24 Jul. 1848. A third man died as a consequence of lockjaw after being 'wounded in the thumb' by Fitzpatrick. See *Armagh Guardian*, 17 Jul. 1848.

encountered Philip Fitzpatrick, who 'was shouting, and exclaimed that he could beat ever a papist in the lane'. Michael Henderson, who, according to one witness, was intoxicated, took umbrage at this and engaged Fitzpatrick in a fight. They were separated by a Patrick Gallery, who had been drinking with the Hendersons, but who declared that 'the man who would strike "Phil" would strike him.' This put a stop to the fight between Michael and Philip. At this point, however, John Henderson intervened and 'exchanged four or five blows' with Fitzpatrick. It was in the course of this fight that Fitzpatrick stabbed John Henderson through the heart with a butcher's knife which he had borrowed some hours earlier. He then approached Michael Henderson again and although the latter pleaded with him a number of times that he had 'already done enough' Fitzpatrick stabbed and killed him as well. After killing both brothers he was heard to declare 'I'm the boy can lay them by.'[98]

There were also cases where individuals responded to an insult or challenge with lethal violence. In Fermanagh in February 1835, John Armstrong, a Protestant, was suspected of the killing of Roger O'Neill, a Catholic. The police believed that this case arose 'in consequence of [a] difference in religion'.[99] On the day in question, John Armstrong was beaten on the road five miles outside Enniskillen by a number of people returning from a funeral. Following the beating, Armstrong ran to the house of a relation and there armed himself with a spade and, along with a friend called Robert Armstrong, went along the road to seek revenge. On the road, they came across a group of Catholics returning from the funeral 'none of whom, as it appeared on the inquest, had any concern in the [earlier] abuse of John Armstrong'.[100] Among this group was Roger O'Neill. Armstrong seems to have singled him out and 'without any provocation whatever' hit him on the head with the spade handle, from which O'Neill died a few days later.[101]

In many of these cases a personal dispute intermingled with wider sectarian tensions within the community to give rise to homicidal violence. This is evident in the killing of William Flynn near Newtownhamilton, Co. Armagh, in October 1847, for which Joseph and John Thompson were indicted at the spring assizes of 1848. Flynn, a Catholic, was returning home one night with a number of people along a public road from a fair when Alexander, Joseph and John Thompson, all Protestants, overtook him. At this point, Flynn left the group he was with and went up to Joseph Thompson and asked 'if he wanted for company'? Thompson replied that

[98] *Armagh Guardian*, 24 Jul. 1848.
[99] NAI, official papers, 1835/352.
[100] *Enniskillen Chronicle and Erne Packet*, 12 Feb. 1835.
[101] NAI, official papers, 1835/352.

he did not 'as he was in a hurry home'. Flynn then asked what 'if he were made wait,' and pushed Thompson into a ditch. Following this, Thompson went up the road to the house of a man called James Henry. There were a number of people in the house, including two policemen. Thompson told those present what had occurred and one of the policemen told him that he could bring Flynn before the court of petty sessions for the assault, but Thompson declared he 'would be revenged of him'. Mrs Henry, who was in the house at the time, 'chided him for the words he made use of in the house, and added that he would not be able to beat any person'.[102]

At this point, a number of people were heard passing the house when Thompson rushed out and the police followed him. The police then heard a voice at the gate of Henry's house declare to William Flynn, 'are you as good a man now as you were to-night before'. Flynn simply replied 'I am'. There was a confrontation, at this stage, the exact nature of which is difficult to ascertain as a number of witnesses claimed that, due to the darkness and the nature of the weather, they were unable to see exactly what was happening. It is clear, however, that during the course of the fight Flynn was stabbed in the heart and died shortly afterwards.[103]

According to Joshua Magee, the county coroner, the locality in which this offence occurred, near Newtownhamilton, was a 'mountainous' area in which 'the people are [...] divided into two hostile factions Orange & Catholic'. He pointed out also that tensions in the locality had been greatly increased in the last twelve months 'since a Catholic named McEllherron lost his life in an affray in [Newtownhamilton], & since that period a deep revengeful feeling prevails & when the people meet they view each other somewhat in the same light, that two hostile armies would'.[104]

III

What do these cases reveal about the relationship between sectarian animosity and violent activity in Ireland at this time? Whether arising from communal, group or individual conflicts, these homicides expose real and significant sectarian tensions and offer clear support to the position that sectarian animosity was a direct cause of violent activity at this time. In particular, the incidents of communal violence demonstrate the ability of sectarian feeling to mobilise large numbers of people, both Catholic and Protestant, in a way that few other issues could, and to provoke violent conflicts which seem to reveal pervasive and real sectarian divisions that are difficult, if

102 *Armagh Guardian*, 6 Mar. 1848.
103 Ibid.
104 NAI, outrage papers, Armagh, 1847/303.

not impossible, to dismiss as unrepresentative of attitudes in the wider culture. Yet, as was demonstrated earlier in this chapter, such animosity rarely gave rise to serious or lethal violent conflict. Such cases as did arise constituted but a small proportion of all acts of lethal violence; based on more qualitative evidence from the Poor Law Commission, it seems that sectarian conflict did not give rise to widespread unrest at this time. Thus, if we assume that widespread and deep-rooted sectarian animosity should give rise to high rates of serious violence, there seems to be an apparent inconsistency between the quantitative data on sectarian homicide and the contextual analysis of particular incidents. Is it possible to explain this apparent inconsistency?

It may be that in many instances and in many areas the conditions for the emergence of violent conflict were not present. The importance of two factors has been noted in incidents of lethal violence. First, the attempt by one side to assert itself over the other and, second, a willingness to respond to a challenge from the opposing side by resorting to acts of violence. In the south of the country there can be little doubt of Catholic self-assertion in this period. The mass demonstrations of the 1820s in favour of Catholic emancipation and in the anti-tithe demonstrations of the early 1830s are obvious examples.[105] Yet, few enough serious or lethal acts of violence arose from sectarian animosity. This may have been due to reluctance among Protestants to rise to such challenges, as it would have placed them in a dangerous and undesirable position, perhaps leaving them exposed to reprisals. Many in the south may have chosen the route of migration to the north of the country or emigration to North America as an altogether safer option.[106] The relative absence of sectarian violence should not lead us, therefore, to underestimate the strength and extent of sectarian animosity in the south of the country. It seems, however, that the conditions for the expression of such animosity in acts of lethal violence were limited.

In the north too, segregated communities and the dominance by one religious grouping over another within specific localities may have served to lessen the likelihood of confrontation. James Denham, esq., a magistrate in Co. Fermanagh, informed the 1835 Poor Law Commission that the parish of Cleenish was 'quiet' because it was 'a Protestant parish [and] the

---

[105] See McGrath 'Interdenominational Relations' and O'Hanrahan 'Tithe War'.

[106] There was a considerable movement of Protestants from the south of Ireland in this period. See Miller, 'The Lost World of Andrew Johnston' p. 223. Miller points out that 'the hemorrhage of southern Irish Protestants [in the pre-Famine period] both resulted from and greatly contributed to the rise of middle-class Catholic political and economic ascendancy in those counties.'

Roman Catholics dare not disturb the country as in the south of Ireland'.[107]
Another magistrate in the county, William Darcy esq., also reported that
the parish of Derryvollan was 'perfectly peaceable' and pointed out that 'the
parishioners [were] chiefly Protestants'.[108] In such instances, the risk and fear
of reprisal may have outweighed the minority group's willingness to react
to the assertion of dominance by the majority. Emigration, as Donnelly and
Clark have pointed out, may also have served to lessen the extent of unrest
generally in the north.[109]

Yet, while local dominance, segregation and wider forces such as
emigration may have contributed to the low rates of lethal sectarian
conflict, they do not of themselves wholly explain them. In some respects,
issues of local dominance simply raise further questions about the role of
violence at this time. For instance, why didn't the assertion of the majority
over the minority involve serious acts of violence? It is also important
not to overemphasise the degree to which these were mutually exclusive
communities. There was still ample opportunity for both communities to
interact in the course of their daily routine, not to mention at fairs and
markets.[110] Moreover, while emigration may have served to lessen the
extent of social unrest it does not of itself explain the low rates of sectarian
violence. It might be expected, for instance, that those who stayed behind
were those who were most committed to staying and meeting any challenge
to their community or religious identity. Moreover, there was, as noted, some

---

[107] Poor Law Commission, *appendix e*, p. 351.

[108] Ibid., p. 352.

[109] Clark and Donnelly, *Irish Peasants*, p. 150.

[110] It is striking how some of the cases in our sample reveal co-operation and sometimes
friendship between individual Catholics and Protestants within particular localities as well
as sectarian animosity. In the case on the island of Innishmore in Co. Fermanagh, the
protagonists, Kenny and Lunny, both lived on the island, which, according to a local land
agent, William Armstrong, contained 'a number of inhabitants [...] of different religious
persuasions; [who had] lived till lately upon very amicable terms, save some trifling
bickering betimes' (*Enniskillen Chronicle and Erne Packet*, 19 Aug. 1824). The evidence
relating to the Macken fight also reveals some ties of friendship and co-operation on a
local level. For instance, Edward Scarlet, son of one of the deceased, pointed out that
Pat Montgomery, one of the accused, 'used to be dining in his house when steward of
Mr Nixon'. John Glass, an Orangeman and a key prosecution witness, stated that he had
known Francis McBrien, one of the accused, 'for a long time, and was on friendly terms
with him'. See *Enniskillen Chronicle and Erne Packet*, 25 Mar. 1830 and 1 Apr. 1830. This
would, in some respects, also be consistent with the view of interdenominational relations
in the north at this time put forward by Elliott. She suggests that while Catholics and
Protestants viewed each other across a sectarian divide, friendships were still formed and
there was a degree of interdependence on both sides. Elliott, *Catholics*, chapter ten. See
also Akenson, *Small Differences*; Madden, *Forkhill Protestants and Forkhill Catholics*; W.E.
Vaughan, 'Ireland c.1870' in *idem* (ed.), *Ireland under the Union, I*, p. 745.

movement of Protestants into Ulster at this time from southern areas of the country, which may have contributed to rather than diminished the extent of sectarian animosity in the province. This would suggest that there were other forces at work in the containment of violent sectarian conflict.

Another key factor may be the effectiveness of outside controls. The ban on party processions between 1832 and 1845 may, for instance, have limited the opportunity for confrontations between the two communities. Yet, while this might partly explain the low rate of homicides arising from communal confrontations it does little to explain the low rate of incidents involving group and individual confrontations. Even a cursory examination of the court records of the time also reveals that the reaction to the imposition of the ban among at least some members of the Protestant community was often to continue with the processions in defiance of the law.

This period, of course, also saw the introduction of a centrally-controlled national police force in Ireland. It may be that the increasing role of the police in patrolling fairs and other large social gatherings served to inhibit the extent and frequency of violence. For instance, Sir Frederic Stovin reported that a fight was prevented at the Enniskillen races in 1835 due to a 'display of force' by the military and a 'large party of police' on the day.[111] Yet the role of the police in imposing outside control should not be exaggerated. The participants in a number of these cases were quite willing to ignore the police. This is evident on a communal level in the actions of the Orangemen in the shooting of Boyle in Armagh in 1845 and, on an individual level, in the actions of Thompson in ignoring the advice of the police in the same county in 1848. Moreover, although the police prevented a confrontation at the race meeting above, a riot did break out following a subsequent meeting, perhaps indicating that the police could postpone but not always wholly prevent sectarian violence. Indeed, the presence of a large number of police did not always prevent a serious clash, rather it could serve to aggravate the situation. For instance, there was a considerable police presence at one of the most serious incidents of sectarian violence in this entire period, the killings at Dolly's Brae in Co. Down in 1849. The actions of the police on this day may have served to aid rather than inhibit violent activity.[112] This is not to suggest that the police were wholly ineffective in controlling sectarian violence, but rather that their effectiveness depended less on a 'display of force' and more on whether the parties involved were willing to cede to their authority. In this sense, the 'display of force' was probably a necessary but not always a sufficient condition for the police to maintain order.

[111] Select committee on Orange lodges, 1835, p. 326.
[112] See Kinealy 'A Right to March?', p. 62.

A more effective control on the extent of violence may have been the role of local magistrates within these areas who could exert an influence over both sides of the community. This is evident in the role of Lord Enniskillen on the morning of the Macken fight, where his intervention helped to defuse a large-scale confrontation. There were also attempts, following the end of the ban on party processions in 1845, by members of the local Protestant gentry to discourage Orange marches in the north of the country.[113] Efforts were also undertaken that year by leading figures within the Repeal movement and the clergy to encourage Catholics not to respond to any provocation arising from Orange marches. Thomas Steele, a prominent figure in the Repeal movement and a close associate of Daniel O'Connell, toured the north of Ireland before the marching season in 1845 and distributed 20,000 copies of an address calling on Catholics not to respond to any provocation arising from Orange processions.[114]

Yet, while prominent figures such as Lord Enniskillen could play a useful role in brokering a settlement between rival groups, it is also clear that such influence was by no means total. There were certainly incidents where the advice of local notables was ignored. For instance, at the Inishmore fight in Co. Fermanagh in 1824 an attempt to prevent a confrontation by a local land agent, William Armstrong, failed. The actions of local magistrates could also serve to aggravate the situation. In the case of the killing of William Lang in Fermanagh in 1835, the group of Protestants involved had originally been detained by the police and their weapons were taken from them. Within a short period of time, however, they had been released on the instructions of a local magistrate and given back their weapons. Shortly after this, the fatal encounter in which Lang lost his life occurred.[115] The efforts of political figures such as Thomas Steele, however well-intentioned, may also have served more to raise suspicions within the Protestant community than to lessen the likelihood of conflict.[116]

Ultimately, the low rate of lethal sectarian violence was due more to conditions and attitudes within these communities than the effectiveness of external controls upon them. There was probably a practical consideration within the communities themselves of the need to maintain stability and a realisation of the inherent dangers and difficulties, both on an individual and communal level, in committing such acts as it might spark off a more

---

[113] Ó Muirí, 'The Orangemen, Repealers and the Shooting of John Boyle', pp. 452–60.

[114] Ibid., pp. 443–50.

[115] Select committee on Orange lodges, 1835, p. 326.

[116] Some within the Protestant community certainly saw Steele's efforts more as an act of provocation than conciliation. See Ó Muirí, 'The Orangemen, Repealers and the Shooting of John Boyle', pp. 454–7.

thorough or large-scale confrontation. There was probably also a wider but not wholly unrelated consideration that lethal violence was simply not an appropriate response to sectarian animosity. In particular, unprovoked sectarian violence was probably not considered legitimate. It is notable, for instance, that, with the possible exception of Fitzpatrick, none of these cases involved planned attempts to kill a member of the other community. When someone was killed it was as a result of injuries sustained in the course of a fight rather than a premeditated decision to kill. This is also reflected in the fact that in the majority of cases those accused of homicides arising from sectarian conflict were either convicted on the lesser charge of manslaughter or acquitted.[117] This is all the more extraordinary when one considers that lethal weapons, in particular firearms, featured prominently in a number of cases. These were, it seems, communities in which a sense of religious difference and sectarian hostility intermingled, interacted and ultimately competed with considerations of local stability and ideas of what constituted legitimate violence.

There were, of course, situations where sectarianism overcame considerations of the need for peaceful co-existence within localities and concepts of legitimate violence. This is most evident in cases where individuals, such as Philip Fitzpatrick, broke ranks and indulged in extreme sectarian violence. Such occasions were, however, exceedingly rare and unrepresentative.[118] It is also evident at times of political change or instability, such as the passing of Catholic emancipation in 1829. Indeed, there can be little doubt of the connection between political instability and violent activity, and it is, perhaps, no coincidence that elections could also witness particular outbursts of serious violent conflict.[119] Yet, even here, violence depended more on the contingencies of particular situations rather than premeditated decisions to engage in acts of lethal violence.

---

[117] See Mc Mahon, *Violence, the Courts and Legal Cultures*, chapter four.

[118] Fitzpatrick was portrayed in the local press as very much an outsider. He had been tried on four occasions previous to this. Questions were also raised as to whether or not he was a Protestant. When he had been committed to gaol on previous occasions he had told the turnkey that he was a Catholic. At the time of his trial for murder, he claimed, however, that he was always a Protestant and had only said he was a Catholic to 'vex' the deputy governor of the prison. The *Armagh Guardian* maintained that he was only a Protestant through marriage and that he was originally a Catholic from Co. Cavan. Whatever the truth of the matter, it is clear that the *Armagh Guardian*, a Protestant newspaper, was keen to distance Fitzpatrick from the Protestant faith. See the *Armagh Guardian*, 22 May, 24 Jul. and 14 Aug. 1848.

[119] Farrell too has noted the relationship between periods of particular political crisis and outbreaks of sectarian violence. See generally Farrell, *Rituals and Riots*, chapters two, three and four.

Violence was more likely to be carried out in a controlled manner and within the context of unwritten rules of appropriate action which may actually have served to enhance rather than disrupt communal stability by simultaneously expressing but also limiting the divisiveness of sectarian animosity (or, in other contexts, factional or political rivalry). Similarly, the use of parades or processions in order to express religious (and/or political) identity, while provocative, also probably served to channel and restrict the assertion of identity in a relatively secure and controlled manner, although by no means a risk-free one.

Finally, it is necessary to reflect more directly on the part played by religious identity and its relationship to violent activity. There can be little doubt that both Catholic and Protestant religious identities generated a considerable degree of sectarian animosity in this period and that such animosity could also lead, albeit rarely, to acts of lethal violence. Could it also be the case that the character of both religious outlooks and the hostility they showed towards each other served to lessen and control violent conflict? This is, to say the least, a dubious claim. It amounts, in a strict sense, to a circular argument claiming that Catholics and Protestants managed to coexist as Catholics and Protestants because they were Protestants and Catholics. Even to claim that by accentuating the 'small differences' between each other they managed to coexist seems a dubious and, ultimately, untestable proposition. Surely, one could equally argue that if they had tried to lessen the significance of these differences it would have led to a more peaceful coexistence. Nor can we understand the low levels of sectarian violence simply in the light of 'deterrence communities' whereby the maintenance of clear differences in religious identity in Ulster somehow acted as a control on violent activity.[120] This approach serves to decontextualise experiences in Ulster from those in the rest of Ireland where similar patterns of violence are found but where sectarian division was not a major factor in the control of violent action. Thus, faction fights followed broadly similar patterns to sectarian group confrontations without the controlling factor of religious division, and ambivalence over questions of identity was more pronounced than in sectarian clashes. It did not, however, lead to radically different experiences of violent conflict. Sectarian violence in Ulster followed broader patterns of violence in Ireland rather than taking on wholly distinctive forms based around 'deterrence communities' rooted in religious difference.

A more likely explanation is that religious identity was itself bound up in and infused with competing considerations of sectarian hostility, community stability and concepts of legitimate violence. In this sense, the relatively low

---

[120] See, for instance, T.K. Wilson, *Frontiers of Violence: Conflict and Identity in Ulster and Upper Silesia, 1918–1922* (Oxford: Oxford University Press, 2010).

rate of sectarian homicide evident in Ireland at this time was rooted less in the maintenance, extenuation or exaggeration of religious difference, but rather was a product of the complex interplay of competing considerations of religious identity, community and ideas of what constituted legitimate action. Such interaction ultimately underpinned the relationship between sectarian animosity and violent activity.

More work needs to be done on both the causes and dynamics of sectarian violence and, in particular, how it was contained and limited over the course of this period. More localised and in-depth studies of particular counties would also be helpful. Yet, based on a study of homicide at least, it is safe to conclude that considerations of local circumstance and wider concepts of legitimate violence meant that while sectarian animosity was a real and pervasive force in Irish society in the first half of the nineteenth century, this did not necessarily make it a particularly violent place or one in which violence was necessarily socially disruptive. It was rather a society in which the extent of both sectarian animosity and violent activity was very clearly controlled within both Catholic and Protestant communities. The picture that emerges, therefore, is not so much of a people bound by or in thrall to the 'madness of party' but rather communities that lived, however imperfectly, with the legacy of their history.

Conclusion

Ireland in the first half of the nineteenth century could be a violent place. In certain areas, in particular Co. Tipperary and, at times, in other locations, rates of homicide could be considerably higher than those found in present-day Ireland and Europe. The nature of some violent activity also suggests that violence could, in certain contexts, come to play a prominent part in the socio-economic, cultural and political life of the country. Pre-Famine Ireland can at times appear, from the perspective of the early twenty-first century, to be an extraordinarily violent place with groups meeting in open combat at social gatherings such as fairs to vent sectarian or factional animosities or at events such as elections to express political rivalries. Indeed, the most striking difference between that time and the present is the incidence of group and collective violence, particularly, though not exclusively, in the early decades of the nineteenth century. The periodic outbreaks of unrest where violence was used to address wider socio-economic grievances particularly relating to land also suggests a society where violence could, at times, become the primary means of dealing with economic and social conflicts. Both agrarian unrest and sectarian violence might easily offer the impression of a country in which violence was a dominant means of dealing with conflict, and undoubtedly helped to feed perceptions of Ireland as a violent society.

Such activity needs to be seen in context, however. The available statistical evidence indicates that, in much of the country and for much of the period under review, the extent of violence was contained. The incidence of homicide was not particularly high; it was comparable, on a national level and in most individual counties, to rates found in other countries at the time and is by no means out of line with rates found in modern-day Europe. There is also little evidence that rates of homicide were much higher in some areas in the nineteenth century than they had been in the eighteenth. The more qualitative evidence drawn from the responses offered to the Poor Law Commission also indicate that violent conflict was by no means ubiquitous or a major source of social unrest.

The centrality of violence in Irish society can also be questioned. While particular acts of violence may reveal underlying conflicts in Irish society, they do not necessarily offer the clearest indication of how these conflicts were usually dealt with. Violence or the threat of violence, while by no means absent, was not central to the regulation and occupation of land. It might, of course, be argued that the study of homicide does not allow for a full picture of violent activity and that intimidation and non-lethal violence imposed a kind of order in which lethal violence was simply unnecessary. This would again place violence and the threat of violence at the centre of economic and social life, but this view is not sustained by the evidence. In many areas, including counties with a reputation for unrest such as Co. Clare, there is little evidence that non-lethal land-related interpersonal violence was common or that there was widespread communal support for such violence or, more generally, that the threat of violence was effective in regulating the rural economy. It is highly unlikely, therefore, that low rates of lethal violence simply reflect the successful imposition of a widespread system of intimidation on Irish communities.

This does not mean, of course, that we should lightly dismiss the significance of agrarian unrest or simply refute its symbolic importance. We need rather to understand the relationship between, on the one hand, outbreaks of agrarian unrest and, on the other, the evidence of a lack of social unrest, without dismissing either as wholly unrepresentative. A central contention of this book is that episodes of unrest can be reconciled with generally low rates of homicide if we accept that, first, unrest reveals much about the underlying conflicts over land and the rural economy in certain parts of Ireland and, second, that the low rates of homicide reflect the ability in many areas to manage and contain such conflicts for long periods of time. They might be seen as two sides of the same coin – reflecting the desire and, at times, the ability to maintain a particular form of order in the face of considerable economic and social challenges. However, the maintenance of order was not generally achieved by a communal conspiracy underpinned by the threat of secret society-inspired violence, but rather through a complex (and unequal) negotiation of interests between landlords, farmers, and labourers which served to contain and control the extent of violent conflict.

There were also real limits to the extent of violent sectarian conflict in pre-Famine and Famine Ireland. Acts of lethal violence arising from sectarian animosity certainly did not constitute a high proportion of homicide cases in this period. There is also considerable evidence to suggest that lethal violence, at least, was not considered an appropriate or legitimate response to sectarian animosity. Such animosity, particularly in the north of the country, was played out in different ways through the assertion of identity in processions and group confrontations where the extent of violence was usually controlled. Politically-motivated lethal violence was also extremely rare – constituting a tiny minority of all cases of reported homicide at this time. The available evidence also indicates that the incidence of faction fighting, while common in some areas, particularly the south and the west in the early decades of the century, was by no means ubiquitous. Ritualised group fighting may, in some respects, have also channelled aggression, restricting it to particular occasions and events and thereby lessening the likelihood of serious interpersonal conflict at other times.

Most acts of lethal violence, of course, did not have their roots in sectarian, political or factional disputes or even in conflicts directly relating to economic issues such as land. On the contrary, many cases arose from personal disputes among men, often over apparently minor matters, and from personal disputes within families. Moreover, the nature of such homicide is by no means out of line with experiences in the present day, suggesting that, while there are obviously differences, there is also some degree of continuity in the patterns of violent activity in Ireland between past and present. The available evidence also indicates that the use of interpersonal violence was not central to personal and familial relationships.

This is not to deny the prevalence of certain forms of violent activity, but rather to make the case that we need to draw a distinction between prevalence and centrality. It is highly likely, for instance, that domestic violence was as prevalent in nineteenth-century Ireland as it is in the present day (when just over one in four of the population report having experienced some form of abuse). It would be a mistake, however, to conclude from this that violent abuse is central to familial and personal relations, that is to say that the use of violence is the fundamental means through which family relations are generally ordered or that it dominates relationships among men or between men and women. To argue that this was the case in pre-Famine Ireland would require much stronger evidence than I have been able to find and, indeed, it is difficult to see how any society could function if the *use* of violence by the majority of the population was the dominant means of communicating and negotiating interests among individuals.

This is not, however, to underestimate the possible impact of the *threat* of violence on interpersonal relations and how vulnerability to both violence and the threat of violence could vary according to age, gender and social position. While all human relationships, however intimate or distant, contain within them the potential for violence, certain sections of the population are undoubtedly more vulnerable to the threat of violence than others. Married women, for instance, might find that the risk of violence increased considerably when they acted or were perceived to act against their husbands' wishes. More generally, men might use the threat of violence to control women's behaviour. The extent of such threats cannot be quantified, but it would be foolish to discount the potential impact on individual lives. Young men might also have to contend with greater levels of threatened violence from their peers than other groups. Thus, the threat of violence as well as actual acts of violence could, in certain circumstances, have a considerable impact on the lives of individuals.

Yet, while acknowledging the variability of vulnerability to violence according to social, gender and age profiles, it would be dangerous to view the potential threat of violence as necessarily central to relationships in Ireland. To do so privileges violence over other means of communication and negotiation among individuals and reduces the complexity of human interaction to a series of threats and counter threats or violent actions and counter actions. Violence is not an inevitable response to conflict, but is rather one means among many of dealing with it. The striking fact about pre-Famine Ireland is how the potential for violence was often carefully managed and controlled and, as in the present, prevented, in the main, from disrupting the prevailing order.

There is, of course, also a need to further explore the nature and meaning of other forms of violent activity – further studies of assault, robbery, rape and infanticide are needed to reach a fuller understanding of the part played by violence in Irish life. Such studies would do much to illuminate the meaning of and attitudes to violence in Ireland. The study of homicide does, nevertheless, offer a significant perspective. It allows us to trace some patterns of violence over time and to draw on viable comparative sources from other countries and periods. This is far more problematic with other forms of violent activity. The classic objection to quantitative studies of homicide is that they cannot reveal the overall level of violence in society. This is, of course, compelling, but can also be highly misleading as it usually seeks to undermine what can, with care, be quantified with allusions to what cannot ultimately be known. In doing so, such objections too easily and perhaps lazily dismiss the importance of homicide as a key to understanding patterns of violent activity. In our context, a low rate of homicide is significant in pre-Famine and Famine Ireland as it offers an indication not of increasing or decreasing levels of violence in general, but of the extent to which violence was contained and controlled over time and the part serious acts of violence could play in social and cultural life.

If pre-Famine and Famine Ireland could, at times, be a violent place it was not, on the whole, a particularly or remarkably violent society and those who lived in Ireland at this time did not inhabit an 'extremely violent world'. The sources of conflict and the means of control could often be delicately balanced and when these controls were called into question or weakened the consequences could be severe. This could, for instance, occur at times of political instability or economic uncertainty. On the whole, however, this was not a society in which violence was the primary or dominant means of self-assertion or one in which relationships were generally characterised by the use of interpersonal violence, but rather one where the extent of violent conflict and the potential for violence was limited, tightly controlled and marginalised within communities.

Why then was Ireland perceived as a violent society? This view of Ireland, which was prevalent in some political writing, traveller accounts and parliamentary reports, was derived, to some extent, from incidents of agrarian, factional and sectarian violence. Particular incidents of unrest were undoubtedly dramatic and, therefore, more likely to garner attention and it is perhaps not surprising that commentators focused on these in their portrayals and characterisations of Irish society. We might then simply see perceptions of Ireland as a violent society as a failure on the part of influential commentators to properly contextualise incidents of unrest or fully understand the broader picture in pre-Famine and Famine Ireland, or as part of a tendency to simply repeat the received wisdom of previous commentators. Yet, explanations of perceptions of Ireland as a violent society which rest solely on the impact of reports of particular episodes of unrest on individual commentators are not wholly satisfactory. There also needs to be at least some recognition of the contexts from which such views emerged and of their political utility.[1]

In pre-Famine and Famine Ireland, the dominant narratives of violence are generally rooted in competing interpretations of Irish society and culture which, in turn, often reflected broader political philosophies.[2] For those who sought to defend both central and local authority from accusations of bias and incompetence, there was a clear advantage in portraying violence in Ireland as simply a product of an inherently unruly and uncivilised people. Writers hostile to demands for political reform in Ireland could argue that violence was not a consequence of political failures, but rather a common feature of Irish life stretching back millennia which had little or nothing to do with British rule in Ireland.[3] In doing so, it was possible to dismiss the genuine points of conflict in Irish society and the need for substantial

---

[1]   A full account of the political contexts in which discussions of violence took place would require a separate study. The following overview is intended simply to highlight some key influences on perceptions of pre-Famine and Famine Ireland.

[2]   The positions outlined here reflect a wider divide in political writing of the period which centred on whether 'Irish character' was due to history ('the result of centuries of oppression and demoralization') or whether it was due to 'primordial, quasi-natural causes' rooted in 'Celtic descent and immemorial habits'. See Roberto Romani, 'British Views on Irish National Character, 1800–1846. An Intellectual History', *History of European Ideas*, 23 (1997), p. 194.

[3]   See, for instance, E.A. Kendall, 'Letter to a Friend on the State of Ireland, the Roman

political reform and to argue that, in such circumstances, only effective repression by the state could maintain order among an unruly population.

There was also undoubtedly a certain political expediency in dwelling on particular incidents of unrest and ideas of Irish exceptionalism in order to garner support for legislative moves to strengthen the coercive powers of the state. Politicians were certainly not slow to combine ideas of Irish exceptionalism and particular moments of unrest to strengthen the case for legislation in Ireland that would not be tolerated in England. This can be seen, to take but one example, in the approach taken by Robert Peel in his attempt to introduce police reforms in the mid-1810s. In making the case for the introduction of the Peace Preservation Force in 1814, Peel emphasised how the 'character and spirit of the governed' in Ireland was 'completely different' from that in England. In Ireland, there was an 'extreme virulence' of spirit operating on the character of the people and he asserted that conditions in Ireland were 'so different' as to warrant measures which would be deemed 'improper' in England. In getting the bill passed, Peel recounted particular moments of extreme violence which, he noted, had the 'due effect upon the minds of English country gentlemen' who ultimately passed the bill without serious opposition.[4] Here, conceptions of national character, ideas of Irish exceptionalism and incidents of agrarian violence could all be combined to reinforce and perpetuate a particular picture of Ireland. Peel's picture, of course, was not plucked from the ether and the tone of his parliamentary address is balanced, but it was nevertheless a partial portrayal of Ireland designed to serve a particular political end and one which built on an image of Ireland as a violent society.

This image, however, was not just useful for those who sought to prevent reform or for those who looked for exceptional powers that would not be tolerated in England. On the contrary, it was more often those who sought reform in Ireland that offered up the image of a violent country. This can be traced in an alternative and somewhat more sophisticated view of Irish society and culture. This interpretation shares the view of Irish violence as a product of an uncivilised and unruly population, but also stresses that the reasons for this state of affairs lies, to some extent at least, in the mismanagement of successive governments and of a corrupt landed interest rather than reflecting any inherent or unceasing tendency on the part of the Irish people to resort to violence. This position is clearly expressed in perhaps the single most influential work on violence in nineteenth-century Ireland,

Catholic Question, and the Merits of Constitutional Religious Distinctions', *Quarterly Review*, 38 (1828), pp. 535–98.
[4]   See Palmer, *Police and Protest*, pp. 201–2.

George Cornewall Lewis's *On Local Disturbances in Ireland.*[5] Rather than wallowing in a form of political fatalism or relying wholly on notions of Irish exceptionalism, Lewis used agrarian violence to make a case for intervention and reform in Ireland. In his view, it was only through intervention by the state that Ireland would join the ranks of other civilised countries within the United Kingdom.[6] In particular, he advocated a particular form of poor law in Ireland based around the workhouse. In making his case, he used agrarian violence to demonstrate the failure of existing policies and to support a critique of landed authority in Ireland. Thus, while Lewis eschewed the notion of Irish exceptionalism and of an inherently violent people, and rejected the need for more coercive legislation, he too found it politically expedient to portray Ireland as a violent society. Like Peel, the picture he presented was safely rooted in incidents of agrarian unrest, but was also a partial one which furthered particular political aims – in this case a poor law policy that would ultimately prove disastrous during the Famine of the 1840s. A similar view of Irish violence as a product of past misrule can also be found, albeit in a more strident form, in the work of the French liberal commentator, Gustave de Beaumont. For de Beaumont, Irishmen were 'lazy, mendacious, intemperate [and] prompt to acts of violence', but he was also keen to point out that he did not attribute this to any 'original or hereditary taint', but rather to the 'most merciless tyranny' arising from seven centuries of British rule.[7] Here again, violence was used to develop and deploy a wider critique of local and central authority in Ireland.

These distinct but, in many respects, complementary views of Irish society, and the political agendas which accompanied them, dominated and shaped discussions of violence in pre-Famine and Famine Ireland and promoted perceptions of Ireland as a violent society. There can, moreover, be little doubt as to their influence at the time and, certainly in the case of Lewis, of their enduring impact on subsequent historical treatments of violence in pre-Famine and Famine Ireland. They were fundamentally political positions (rooted in particular political philosophies) which drew on and misused history and ideas of national character to further certain

---

5   Lewis, *On Local Disturbances.*
6   For Lewis, in Ireland, civilisation and improvement would have to 'descend from above' as they could not be expected to emerge from the inner workings of Irish communities. Unlike England and Scotland, Ireland was still 'clay under the potter's hand' – the elements of society were still 'floating in chaos' awaiting the firm 'hand of power to fix and fashion them' (Lewis, *On Local Disturbances*, v–vi).
7   de Beaumont, *Ireland: Social, Political and Religious*, pp. 193–4. De Beaumont drew on Lewis's work when discussing patterns of violence in Ireland.

political interests, and were not ultimately concerned with reaching any viable understanding of violence in Ireland or, indeed, Irish life.

The perception of pre-Famine and Famine Ireland as a violent society should not then be understood solely as a product or true reflection of the extent of violent activity in the country. It is due, in part, to the failure of prominent commentators to fully contextualise unrest and to fully investigate broader conditions in the country. There was also undoubtedly a certain political utility in portraying Ireland as a violent society. For those who wanted to defend government policy in pre-Famine and Famine Ireland against accusations of mismanagement, prejudice and exploitation or who wanted to pursue more coercive policies, there was a convenient logic in arguing that the forces of the state had to contend with an unruly population who had no hesitation in resorting to often extreme violence. The advocates of coercive legislation and the opponents of political reform could also cling to and propagate perceptions of Ireland which saw violence as an enduring feature of life deeply rooted in the Irish past. Conversely, the portrayal of Ireland as a violent society was also attractive to those who were highly critical of long-standing government policies in Ireland. Incidents of agrarian unrest could easily be mobilised to offer a critique of local and central authority. The prominent voices offering such critiques, however, rarely offered a particularly compelling analysis of the difficulties facing the country, but more often sought to pursue their own agendas through the highlighting of periodic outbursts of unrest. Thus, those from often strongly-opposed political positions could find clear comfort in the idea of Ireland as a violent society. In doing so, they provided a distorted picture of the nature of Irish society and culture.

Ireland and the history of violence in the West

Can we locate pre-Famine and Famine Ireland within a wider history of violence in both Europe and the broader western world? There are distinctive features to the Irish experience. Questions of land and sectarian animosity provided a greater spur to violent activity than in other parts of the United Kingdom in the nineteenth century. The extent of group violence was also probably greater than elsewhere in western and northern Europe (though we await a genuine comparative study to establish the real extent of the differences). But such violence was not the dominant form of violent activity on the island – acts of both land-related and sectarian lethal violence were relatively rare manifestations of a rare phenomenon. Outbreaks of violent activity by agrarian secret societies were by no means ubiquitous and, indeed, were, if anything, restricted to particular periods and certain areas of the country. It is also apparent that, in general, experiences of lethal interpersonal violence were not radically different from other European and North American countries, both in the nineteenth century and in the present day. The rates of homicide in pre-Famine and Famine Ireland would, if we allow for improvements in medical care, compare very favourably to many countries in Western Europe and North America in the early twenty-first century. The nature of the majority of conflicts which gave rise to lethal violence are also broadly similar to those found in the present day – with a high proportion of cases involving disputes over seemingly trivial altercations among men and violent conflicts over personal relationships within families. Indeed, the extent and nature of lethal violence in pre-Famine and Famine Ireland fits very comfortably within patterns found in contemporary western societies and there is little here to suggest that such patterns were the product of a distinctive Irish tradition of violence. One might even begin to question whether being 'Irish' (rather than simply living on the island) had any real influence over the patterns of violence in Ireland. There is, in essence, little evidence to support claims of Irish exceptionalism when it comes to the history of interpersonal violence.

How then might we understand the history of interpersonal violence in Ireland within a broader history of violence in Europe and beyond? Understandings of the history of violence in Europe have been profoundly influenced by the concept of a civilising process in the light of which low rates of lethal interpersonal violence are seen as the product of greater state intervention, changing conceptions of personal honour and increased levels of 'affect control' since the late middle ages.[8] It has been argued that we can also understand patterns of interpersonal violence in Ireland over the last two hundred years or so in the context of a wider European civilising process. Ian O'Donnell, for instance, points to marked differences in homicide rates between the 1840s and 1950s and also draws attention to certain differences in the contexts in which lethal violence arose in the nineteenth century and the present day.[9] Yet, the idea that changes can be understood as part of a broad civilising process that has imposed higher levels of self-control on the general population is not sustainable. To argue, based on a comparison between homicide rates in pre-Famine and Famine Ireland and the 1950s, that there has been a radical change in levels of self-control in Irish society over the course of the last two hundred or so years is to offer too narrow a view of the available statistical evidence. Homicide rates in the pre-Famine era, as noted earlier, are not radically different to rates in the present day

---

[8]   See, for instance, Spierenburg, *A History of Murder*.

[9]   See O'Donnell's two articles, 'Lethal Violence in Ireland' and 'Killing in Ireland at the Turn of the Centuries'.

and it is the exceptionally low rates in the mid-twentieth century that are out of kilter with the rates in the nineteenth century and the present. The rate in the Republic of Ireland in the 1950s of 0.35 per 100,000[10] and the rates in Northern Ireland (not exceeding 0.5 per 100,000 throughout the 1950s)[11] were amongst the lowest national homicide rates in recorded human history and would appear low when compared to most other countries in Europe (and beyond) in any period. The changes in the contexts in which homicide cases arise, between the nineteenth century and the present day, also do little to support the view that the history of violence can be understood in the light of a wider civilising process. There are, of course, changes. There is, for instance, a decline in rural land-related homicides and a rise in more recent decades in urban homicides related to organised crime. Both forms of violence, however, constitute only a minority of cases in both periods and it would be misguided to argue that the violence arising from organised crime somehow reflects a more instrumental use of violence or requires a greater degree of self-control in its execution than the agrarian violence of the nineteenth century. The change rather reflects the diminution of one set of conflicts and the emergence of another. There is also a broader continuity in the incidence of petty personal disputes among young men and domestic homicides which dominates the patterns of lethal violence. It is, if anything, the similarities in the extent and nature of lethal violence that are most striking when we compare cases from the early and mid-nineteenth century with the present day.

It may, of course, be that pre-Famine and Famine Ireland had already taken on the trappings of a modern society and that the forces identified by advocates of the civilising process thesis were already in place or were at least beginning to develop and influence the nature of Irish society by the early 1800s. This is a more plausible argument. There was an increase in state and church intervention in the lives of ordinary people in early nineteenth-century Ireland and, more broadly, there were a range of social and cultural changes such as greater integration in the market economy, the spread of literacy and growing engagement in political activity which might indicate the development of a more modern and, therefore, in the view of some, a less violent society.

In those counties for which we have data covering the first fifty years

---

[10] O'Donnell, 'Lethal Violence in Ireland', p. 677.

[11] These were, of course, to rise dramatically in the context of the political conflict in the 1970s – reaching an all-time high of 24.58 per 100,000 in the early 1970s – actually exceeding the highest rates found on either a national or county level in pre-Famine and Famine Ireland. See *Homicide Statistics*, House of Commons research paper 1999/56, p. 14.

of the century, there is, however, little evidence of any radical change in the extent or nature of lethal interpersonal violence. What is also striking about the Irish case is that homicide rates were also low in some areas in which interventions by church and state as well as broader social and cultural changes were least keenly felt in the pre-Famine era. Moreover, if we understand agrarian unrest, as some historians do, as the product of the intrusion of the market economy into pre-Famine Irish society, it might even be argued that it was the forces of modernity which disrupted the nature of Irish society and led to the most pronounced outbreaks of violent activity in that period. At least some of the major incidents of lethal violence in this period also involved either a clash with or the intervention of the newly-established police force, most notably the killings at Carrickshock in 1831 and at Dolly's Brae in 1849. It is unlikely, then, that low homicide rates were the product of an encroaching modernity.

Although it must be conceded that we simply do not know enough about the forces which shape the lives and self-perceptions of men in modern Ireland, there is also little evidence to suggest that profound or radical changes in concepts of male honour or, more broadly, masculinity (if such have occurred) have had a radical impact on practices of lethal violence among men. Again, if we allow for medical care, the rates of lethal interpersonal violence are probably lower in the 1830s and 1840s than in the present day.

On the whole, there is limited support for the idea that low homicide rates in Ireland can be explained by the erosion of family, tribe, tradition and religion by the forces of individualism, cosmopolitanism, reason and science. Indeed, it is highly doubtful that even by the mid-twentieth century the exceptionally low rates of homicide in Ireland can be understood as reflecting the triumph of the forces of modernity or civility over those of tradition. The mid-twentieth century was, if anything, a time when the forces of family, tribe, tradition, and religion appear in the ascendant.

This is not, of course, to offer some sentimental or dewy-eyed defence of traditional Ireland. Low rates of homicide, even the exceptionally low rates of the 1950s, should not lead us to complacently conclude that Ireland was somehow a wholly peaceful and contented land. In the 1950s, low homicide rates could clearly exist alongside episodes of horrific, sometimes institutionalised, violent abuse. This should not, however, lead us to dismiss or privilege one phenomenon over the other in our understanding Irish society or to see them as necessarily contradictory. They can be seen as two sides of the same coin – reflecting a marked desire and ability to contain, control and marginalise 'deviant' behaviour that might threaten the prevailing order. Violence could be used to marginalise and against the marginalised, but it was itself contained, controlled and prevented from taking on a central, dominant or too disruptive position in Irish society. There is, in other words, a distinction to be made between a peaceful land and a quiet country. Comfort, safety and ease for some could co-exist with and, in some circumstances, be linked to the marginalisation and abuse of others.

There is also little in this picture to support the idea of emerging sensibilities of civility or of new forms of interaction which radically transformed the practice of violence. Distinctions between modern and traditional societies, or between civilised and less civilised societies, carry little weight or explanatory value when it comes to the history of interpersonal violence in Ireland. Low rates of violence do not depend on modernity or tradition, but rather on the nature and shape of particular communities and how those communities relate to and interact with wider national and international circumstances. It is in those areas, whether 'modern' or 'traditional', where communities feel under serious threat or where they begin to falter or even fail, that we see the highest levels of violence in Ireland – be that Tipperary in the pre-Famine period or, for different reasons, north inner-city Dublin in the present day. Any attempt to locate the history of violence in Ireland since 1800 within a broader civilising process or transformation in gender roles is misguided.

A possible alternative explanation is provided by Randolph Roth. For Roth, there are four key correlations which underpin low rates of interpersonal violence:

1. The belief that government is stable and that its legal and judicial institutions are unbiased and will redress wrongs and protect lives and property.
2. A feeling of trust in government and the officials who run it, and a belief in their legitimacy.
3. Patriotism, empathy, and fellow feeling arising from racial, religious, or political solidarity.
4. The belief that the social hierarchy is legitimate, that one's position in society is or can be satisfactory and that one can command the respect of others without resorting to violence.[12]

Can this model be applied to Ireland? It is certainly the most sophisticated model for understanding patterns of interpersonal violence in that it eschews any tendency to draw a 'sharp line between premodern and modern states and personalities'.[13] It is clear too that homicide rates in Ireland could rise

[12] Roth, *American Homicide*, p. 18.
[13] Ibid., p. 12.

at times of political instability when the position of the government was openly questioned. There was, for instance, a marked increase in violence in Ulster in 1829 when the contentious issue of Catholic emancipation came to the fore in Irish political life. Many members of the Protestant community expressed clear disapproval of government action and there was a widespread sense of betrayal at the passing of the act. A key theme in the emancipation campaign was also the open questioning by prominent members of the Catholic community of the impartiality of the judicial system in dealing with Catholics accused of crimes – accusations which were borne out in cases following a summer of violence in Ulster in 1829. Such moments offer support to a theoretical framework which locates a greater tendency towards interpersonal violence in circumstances where trust in the organs of the state is weak and where political and social instability provides a spur to violent activity.

Yet, while Roth provides a valuable model for tracing fluctuations in rates which should be applied in future studies of homicide rates over time, it leaves us with some questions when we use the model to try and explain the fundamental characteristics which underpin the generally low rates of homicide in nineteenth-century Ireland. Historians of pre-Famine and Famine Ireland would struggle to assert that the above four correlations applied on the island at the time, even in areas that had very low homicide rates.

Government in pre-Famine and Famine Ireland is often seen as unstable and accusations of bias on the part of the state in administering justice were common. The legitimacy of constitutional arrangements on the island were also continually questioned throughout this period and fellow feeling was more likely to rest within religious and political divisions than be located in a sense of national solidarity across communities. The legitimacy of social hierarchy is hard to trace, but there is sufficient evidence that many remained unsatisfied with their social position and that landed authority, in particular, enjoyed an ambiguous place in Irish life at best. This makes it difficult to understand completely the situation in pre-Famine and Famine Ireland in the light of Roth's model.

What circumstances, then, led to low rates of lethal interpersonal violence in pre-Famine and Famine Ireland? Low homicide rates do not reflect the absence of serious conflicts in Irish society. There were many sources of potential conflict arising from economic, social, cultural and political life which could, and, at certain times, did, lead to violent action. The fact that rates of lethal violence were relatively low indicates, however, that relatively sophisticated means were developed to deal with conflict and ensure that violent action was kept within clearly-defined limits.

How was this achieved? Low rates of lethal interpersonal violence are usually attributed not simply to individual self-control but also to effective policing by the state, the churches and local communities and it is necessary, therefore, to reflect more directly on the impact of these forces on the control of violent activity.

Were low rates of homicide a reflection of effective external controls imposed by the state and the churches on Irish communities? It would be a mistake to see low rates of homicide as simply the product of the effective repression of an unruly population brought about by greater intervention by the state in the realm of law and order. A number of counties, for instance, had low homicide rates prior to key law and order reforms (such as the introduction of the county constabulary in the early 1820s) and the introduction of policing had a limited impact on patterns of lethal violence thereafter. As noted earlier, the introduction of policing could also exacerbate conflicts and lead to serious outbreaks of violence. Thus, it would be simplistic to see the low rates of lethal violence as simply a product of increased intervention and effective repression by the forces of the state in the pre-Famine period.

It is also highly unlikely that we can attribute low rates of lethal violence in Ireland to any clear or consistent intervention or even civilising mission by church bodies or, more broadly, to the effect of adherence to orthodox religious beliefs. There is, in particular, little evidence of any neat correlation between adherence to religious orthodoxy and low rates of lethal violence. In some areas of the west and north of the country where homicide rates were relatively low, orthodox religious practice was far from deeply ingrained in the general population. It is also difficult to claim that religiously-inspired movements such as the Temperance campaigns of the 1840s brought any real change in levels of lethal interpersonal violence. Moreover, those who argue most strongly for the effectiveness of clerical control in the post-Famine era generally claim that clerical authority in the years before the Famine was less than total and that it is likely that ordinary people were willing to defy clerical instruction. It is unlikely therefore that the low homicide rates simply reflect a fear of clerical sanction. Religious belief could also clearly contribute to and, indeed, underpin the sectarian divisions which led to some of the most serious single outbreaks of violence on the island in the decades before the Famine. In this sense, religious belief contained within it the potential for violence and the desire to avoid it. To see it as simply an inhibitor of violent activity would be naïve. There was also no radical change in homicide rates, on a national level, in the fifty years after the Famine when both clerical influence and the relative strength of the police increased considerably. As O'Donnell clearly demonstrates, aside from a dip in the 1860s, homicide rates were generally consistent despite the changes occurring in other areas of Irish life.[14] Neither the criminal justice system nor the churches were the ultimate agents of control.

The interaction of ordinary people with these institutions and their willingness to use them was, however, of greater significance. This is most obvious in the case of the courts, which were utilised at all levels, from petty sessions to the assize courts, to deal with a wide range of both minor and major conflicts. Control, in this sense, was driven as much from the bottom up as from the top down through the active participation of ordinary people in the prosecution of violent crime and the pursuit of civil claims. In the case of homicide, as I demonstrate in a forthcoming book, it was the active policing and prosecution of violence by ordinary people both inside and outside the official legal system that often played the crucial role in containing and controlling violent activity.[15] The more informal influence of the clergy is more difficult to identify than that of the courts, but interventions by the clergy undoubtedly served to lessen the need to resort to violence amongst individuals. This, however, probably depended less on the imposition of clerical norms or religious orthodoxy on an unruly population than the demand within communities for effective arbiters in interpersonal conflicts. In this sense, religious adherence and the willingness to resort to the law reflected rather than drove a desire to contain and control violence.

The controls on violent activity were, then, largely developed within communities which, in turn, used the agents of the state and the churches to impose a kind of order. Other means of dealing with conflict within communities, aside from recourse to the courts and the clergy, are far more difficult to trace. There are, however, hints of them. They can be seen, for instance, in the often complex dealings surrounding land use which sought to ensure that conflicts of interest did not become conflicts of violence. They can also be traced in the negotiations surrounding sectarian confrontations where individuals drew on their local connections and knowledge to try and ensure that more serious acts of violence did not occur. They can be detected also in the forms that violence itself took on. Violence, indeed, could play a role in its own control – the use of set-piece confrontations and group fights to express factional and sectarian tensions, for instance, served, within broadly accepted rules of engagement, to keep the extent of

14   O' Donnell, 'Lethal Violence', p. 677. The rates for the post-Famine period are as follows: 1851–60: 1.94 per 100,000; 1861–70: 1.55 per 100,000; 1871–80: 1.86 per 100,000; 1881–90: 2 per 100,000; 1891–1900: 1.86 per 100,000.

15   For an account of popular participation in the prosecution of serious violent crime, see Mc Mahon, *Violence, the Courts and Legal Cultures*. See also Mc Mahon, 'The Courts of Petty Sessions'.

violent conflict under control. They might also be detected in the complex negotiations (sometimes, but not always, violent) that must have occurred within families over resources, behaviour and interests. It is possible also to see in the acute sensitivity to insult in some individual homicide cases, however exaggerated in conflict situations, a deep and profound sense of appropriate behaviour which underpinned social interaction. This was a society, it seems, where there were many unwritten rules which governed, shaped and controlled individual action. Indeed, studies of Irish folklore from the period reveal cultural attitudes in which self-assertion was often seen as disruptive and detrimental to the individual while 'humility and obedience' was generally lauded and rewarded.[16] It is likely, too, that social position was based more on economic than physical strength and it is not hard to imagine how personal status and norms of behaviour were reinforced more by the blithe or, at times, pointed verbal dismissals of the pedigree, position and actions of others rather than through overt and ostentatious displays of physical prowess.

Low rates of homicide might then be explained as the product of the use by ordinary people of a variety of tools of conflict negotiation – the police, the magistracy, the courts, the clergy, communal strategies and, more broadly, adherence to accepted rules of social interaction – to keep the extent of violence within certain bounds and limits. This should not, however, be taken to suggest that these were highly cohesive communities with little by way of economic, social and cultural conflicts. On the contrary, the conflicts are obvious but they seem, for the most part, to have been skilfully managed. In fact, the negotiation of conflict generally reveals the profound inequalities and divisions in Irish life, but also the sophisticated ways in which relations of power within and between communities were expressed and dealt with without recourse to serious acts of interpersonal violence. It was, as it would later be, a quiet country rather than a peaceful land.

These tools for conflict negotiation were not, of course, fail safe. In the face of rapid innovation and widespread insecurity, they could falter. This is most obvious in Co. Tipperary, where disputes over land often provoked by opportunistic landlords led to high rates of lethal violence, or in Ulster where outbreaks of sectarian conflict occurred when local conditions were disrupted by significant political change on a national level, such as in 1829.

---

16   Thuente, 'Violence in Pre-Famine Ireland', p. 131. Thuente suggests that, in their cultural attitudes to violence, the Irish peasantry 'equivocated between the choice of passive submission and violent protest'. A different picture emerges from our study. It was not passive submission or violent protest that defined Irish society and culture, but rather the active negotiation of interests and conflicts, sometimes with violence, often without. See Thuente, 'Violence in Pre-Famine Ireland', p. 147.

There were, indeed, moments when the movements were quick and sudden in the country. In the main, however, violence was contained. This was not a society in which violence was accepted as the dominant means of resolving conflict or, indeed, as a primary means of asserting either personal or familial status, nor even as a prominent means of recreation, but rather one in which consistent efforts were made to marginalise and contain violent activity to ensure that it did not disrupt the prevailing social order.

Low homicide rates are thus a product of the interaction of individual interests with the ability of families and communities, often with the aid of the state, to contain, control and marginalise conflict. Given the very real fault lines and potential for violent conflict in economic, social and political life, the low homicide rates in pre-Famine Ireland can be seen as a singular achievement of familial and communal controls over individual behaviour. Indeed, in a period of rapidly expanding population as well as often considerable instability in economic life, these controls proved highly effective. The costs in other areas of Irish life of that achievement are, of course, less easily quantified and were undoubtedly damaging to individual lives.

What then does Ireland ultimately tell us about the history of violence? It points to the substantial and sophisticated means by which interpersonal violence is contained, controlled and marginalised in European and, more broadly, western cultures. It does this, however, without leading to the assertion that European and western cultures in the modern era provide the most effective social and cultural models for the control or marginalisation of violent activity. Areas of pre-Famine Ireland do not fit neatly into the categories set out by those who view low rates of homicide in the present as a product of distinctively modern forms of economic, social, political and cultural life.

The Irish experience also points to high levels of continuity in the extent and nature of interpersonal violence with fluctuations and variations reflecting the often subtle changes in the nature and location of conflict rather than radical shifts in levels of individual self-control or as a reflection of the benefits of modernity. The Irish case indicates that the history of violence in modern Europe might not be best understood as involving a move in violent activity from the centre to the periphery of social and cultural life, but may more profitably be understood as reflecting 'shifting degrees of marginality' in violent action which, depending on circumstances, might push violence either closer to or further away from the centre of everyday life. It is the charting of such shifts across time and space which should be the main focus of future research. In Ireland, this must involve a focus not simply on explaining changes in Irish society, but also the strong currents of continuity in the social and cultural life of the country and the often profound similarities shared with other countries in Europe and the broader western world.

Finally, what does the history of violence ultimately tell us about Ireland? Pre-Famine and Famine Ireland is often seen as 'a rough and sometimes brutal society'[17] – a time and place where both church and state struggled to contain and manage the forces that threatened the prevailing order. Ireland after the Famine, in contrast, is regarded as an altogether more ordered and orderly society in which individual and social discipline became increasingly central to life on the island. Indeed, images are often conjured of different societies sharing a country but divided in time by a catastrophe. This contrast has led some to conclude that Irish social and cultural life was radically different after the Famine. In the words of one historian, Ireland was 'thoroughly transformed'[18] in the decades after 1850; in those of another, Ireland was 'altered beyond recognition'[19] and, for another, the Famine was probably the 'great cultural break in modern Irish history'.[20]

While there were undoubtedly profound changes in Ireland after the Famine, the history of lethal interpersonal violence provides a different perspective. It points to deeply-rooted continuities in the nature of Irish social and cultural life – in particular, a desire and, more importantly, a profound ability, on the part of family and community in conjunction with the agents of the state, to restrain and control individual behaviour to ensure that social order was maintained. Despite its reputation as an unstable and somewhat chaotic society, pre-Famine and Famine Ireland contained within it sophisticated and complex means by which individual behaviour was shaped and rendered subservient to wider familial and communal interests. In this sense, the controls on individual behaviour which shaped the nature of post-Famine society had deep roots in the pre-Famine period and there are profound continuities in behaviour which stretch across the centuries and remain to the present day. Within the history of interpersonal violence, any neat or simple distinction between pre- and post-Famine Ireland dissolves in the face of larger continuities.

Ireland has long been a 'still quiet country'.

---

[17] Timothy J. Meagher, *The Columbia Guide to Irish American History* (New York: Columbia University Press, 2005), p. 227.

[18] K.A. Miller, *Emigrants and Exiles: Ireland and the Irish Exodus to North America* (Oxford: Oxford University Press, 1985), p. 131.

[19] Alvin Jackson, *Ireland, 1798–1998: War, Peace and Beyond* (Oxford: Wiley-Blackwell, 2010), p. 80.

[20] Ó Ciosáin, *Print and Popular Culture in Ireland*, p. 3.

Appendix one
Methods and sources

A quantitative analysis of homicide is by no means an unproblematic exercise. Both historians of crime and criminologists have long recognised the difficulties involved in the use of official records of crime as indicators of wider patterns of criminal behaviour, and any study of homicide depends on the availability and reliability of official sources. It is necessary, therefore, to reflect on some of the main methodological problems involved in using the available sources for a study of crime in general and of homicide, in particular, in Ireland from 1801 to 1850.

Methods

Is it possible to understand wider patterns of criminal activity through an analysis of criminal statistics? There is no shortage of debate on this issue within the existing historiography. While there are a number of different approaches, broadly speaking, there are two views on the question: (a) those who argue that statistics can, in certain circumstances, provide an insight into actual criminal activity, and (b) those who reject this argument and claim that criminal statistics can only be used to gain an understanding of the interests, priorities and assumptions of the authorities.[1]

In the context of the nineteenth century, V.A.C Gatrell provides perhaps the most sophisticated defence of the first position by adopting what might be termed a (qualified) positivist approach. From this perspective,

---

[1]   For an overview of the debate surrounding the use of criminal statistics, see Clive Emsley, *Crime and Society in England 1750–1900* (3rd ed., Harlow: Pearson Education Limited, 2005), chapter two. See also Xavier Rousseaux, 'From Medieval Cities to National States, 1350–1850: The Historiography of Crime and Criminal Justice in Europe' in Clive Emsley and L. A. Knafla (eds), *Crime History and Histories of Crime: Studies in the Historiography of Crime and Criminal Justice in Modern History* (Connecticut: Greenwood Press, 1996), pp. 3–32.

crime statistics, while by no means a wholly accurate reflection of actual crime *levels* are, if interpreted judiciously, the best available indication of *patterns* of criminal activity.[2] Gatrell acknowledges that 'crime rates cannot tell us how much crime [...] is committed in society.'[3] This is due not only to the fact that there are limits to the capacities of the authorities in detecting and recording crime, but also because the priorities, interests and assumptions of the authorities themselves can impact in significant ways on the pattern of recorded crime. This, of course, raises serious difficulties in using the statistics in order, for instance, to assess long-term trends. Changing priorities may impact upon the levels of recorded crime, or the levels of crime recorded, thereby offering a false picture of the actual state of criminal activity.

While acknowledging these problems, Gatrell claims, however, that an understanding of the pattern of criminal activity can be achieved. He argues that factors such as 'changes in public opinion, judicial attitude, police practice, and legislation' can be taken into consideration, but that these should not be seen, at least in the context of some 'critically important and more serious offences', as distorting 'the real incidence of the offence'.[4] Among these more serious offences he includes serious thefts and acts of violence such as murder and manslaughter.

This broadly positivist approach is not without its critics. Rob Sindall, in his analysis of the English criminal statistics in the nineteenth century, is both highly critical of Gatrell and, indeed, anyone who attempts to draw conclusions about crime based on criminal statistics.[5] He claims that those who adopt this approach are engaged in a disingenuous exercise whereby they admit to the faults in their sources and then carry on regardless to reach conclusions based on them. As he puts it, 'to admit to [...] a deficiency and then proceed on the basis that the admission has neutralized its own

---

[2] Gatrell's study is based primarily on government compiled and published statistics from the nineteenth century. See Gatrell, 'The Decline of Theft and Violence', esp. pp. 241–52. Zehr adopts the same approach to similar sources in France and Germany. He argues that 'crime indexes are not random variables' and that a close examination of the available records can reveal 'recurrent and comprehensible patterns [...] which cannot be attributed simply to biases in the records or the activities of the agencies who complied them' and, therefore, reflect, to some degree, the 'reality' of social conditions. See Zehr, *Crime and the Development of Modern Society*, p. 15. The same approach is also evident among those who rely on non-government sources such as court records; see Beattie, *Crime and the Courts*, p. 10.

[3] Gatrell, 'The Decline of Theft and Violence', p. 243.

[4] Gatrell, 'The Decline of Theft and Violence', p. 248.

[5] Rob Sindall, *Street Violence in the Nineteenth Century: Media Panic or Real Danger?* (Leicester: Leicester University Press, 1990), chapter two.

negative import is pointless.'[6] For Sindall, if criminal statistics can reveal anything it is simply the interests and concerns of those who are responsible for their compilation. The more particular criticisms levelled at the use of the English statistics by Sindall and, more recently, Howard Taylor, would also seem to add further weight to the argument that any faith in these sources to reflect levels of criminal activity is misplaced.[7]

Sindall's critique, however, offers a somewhat unfair characterisation of the more sophisticated versions of the positivist approach. This approach does not simply entail admitting to and then dismissing the problems with the available sources. On the contrary, it involves confronting these problems and attempting to address them and the extent to which they may, in a particular context, impact upon the use of the statistics as a guide to wider social behaviour. If such problems are found to be insurmountable then the sources should obviously not be used. This may be in situations where it is evident that there has been deliberate manipulation of the data by the authorities to suit their own interests or where the collection and/or collation of the data was clearly inefficient or incompetently carried out to such an extent as to render them unviable. It should not, however, be assumed *a priori* that the sources are wholly defective. This is especially so given that new and more sophisticated techniques can and are being developed to deal with at least some of the more obvious problems with crime statistics.[8]

Nor should the use of criminal statistics entail the kind of 'all or nothing' approach that Sindall seems to favour. His critique implies that if statistics cannot reveal the whole truth about every criminal incident, then they should not be employed at all except, perhaps, to offer some impression of 'middle class' impressions of crime. By doing so, however, Sindall excludes other interpretations of the data and effectively enshrines the 'middle class' view of crime as the only possible perspective that can be analysed cogently. Thus, we must sacrifice what may be gleaned about wider social experiences of crime because the data does not meet a standard of absolute truth. This seems to be an extreme reaction to what may be significant but not necessarily insurmountable difficulties. We need to be aware of the potential problems involved in using criminal statistics and be modest in the

---

6   Sindall, *Street Violence*, p. 24.
7   See Sindall, *Street Violence*, pp. 16–23 and Taylor, 'Rationing Crime'. Taylor's criticisms are discussed in greater detail in chapter one. See also John E. Archer, 'Mysterious and Suspicious Deaths: Missing Homicides in North-West England (1850–1900)', *Crime, Histoire & Sociétés / Crime, History & Societies*, 12.1 (2008), pp. 45–63.
8   Monkkonen, 'New Standards'. See also Randolph Roth, 'Homicide in Early Modern England 1549–1800: The Need for a Quantitative Synthesis', *Crime, Histoire & Sociétés/ Crime, History & Societies*, 5.2 (2001), pp. 33–67. See also Roth, 'Yes We Can: Working Together toward a History of Homicide'.

claims we make when using them. We should not, however, abandon them altogether unless there are clear and very compelling reasons for doing so.

Another and somewhat more theoretical challenge to the positivist approach is provided by Jason Ditton. Ditton's critique of criminal statistics is not that they are technically flawed, incomplete or even biased; it is that they are wholly determined by 'control' and simply cannot reveal anything about the behaviour of the offender(s). A crime, for Ditton, cannot be said to have occurred either logically or legally until the guilt of the alleged offender has been determined in a court of law. It is, therefore, the reaction to and control of an activity that creates the crime, not the activity itself. Moreover, he points out that 'the presence of the offender is neither a necessary nor a sufficient condition for the finding that a crime has been committed' (e.g. where a person is convicted for an offence that they were *not* involved in). Thus he concludes that criminal statistics (even if based on the conviction rate) cannot be used to gain any indication of the behaviour of the offender. Ditton reaches this conclusion because, as he puts it, 'there is no resource available to demonstrate that some "crime" is, after all committed by offenders, once the slightest shadow of doubt exists [...] that the empirical basis of the observation might be an artefact of the *process* (rather than the *object*) of that observation'.[9]

This is a flawed and ultimately self-defeating position. It does not require a particularly sophisticated epistemological analysis to realise that it is difficult, if not impossible, to conceive of any process of observation that does not include the 'slightest doubt' that the empirical basis of the observation may be an artefact of the process rather than the object of that observation. That the existence of such a doubt should be the grounds for rejecting the process of observation is an extreme reaction, which, if taken to its logical conclusion, would preclude the observation of any 'object'. Surely, the fact that such doubt exists should lead not to the outright rejection of the process but rather to an exploration of how the process works and what conclusions can be drawn from it.

In the context of a study of crime, this involves an examination of the many potential elements, such as those outlined by Gatrell, which may contribute to the production of criminal statistics. In doing so, the actions of offenders cannot be dismissed and it is the relationship between such actions and their treatment by the criminal justice system that should be seen as integral to the production of criminal statistics.[10] In sum, while any

---

[9] See Jason Ditton, *Controlology: Beyond the New Criminology* (London: Macmillan, 1979), pp. 7–24.

[10] A similar point emerges in Douglas Hay, 'War, Dearth and Theft in the Eighteenth Century: The Record of the English Courts', *Past & Present*, 95 (1982), p. 158.

quantitative analysis of crime must rely on sources that are dependent on the priorities and interests of the authorities, this does not necessarily imply that such priorities and interests wholly determine the nature of the sources.

Sources

Historians have tended to rely on two kinds of sources for the quantitative analysis of homicide. First, there are sources, such as coroners' inquests and police reports, that purport to reflect the number of *detected* homicides. These are generally regarded as the most reliable sources for assessing levels of homicide.[11] Second, there are court-based records that offer information on the number of *prosecuted* homicides. These tend to be employed when sources for the rate of *detected* homicide are unavailable.[12] Both of these types of sources are available, albeit in limited and varying forms, for Ireland in the first half of the nineteenth century. There are police reports of serious crime from the late 1820s onwards and court-based records for most of the period under review. Is it possible to base an analysis of the rate of homicide in Ireland in the first half of the nineteenth century on these sources?

Police statistics

The police statistics were a product of the substantial reforms in policing in Ireland in the first half of the nineteenth century. Over the course of the first fifty years of the nineteenth century, the role and position of the police was to change almost beyond recognition – moving from an essentially local force, made up of semi-professional baronial constables, to a centrally-controlled and armed one consisting of over 11,000 men by the late 1840s. Indeed, by the early 1850s the country had an extensive network of over 1,500 constabulary stations spread throughout the country.[13]

The statistics generated by the constabulary come in two main forms: (a) those compiled by the provincial police forces from the late 1820s to the beginning of 1837, and (b) those compiled, from 1837 onwards, by

11 This is a long-standing position within the criminological literature. See, for instance, Thorsten Sellin, 'The Significance of the Records of Crime', *Law Quarterly Review*, 65 (1951), pp. 489–504. Sellin argues that 'the value of criminal statistics as the basis for the measurement of criminality in geographic areas decreases as the procedure takes us farther away from the offence itself'. This view has been adopted in much of the historiography. See, for instance, Spierenburg, 'Long-Term Trends'.

12 Much of the quantitative analysis of crime in early modern England has, for instance, been based on court records. See, for example, Beattie, *Crime and the Courts* and Hay, 'War, Dearth and Theft in the Eighteenth Century'.

13 For a map indicating the geographical spread of these stations, see Palmer, *Police and Protest*, p. 519.

the central administration in Dublin based on the reports sent in by the police throughout the country. These sources have been utilised in studies of crime in nineteenth-century Ireland,[14] and from the perspective of our study they can be used, with some qualifications, to gain an indication of the rate and geographical spread of homicides known to the police throughout the country.

Table 6.1 A comparative analysis of police statistics in two Irish counties, 1833–50

County	Number of incidents recorded in the police statistics	Additional incidents found in other sources	Combined total
Fermanagh	29	9	38
Kilkenny	115	37	152

There were, however, some flaws in the manner in which the cases were actually recorded by the police. This is evident if we compare the figures drawn from the police statistics with the surviving police reports sent to the government, remaining court records and newspaper reports from individual counties. Table 6.1 shows the results of such an analysis based on the records for two counties, Co. Fermanagh and Co. Kilkenny, for which there are adequate surviving sources. It reveals that in both counties close to a quarter of known homicides were not recorded in the official returns – thirty-seven out of 152 cases in Kilkenny and nine out of thirty-eight in Fermanagh.[15]

---

[14] For example, see McCabe, 'Law, Conflict and Social Order', chapter three; Andres Eiriksson, 'Crime and Popular Protest', chapter four; Connolly, 'Unnatural Death in Four Nations'; O' Donnell, 'Lethal Violence' and *idem*, 'Unlawful Killing'. For a discussion of the available sources for a study of crime in nineteenth-century Ireland, see Brian Griffin, *Sources for the Study of Crime in Ireland, 1801–1921* (Dublin: Four Courts Press, 2005).

[15] This table was compiled using the following sources: National Archives of Ireland, *Irish crime records*; Chief secretary's office, monthly returns of outrages reported by the constabulary, 1841–49 (NAI 3/7/2); Home Office papers, 1839/100/261, 1840/100/262; NAI, official papers, 1838/154/317 and 1842/83; Public Record Office of Northern Ireland (hereafter cited as PRONI), Co. Fermanagh grand jury bill book, 1792–1861, Fer 4/8/1; NAI, crown books for the Co. Kilkenny assizes, 1832–46 and 1846–52, 1D/57/24 and 1D/57/25; NAI, outrage papers, Co. Kilkenny and Co. Fermanagh, 1835–50; *A return of all crimes and outrages reported by the stipendiary magistrates and officers of police in Ireland, to the inspector general of police, or to the Irish government, as having been perpetrated in their respective districts from the 1st of January 1836 to the 12th December 1837; distinguishing such crimes and outrages as were contained in the usual monthly reports, and such as were specially reported*, H.C. 1837–38 (157), xlvi, 427; *A return of outrages reported to the constabulary office, Dublin, as having occurred during the five months commencing September 1836*, H.C. 1837 (212), xlvi, 293; *A return of outrages*

In some instances, it was probably felt that the case, although prosecuted as a homicide, was different from the other cases and was, therefore, not included in the returns. This occurred in situations where the accused was charged with a homicide arising from medical negligence or reckless driving or, in some cases, where the accused was adjudged to be insane.

Of the thirty-seven additional incidents in Kilkenny there were ten such cases – six involving medical negligence, three involving reckless driving and one insanity case. In Fermanagh, there were three cases – two involving reckless driving and one case where the accused was deemed to be insane. The exclusion of these kinds of cases from the returns does not, however, unduly impact upon any conclusions that may be made concerning the experience of interpersonal violence in this period as they were rare and can, to some degree, be seen as different from the overwhelming majority of reported cases. Certainly the cases arising from reckless driving and medical malpractice are more an index of incompetence and negligence than of violent conflict.

The reasons for the exclusion of the other 'missing' homicides are not so clear. Some of these cases were probably deliberately excluded from the figures because they were considered doubtful. This is apparent, for example, in a case from the Fermanagh summer assizes in 1836 where two young Protestant gentlemen, Arthur Irvine and Arthur Forster, were prosecuted for the manslaughter of a poor Catholic man, Robert Farnan. Although prosecuted as manslaughter, this case was not included in the police figures for that year. This may, of course, have been a simple oversight on the part of the police in compiling the figures. But this seems unlikely as the case involved two prominent members of the local gentry and it managed to generate not only a good deal of correspondence between the police and the government but also a degree of controversy in the county as a whole. It is more likely that the police considered the case doubtful and may also have been influenced by the social standing of the accused in deciding not to include the case in the returns. Both of the accused were also acquitted at the subsequent trial.[16]

reported to the constabulary office, Dublin, as having occurred during the months of January and February last, H.C. 1837–38 (214), xlvi, 457; *summary of outrages for Ulster, Leinster, Munster and Connacht*, official papers, 1833/ 153, 154, 154a and b; *summary of outrages for Ulster, Leinster, Munster and Connacht*, official papers, 1834/385, 386, 387, 388, 389, 525, 526, 527, 528; *summary of outrages for Ulster, Leinster, Munster and Connacht*, official papers 1835/351, 352, 353, 354, 355; *summary of outrages for Ulster, Leinster, Munster and Connacht, January to June*, official papers, 1836/116, 117, 118, 119. The following newspapers were also used in this study: *Enniskillen Chronicle and Erne Packet*, *The Kilkenny Moderator*, and *The Kilkenny Journal*.

16   See NAI, outrage papers, Co. Fermanagh, 1836/5x9; *Enniskillen Chronicle and Erne*

The extent to which this occurred should not be exaggerated. There is little evidence that the police or government consistently excluded a significant number of alleged incidents of homicide from the returns. The omissions also seem to be more a feature of the pre-1837 returns than those compiled in later years by the constabulary office in Dublin. In my analysis of homicide in Co. Kilkenny between 1833 and 1850, of the other twenty-seven 'missing' homicides, eighteen occurred in the four years leading up to 1837. In Fermanagh, only two of the other six missing cases occurred in the period after 1837 (one in 1838 and one in 1839). Indeed, the police figures for Fermanagh in the 1830s are lower than those drawn from the court records over the same period.[17] For the most part, these omissions were probably the result of simple inefficiency.

The problems with the pre-1837 statistics were clearly recognised by the government of the day. In 1839, Thomas Drummond, under-secretary 1835–40, claimed that the pre-1837 returns made by the provincial police forces 'were not made out with that accuracy which would admit of a safe deduction being made for a comparison of past and present times; indeed it cannot be said that a perfectly satisfactory comparison can be made beyond the commencement of 1837'.[18] To say that no comparison between the pre- and post-1837 homicide figures can be made is an overstatement. We should, however, be careful when using the pre-1837 figures and treat them as underestimates. While not perfect, the returns after 1837 appear more reliable and, perhaps more importantly, consistent.

The next problem that needs to be addressed is that of the so-called 'dark figure', which refers to those acts that never come to the attention of the authorities. Given the dominant view in much of the historiography of nineteenth-century Ireland, that the legal system was rejected by the mass of the people, it might be argued that any conclusions based on official sources would be questionable. Yet the extent of this problem, at least in the context of the police statistics, should not be exaggerated. There were undoubtedly some incidents that were successfully concealed from the police,[19] but as

---

Packet, 21 Jul. 1836.

[17] Compare, for instance, the figures for Co. Fermanagh, 1831–40, in Table 1.2 and those in Table 1.3 above.

[18] Crime and outrage committee, *Minutes of evidence, 1839*, p. 1077.

[19] Although it is obviously well-nigh impossible to cite cases that were successfully concealed from the authorities, some indication of the difficulties that might be encountered may be seen in a case which arose in Queen's Co. in 1832. In April of that year, a 'very unoffending individual, named Cleary, gardener to John Steel esq.' died after being beaten at the fair of Rathdowney. Steel and his brothers 'having heard that some persons were about to remove the body to Galmoy church-yard, in the County of Kilkenny, to prevent, if possible, the holding of an inquest, instantly dispatched one of their best horses and

McCabe has pointed out, circumstances in Ireland, at least in the 1830s and 1840s, were not particularly conducive to the widespread concealment of acts of lethal violence from the authorities.

The police were very active and thorough in investigating suspicious deaths that occurred in their districts, and it would have been difficult to conceal a high number of acts of lethal violence from them. When they heard about a suspicious death they usually investigated it immediately, and if it was believed to be a homicide they would, at least from the late 1830s onwards, consistently report it as such to the Dublin administration, usually within twenty-four hours. The central administration also put considerable pressure on the constabulary to investigate and report every incident of serious crime. Indeed, a police officer who failed to report a case could face severe consequences. When the homicide of Richard Connell was reported in December 1839, the government were incensed that the original assault committed on Connell in November of that year had not been reported to them and wanted an explanation otherwise the officer responsible would be deemed 'unfit to hold his present position'.[20] In fact, the government's interest even extended to cases where it was suspected that the deceased had come by his/her death from 'natural' causes such as the 'severity of the weather'.[21] Another factor which McCabe notes is the role of priests, who, he points out, would probably have had knowledge of any suspicious death and would, more than likely, have passed this information on to the authorities.[22]

Local officials and clerics were not the only ones concerned with seeing a prosecution in cases of homicide. Ordinary people also played an active part in reporting homicides, and it is unlikely that a significant proportion of victims would have been so devoid of friends and family that many suspicious deaths would go by unnoticed and unreported. The available

had H.P. Delaney, esq. [coroner] on the spot without loss of time. The deceased was, in the mean time, hastily removed and only that Captain Steel and his brothers came promptly to the aid of the coroner no investigation could have taken place'. Even when an inquest was held, 'intimidation [was] the order of the day, it was manifest that no evidence could then be looked for' and the coroner was forced to adjourn the inquest. The inquest was held a number of days afterwards and 'occupied three days, when after a labourious and patient examination of very reluctant witnesses, two persons named Daniel Phelan and Kyran Connors were committed for the homicide to the gaol of Maryborough, on strong circumstantial evidence'. See *Leinster Express*, 28 Apr. 1832.

20   NAI, outrage papers, Co. Kilkenny, 1839/10330.

21   There are numerous examples of this in the police reports, particularly in the winter months. The activities of the police in investigating suspicious deaths are apparent from an examination of the surviving police reports.

22   See McCabe, 'Law, Conflict and Social Order', p. 307.

evidence from the four counties which constitute the main focus of our study certainly suggests that the overwhelming majority of recorded homicides were initially reported to the police by ordinary people. The homicide could, for instance, be reported by those who were related to the deceased. In Armagh, in May 1839, Michael McCresh immediately 'ran into Crossmaglen and brought the Priest [and] went next for the police' following the killing of his brother Brian in a dispute over land. His father, Peter McCresh, also gave information to the police.[23] At other times, the homicide was reported by the neighbours of the deceased. In 1840 in Queen's Co., a Mathew Bryan was charged with the murder of his mother. In this case, his neighbours sent for the police immediately they heard of Bryan's attack on his parent.[24] Friends and employees of the deceased could also play their part. In Co. Kilkenny in 1836, Patrick Dowling died as a consequence of being hit behind the ear with a loaded whip. Initially, the attack seemed to have little adverse effect, but when Dowling's condition deteriorated, 'his friends [...] communicate[d] the circumstances to the police.'[25]

In other cases, the homicide was reported by those who came upon the scene, but who had no apparent connections with either the deceased or the accused. For instance, in Co. Kilkenny in September 1837, Patrick Shiel, a small farmer, discovered the body of John Nonnan while he and his wife were crossing a stream near their house. Shiel 'immediately went for the police' who were able to gather evidence at the scene. This led to the subsequent arrest and trial of John Cleary for the murder.[26] In Queen's Co. in November 1847, John Bailey, a night watchman on the railway, discovered a body near the railway works and immediately 'gave notice to the station master and the nearest magistrate'.[27] Such incidents suggest that the authorities could enjoy a good deal of co-operation from ordinary people in detecting homicides. Indeed, and as McCabe also points out, there was 'little police concern' that acts of lethal violence were being actively concealed from them.[28]

Another problem with the sources is that they are influenced by the process by which particular incidents and allegations were dealt with and

---

[23] *Belfast Newsletter*, 2 Aug. 1839.
[24] *Leinster Express*, 7 Mar. 1840.
[25] NAI, outrage papers, Co. Kilkenny, 1836/106.
[26] *Belfast Newsletter*, 20 Mar. 1838.
[27] *Leinster Express*, 11 Mar. 1848.
[28] McCabe, 'Law, Conflict and Social Order', p. 307. McCabe estimates that 'communal non-cooperation' was a factor in only three per cent of cases in a sample of reported homicides in pre-Famine Co. Mayo and believes that, on the whole, ordinary people were willing to report cases. See also Mc Mahon, *Violence, the Courts and Legal Cultures*, chapters one and two.

understood by the authorities. This process was obviously dependent on the subjective and, potentially erroneous, decisions of bodies such as the police and, more importantly, perhaps, coroners' inquests.[29] It might be, for instance, that coroners' juries deemed particular incidents not to be cases of felonious homicide but rather acts of justifiable homicide if they were sympathetic towards the alleged perpetrator. This problem should not be overstated however. The proportion of cases in which a coroner's inquest deemed an incident to be an act of justifiable homicide was miniscule – amounting to a mere 0.39 per cent of all verdicts given in the period from 1831 to June 1841, while verdicts of murder and manslaughter accounted for 11.58 per cent.[30] Thus, the exclusion or inclusion of cases of justifiable homicide from the overall homicide figures would have little bearing on the overall rates of homicide in Ireland at this time.

Another and potentially more serious problem might be that coroners' inquests were simply incompetent in carrying out their duties. Some commentators of the day felt that a lack of medical expertise at coroners' inquests could lead to erroneous judgments and, in particular, that there could be a failure to recognise that a homicide had actually occurred.[31] There were also a number of acts introduced to reform the system in this period.[32] Yet, while there were complaints about the efficiency of coroners' inquests and, on occasion, the conduct of coroners, there is no evidence of widespread dissatisfaction, certainly not on a local level or on the part of the police, with the verdicts given by coroners' juries.[33] At some coroners' inquests at least, juries also showed an ability to look beyond the obvious explanation for a suspicious death. For instance, an inquest was held in Fermanagh in 1815 on the body of James Rutledge. At first it was believed that Rutledge had met his death after the wall of a cowshed had fallen on him, but 'on strict investigation of the circumstances, however, the jury had reason to suspect that this was only a stratagem of the murderer to make

---

[29] On the role of the coroner and of the coroner's inquest, see W.E. Vaughan, *Murder Trials*, chapter two and Mc Mahon, *Violence, the Courts and Legal Cultures*, chapter one.

[30] *Abstract of the deaths on which inquests were held in each year, for the ten years ending 6th June 1841 in the Report of the commissioners appointed to take the census of Ireland for the year 1841 with appendix and index*, pp. 192–3, H.C. 1843 (504), xxiv, 1.

[31] Such criticisms came largely from the medical press. Similar criticisms were also made in England at this time. See Brian Farrell, *Coroners: Practice and Procedure* (Dublin: Round Hall Sweet & Maxwell, 2000), pp. 25–6.

[32] Coroners' inquests were subject to four acts of Parliament between 1829 and 1846. See Farrell, *Coroners*, pp. 21–7 and Vaughan, *Murder Trials*, pp. 42–4.

[33] I have not come across a case in my sample where the police expressed surprise at or disapproval of a verdict of a coroner's jury. This is not to suggest necessarily that such cases did not arise, but rather that they were rare.

the death appear accidental.' The jury found that death was caused by a blow to the back of Rutledge's head 'which was supposed to be inflicted by a hatchet, or some other edged instrument, and which was doubtless the immediate cause of death'.[34]

Other reasons, aside from a lack of expertise, could contribute to the under-recording of homicide cases. Taylor has argued, in the context of the English police statistics in the nineteenth century, that the police deliberately sought to downplay the number of murders in order to avoid the costly business of launching a murder investigation.[35] In an Irish context, there are, as we have seen, definite question marks over the manner in which *detected* homicides were recorded, but there is no evidence of a consistent or deliberate plan to under-record or manipulate in any way the levels of reported homicide. Given the Dublin administration's obsession with questions of law and order, there would have been little will or inclination to let a homicide go unpunished in order to avoid the expense of prosecution. If anything, the view would have been quite the opposite at this time.[36]

Finally, we need to confront the fact that statistics based on the number of *detected* homicides may include 'offences subsequently determined not to be homicide'.[37] This problem cannot be answered simply with reference to the available sources. Even if it were possible to trace every case through the court system to see if the case ended in a conviction or not, this obviously would still not resolve the issue because although an acquittal could mean that no homicide was committed, it could also mean that a homicide occurred but that the person being tried was not guilty of committing it.

---

[34] *Enniskillen Chronicle and Erne Packet*, 15 Feb. 1815. No medical officer attended the inquest.

[35] Taylor, 'Rationing Crime'.

[36] The interest of the government in seeing that cases were properly investigated, reported and brought before the courts is reflected in the case of William Walsh. In Co. Kilkenny in October 1840, a young female child called Austice Gahan was killed after being run over by a horse that was ridden by Walsh. The police believed that the case was an accident and did not report it. However, reward posters were put up in the locality offering a reward of £20 for information on the incident. These posters came to the attention of the government and they wrote to the police asking why the case was not reported. The police claimed that they had not reported it because they believed it was an accident, but the government insisted that they wanted a report sent of all fatal accidents in the district. Walsh was also committed to abide his trial at the spring assizes of 1841, although, at the assizes, the crown solicitor decided not to send the case before the grand jury. Thus, even though the case was deemed an accident by the police, due to government interest, the case still came before the courts. NAI, outrage papers, Kilkenny, 1841/917/17721/17127.

[37] See Philip White, 'Homicide' in M.A. Walker (ed.), *Interpreting Crime Statistics* (Oxford: Clarendon Press, 1995), p. 130. White calculates that in modern-day England and Wales fifteen per cent of cases are later found not to be homicides.

In this sense, neither the rate of detection or conviction necessarily supplies unproblematic or complete data on the number of actual homicides. Yet, once again, the extent of this problem should not be overstated. An analysis of homicide cases in a number of counties reveals that cases were rarely found not to be homicide at a later stage of the criminal process. Indeed, it was relatively rare for the defence to argue that a case was not a homicide.[38] The rate of detection, therefore, while by no means ideal as an indicator of levels of lethal violence, is still perhaps the most viable source for such an exercise as it provides the widest available sample of incidents. On the whole, the police statistics, at least from 1837 onwards, provide a relatively dependable and consistent base upon which to construct a viable statistical analysis of homicide rates. The pre-1837 statistics are obviously less reliable and must be treated with greater caution.

Court-based records

The other two 'official' sources at our disposal are both court-based records, namely the published government statistics of committals for trial and the original court records. The former have been used by historians to assess the rates of homicide in Ireland in the first half of the nineteenth century. Palmer, for instance, has compared the number of committals for homicide in Ireland in the 1820s with those from England and concluded that 'the murder rate in Ireland continued to be alarmingly high and the contrast to England stark'.[39] This approach, however, can be seriously misleading. In the context of homicide prosecutions, the main drawback of the official government figures is that they are based on the *number of people indicted for homicide* rather than the *number of homicide cases*. This can result in a somewhat distorted impression of the actual level of homicide cases before the courts. For example, Maxwell Hamilton, the crown solicitor on the north-east assizes circuit, pointed out that while the government statistics showed that nineteen people had been indicted for murder there were only two cases of murder in Co. Louth in 1838.[40] Hamilton also pointed out that when 'a man is indicted, perhaps for murder; that indictment may be withdrawn at the assizes, and subsequently an indictment for manslaughter

---

[38] From a sample of 141 cases drawn from three counties (Co. Armagh 1807–50, Co. Fermanagh 1811–50, and Queen's Co. 1832–50) there were only eighteen (12.76 per cent) in which the defence put forward such arguments.

[39] Palmer, *Police and Protest*, p. 271.

[40] Crime and outrage committee, *Minutes of evidence, 1839*, p. 768. Hamilton also points out that a case which occurred on the borders of counties Louth and Monaghan in which fifteen people were committed to gaol for trial was included in the returns for both counties because the prisoners had been transferred from the Louth prison to the Monaghan prison while awaiting trial.

sent to the grand jury, both those indictments would then appear in the return, the indictment for murder, and the indictment for manslaughter'.[41] Such flaws in the government statistics suggest that they are simply an inadequate source for the quantitative analysis of homicide.[42]

Given that the government statistics are flawed sources for homicide prosecutions, we are left with the original court records as our remaining 'official' source for the incidence of homicide in the early part of the nineteenth century. This is a less than ideal situation. The most glaring problem is that the majority of the court records were destroyed in 1922.[43] This means that we cannot attain a truly comprehensive countrywide picture of homicide cases for the early decades of the century. Moreover, those sources that survive do not always provide the most accurate picture even of the number of cases that came before the courts.

There are two main types of surviving court records: crown books and grand jury indictment books. Of these two, the former are by far the more reliable, useful and comprehensive. They provide basic information on the offence (including the name of the deceased, when and where the offence is alleged to have occurred and the weapon or mode of killing employed), the names of the defendants (and whether or not they were held in custody, on bail or whether they were amenable to justice in the first instance),[44] the names of the prosecution witnesses, the verdict and sentence. The crown books represent the best source for any quantitative analysis of homicide prosecutions (and criminal prosecutions generally) in our period.

The other available records are the grand jury books. It was the role of the grand jury to decide, based solely on the evidence for the prosecution, whether or not a case should be sent for trial. The information provided by these books is far more basic than the crown books. They generally record the offence, the name of the accused, whether or not the grand jury deemed it worthy of a criminal trial and, sometimes, the names of the prosecution witnesses. They do not, however, provide information as to who the victim

41 Crime and outrage committee, *Minutes of evidence 1839*, p. 715.
42 For the rates of homicide based on these sources, see, however, McCabe, 'Law, Conflict and social Order', p. 57.
43 An indication of the records lost at this time may be gleaned from Herbert Wood, *A Guide to the Records Deposited in the Public Record Office of Ireland* (Dublin, HMSO, 1919). For an account of the events surrounding the destruction of the records, see Ronan Keane, 'A Mass of Crumbling Ruins: The Destruction of the Four Courts in June 1922' in Caroline Costello (ed.) *The Four Courts: 200 Years: Essays to Commemorate the Bicentenary of the Four Courts* (Dublin: Incorporated Council of Law Reporting for Ireland, 1996), pp. 159–68.
44 Even if a defendant was not in custody or out on bail his/her name was still included in the crown book.

was or when and where the offence is alleged to have occurred or any indication of the final outcome of the case. Despite the rudimentary nature of the information provided – these records are still useful, especially when they are combined with and compared to newspaper reports of criminal trials. By tracing the names of defendants in the original grand jury books through the available newspaper sources, it is possible, to some extent at least, to expand upon and amend the information provided by the original records.

The figures for *prosecuted* homicide used in this study were compiled using the grand jury books for Co. Armagh (1801–50), Co. Fermanagh (1801–50), Co. Tyrone (1801–9 and 1814–50) and Queen's Co. (1821–50). These sources are also supplemented with information from local newspapers. I have also gathered data from the crown books for Co. Kilkenny (1833–50).[45]

The count itself generally includes all homicides that appeared in the court books. I have not, however, included cases of attempted murder, conspiracy to murder or soliciting to murder, or cases of infanticide where these could be clearly identified. There were also some complicating factors in counting the number of incidents in the grand jury books.

In his quantitative analysis of the grand jury books of Armagh and Tyrone for the period 1732–1801, Neal Garnham engages in a direct count of every incident of murder recorded in the grand jury book and assumes, not unreasonably, that each incident prosecuted represents a separate incident. For example, in the period 1742–51 nineteen murders were recorded in the book and each one of these is taken to represent a separate incident.[46]

There are, however, definite difficulties and pitfalls in applying Garnham's methodology to these sources, for the nineteenth century at least. It is necessary when examining these sources to amend the figures to take account of several factors. There are some cases where the same defendant is listed in the court book as being charged with both murder and manslaughter. The reason for this is relatively straightforward – the grand jury could, after assessing the evidence of the prosecution witnesses,

45 The following court records were examined: PRONI, Co. Fermanagh grand jury bill book, 1792–1861, Fer 4/8/1; PRONI, Co. Armagh grand jury bill books, 1797–1822, 1823–33 and 1833–58, Arm 1/2A/1, Arm 1/2A/2 and Arm 1/2A/3; PRONI, Co. Tyrone grand jury bill books, 1745–1809 and 1814–99, Tyr 4/2/1 and Tyr 4/2/2. NAI, crown books for the Co. Kilkenny assizes, 1832–46 and 1846–52, 1D/57/24 and 1D/57/25 and NAI, Queen's Co. grand jury bill book, 1818–1882, 1D/60/14. The following newspapers were used in this study: *The Enniskillen Chronicle & Erne Packet, The Belfast Newsletter, The Banner of Ulster, The Northern Whig, The Leinster Express, The Newry Telegraph, The Kilkenny Moderator, The Kilkenny Journal, The Armagh Guardian, The Strabane Morning Post* and *The Fermanagh Mail.*
46 Garnham, *The Courts, Crime and the Criminal Law*, p. 175.

decide that the case did not warrant a charge of murder, and decide that the accused should be tried for manslaughter instead. I have only counted these cases once. Also, where it is evident that the same defendant appears in the court record twice for the same offence (which usually occurs when a case is postponed to a subsequent assizes) I have counted one case. Similarly, I have amended my figures using local newspapers to avoid, where possible, counting the same offence and defendants more than once. For instance, the murder of Patrick Moley in June 1818 appears six times in the Armagh grand jury book – four times in 1819 and once each in 1821 and 1825 with different defendants in each case. There is little or no indication in the grand jury book that there is a connection between the six different cases in the records for 1819, 1821 and 1825. Such cases can obviously lead us to overestimate the number of homicide cases before the courts. By tracing the cases through our newspaper sources, however, it has been possible, to some extent at least, to avoid counting offences more than once in the homicide count. There are also some incidents (thankfully infrequent) where the newspapers have reports of trials in their respective counties for which there is no record in the grand jury books. These cases have also been added to the homicide count. This method of amending the information in the original court records is, of course, less than ideal as it means we have to depend on the availability of newspapers for the years under review and rely on the often limited coverage of court sittings in the surviving papers. Thus, such amendments must be somewhat partial – more viable in some years and some places than others.

The figures based on the Fermanagh grand jury book can be regarded as an accurate reflection of the number of *prosecuted* homicides. This is due to both the accuracy and consistency of those who entered the details into the grand jury book and also the availability of corresponding newspapers sources for forty of the fifty years covered by the book. This has allowed me to make the type of amendments outlined above where necessary. The figures gleaned from the grand jury book of Queen's Co. are also reasonably reliable, at least from the 1830s onwards, due to good newspaper coverage between 1832 and 1850. The figures for Armagh may be regarded as somewhat less reliable. The entries made in the Armagh grand jury book can, on occasion, serve to distort the real level of cases being prosecuted and can lead to an overestimation of the number of homicides before the courts. The newspaper coverage, while reasonable, is also less satisfactory than that available for Fermanagh. The least reliable figures are those gleaned from the Co. Tyrone books. The books themselves are in a less than ideal condition and there are limited newspaper sources with which to test their reliability, meaning it is possible that the figures gleaned from these books are overestimates of the actual level of homicides before the courts.

Yet, while we must abandon claims to total accuracy, this perhaps unconventional and 'hybrid' method of compilation is probably the most appropriate available method of ascertaining the rate of prosecuted homicide from the grand jury books. It may not provide a wholly accurate account of the level of prosecuted homicide, at least in the case of Armagh and Tyrone, but it can offer a broad indication of general trends in the respective counties.

Appendix two
Homicide and motive

The question of motive is a rather difficult one to address as homicides can be and generally are classified in a variety of different ways. As Wilson and Daly have pointed out, 'the prevailing criminological conception of motives in homicide is a wooly amalgam of several potentially independent dimensions: spontaneity versus premeditation, the victim–offender relationship, and only a relatively small dose of [...] substantive issues.'[1] The solution offered by Wilson and Daly is to try and isolate the substantive issue and to make it the primary focus of inquiry. While this is a perfectly valid approach, there are risks involved in privileging one factor over another when attempting to understand the motives behind violent activity. In some cases, the substantive issue can be the most significant factor. This is evident, for instance, in homicides involving robbery where it is generally the desire to take the victim's property that is central to the act rather than necessarily the relationship between the parties. In other cases, it is the relationship between the parties that is to the fore. For instance, in cases of spousal homicide, the act may arise from a relatively minor argument, but its real motivation may lie somewhat deeper in the relationship between husband and wife.

Thus, in some cases, it is clearly the relationship between the parties that is the primary cause of the dispute and it is the tension within this relationship that elevates the substantive issue to a position of significance. In other cases, it is the substantive issue which upsets or disrupts the relationship between the parties. To exclude either of these factors would be a mistake, but in order to classify the cases it is necessary to emphasise or privilege what we believe to be the dominant element in the act. This is, of course, by no means a foolproof method of classification and is obviously quite a subjective exercise. It is, however, a necessary one if any wider understanding of the contexts in which these homicides occurred is to be

---

[1] Daly and Wilson, *Homicide*, p. 173.

reached. The discussion here will focus on the four main categories of cases which are dealt with in this book, namely, personal disputes, personal family disputes, land-related disputes and, finally, disputes arising from sectarian animosity.

Personal disputes are defined as those which arise primarily from the relationship between the protagonists and where the substantive issue (e.g. an insult which sparks off a confrontation) is deemed to be of lesser importance. I have also included cases in this category where the substantive issue has no clear or direct connection to any wider economic, political or sectarian consideration. The category of personal family homicides includes those cases where it is clear that the parties were related *and* where, similar to personal disputes among non-relatives, the case did not arise directly from any wider economic, political or sectarian motive. This means, for instance, that disputes among siblings over land are not included in this category but rather treated as land-related cases. A relatively broad definition has been applied to the category of land-related homicides to include cases arising from eviction, conflicts over the possession of disputed land, disputes over access to land and cases which stemmed from the payment or non-payment of rent. The category of sectarian homicides includes all reported incidents which are identified as sectarian by the police and magistrates in their reports and also cases where sectarian animosity is explicit or can reasonably be implied as a key motivation of one or more of the parties involved based on evidence in the available sources. Table 7.1 is based on national samples for Ireland from 1843 to 1845 and 1847 to 1849. Table 7.2 is derived from long-term studies of four counties, Co. Armagh and Co. Fermanagh in the north, and Queen's Co. and Co. Kilkenny in the south of the country.

Sources

The 1843–5 sample is based on a total of 417 cases reported by the police throughout the country between January 1843 and December 1845. Chief Secretary's office, constabulary returns, monthly returns of outrages, 1843–45, National Archives of Ireland (NAI), 3/7/2.

The Famine sample is based on a total of 261 cases reported by the police for the following months: (a) March, April, July, August, October and December 1847; (b) February, August, October, November and December 1848; (c) July, August and November 1849. Chief Secretary's office, constabulary returns, monthly returns of outrages, 1847–49, NAI, 3/7/2.

The county-based samples are based on an investigation of outrage papers (police reports) for the four counties between 1835 and 1850 held in the National Archives of Ireland, and reports of homicides found in contemporary newspapers as well as data gleaned from the following court records: Public Record Office of Northern Ireland (PRONI), Co. Fermanagh grand jury bill book, 1792–1861, Fer 4/8/1; PRONI, Co. Armagh grand jury bill books, 1797–1822, 1823–33 and 1833–58, Arm 1/2A/1, Arm 1/2A/2 and Arm 1/2A/3; NAI, crown books for the Co. Kilkenny assizes, 1832–46 and 1846–52, 1D/57/24 and 1D/57/25 and NAI, Queen's Co. grand jury bill book, 1818–1882, 1D/60/14. The following newspapers were used in this study: *The Enniskillen Chronicle & Erne Packet*, *The Banner of Ulster*, *The Belfast Newsletter*, *The Northern Whig*, *The Leinster Express*, *The Newry Telegraph*, *The Kilkenny Moderator*, *The Kilkenny Journal*, *The Armagh Guardian*, *The Strabane Morning Post* and *The Fermanagh Mail*. The more long-term study of Co. Fermanagh is due to the availability of better and more consistent records for that county.

Table 7.1 Motives attributed to reported homicides in pre-Famine and Famine Ireland

Motive/type of dispute	Ireland 1843–5	Ireland 1847–9
Personal disputes	112	53
Personal family disputes	48	35
Land	65	33
Property/ money/ execution of a decree etc.	45	35
Robbery	12	37
Participation in a criminal prosecution	9	9
Maintenance of order	4	1
Sectarian	7	9
Political	2	1
Faction	9	0
Work/ business	17	6
Dispute arising from a sporting event	21	1
Sexual assault	3	0
Unknown	50	32
Miscellaneous	13	9
Totals	417	261

Table 7.2   Motives attributed to reported homicides in four Irish counties

Motive/type of dispute	Armagh 1835–50	Fermanagh 1811–50	Kilkenny 1835–50	Queen's Co. 1835–50
Personal disputes	23	21	25	19
Personal family disputes	15	14	13	11
Land	10	3	17	8
Property/ money/ execution of a decree	9	6	2	7
Robbery	0	1	4	2
Participation in a criminal prosecution	0	1	0	2
Maintenance of order	0	1	1	0
Sectarian	9	11	0	1
Political	0	0	1	1
Faction	0	2	2	4
Work/ business	1	0	3	0
Disputes arising from sporting contests	0	0	5	3
Sexual assault	0	0	1	0
Medical negligence	0	1	6	0
Reckless driving	3	2	3	2
Unknown	20	12	26	18
Miscellaneous	1	0	5	0
Totals	91	75	114	78

Bibliography

Manuscript sources

(a) National Archives of Ireland
Chief Secretary's office: Irish crime records, official papers, convict reference files, monthly
  returns of outrages, outrage papers.
Crown books for the Co. Kilkenny assizes, 1832–46 and 1846–52, 1D/57/24 and 1D/57/25.
Queen's Co. grand jury bill book, 1818–82, 1D/60/14.

(b) National Library of Ireland
Return of the number of offences reported as having been committed in the Dublin police
  district (1841–50).
Home office papers.

(c) Public Record Office of Northern Ireland
Co. Armagh grand jury bill books 1797–1822, 1823–33 and 1833–58, Arm 1/2A/1, Arm
  1/2A/2 and Arm 1/2A/3.
Co. Fermanagh grand jury bill book, 1792–1861, Fer 4/8/1.
Co. Tyrone grand jury bill books 1745–1809 and 1814–99, Tyr 4/2/1 and Tyr 4/2/2.

Parliamentary papers

*Report from the select committee appointed to examine into the state of the disturbed counties in
  Ireland; into the immediate causes which have produced the same, and into the efficiency of
  the laws for the suppression of outrage against the public peace, with the minutes of evidence,
  appendix and index,* H.C. 1831–32 (677), xvi, 1.
*A return of the number of offences against the law, which have been committed in Ireland, during
  the years 1831–32, so far as returns of such offences have been made to the Irish government;
  specifying the general nature of the offences, and the counties or places in which they have
  occurred,* H.C. 1833 (80), xxix, 411.
*First report of His Majesty's commissioners for inquiring into the condition of the poorer classes
  of Ireland,* app. a, H.C. 1835, xxxii, (369).
*Report from the select committee appointed to inquire into the nature, character, extent and
  tendency of Orange lodges, associations, or societies in Ireland, with the minutes of evidence,*

197

and appendix, p. 113, H.C. 1835 (377), xv, 1.

The third report of the select committee appointed to inquire into the nature, character, extent and tendency of Orange lodges, associations or societies in Ireland, p. 72, H.C. 1835 (476), xvi, 1.

Poor inquiry (Ireland): appendix (E) containing baronial examinations relative to food, cottages and cabins, clothing and furniture, pawnbroking and savings' banks, drinking and supplement containing answers to questions 13 to 22 circulated by the commissioners, H.C. 1836, xxxii, [37], 1.

Poor inquiry (Ireland): appendix (F.) containing baronial examinations relative to con acre, quarter or score ground, small tenantry, consolidation of farms and dislodged tenantry, emigration, landlord and tenant, nature and state of agriculture, taxation, roads, observations on the nature and state of agriculture and supplement containing answers to questions 23 to 35 circulated by the commissioners, H.C. 1836 (38), xxiii, 1.

A return of outrages reported to the constabulary office, Dublin, as having occurred during the five months commencing September 1836, H.C. 1837 (212), xlvi, 293.

A return of all crimes and outrages reported by the stipendiary magistrates and officers of police in Ireland, to the inspector general of police, or to the Irish government, as having been perpetrated in their respective districts from the 1ˢᵗ of January 1836 to the 12ᵗʰ December 1837; distinguishing such crimes and outrages as were contained in the usual monthly reports, and such as were specially reported, H.C. 1837–38 (157), xlvi, 427.

A return of outrages reported to the constabulary office, Dublin, as having occurred during the months of January and February last, H.C. 1837–38 (214), xlvi, 457.

Minutes of evidence taken before the Select Committee of the House of Lords appointed to enquire into the state of Ireland since the year 1835 in respect of crime and outrage, which have rendered life and property insecure in that part of the empire, and to report to the house, H.C. 1839 (486), xi, xii, 1.

Twentieth report of the inspectors general on the general state of the prisons of Ireland, 1841, appendix no. 2, H.C. 1842 (377), xxii, 117.

Twenty-first report of the inspectors general on the general state of the prisons of Ireland, 1842, appendix no. 2, H.C. 1843 (462), xxvii, 83.

Abstract of the deaths on which inquests were held in each year, for the ten years ending 6ᵗʰ June 1841 in the Report of the commissioners appointed to take the census of Ireland for the year 1841 with appendix and index, pp. 192–3, H.C. 1843 (504), xxiv, 1.

Twenty-second report of the inspectors general on the general state of the prisons of Ireland, 1843, appendix no. 2, H.C. 1844 (535), xxviii, 329.

Report from Her Majesty's commissioners of inquiry into the state of the law and practice in respect to the occupation of land in Ireland, p. 42, [605], HC 1845, xix, I.

Report from Her Majesty's commissioners of inquiry into the state of the law and practice in respect to the occupation of land in Ireland, part i [606], HC 1845, xix, 57.

Report from Her Majesty's commissioners of inquiry into the state of the law and practice in respect to the occupation of land in Ireland, part ii, [616], HC 1845, xx, I.

Twenty-third report of the inspectors general on the general state of the prisons of Ireland, 1843, appendix no. 2, H.C. 1845 (620), xxv, 231.

Report from Her Majesty's commissioners of inquiry into the state of the law and practice in respect to the occupation of land in Ireland, minutes of evidence, part iii, [657], HC 1845, xxi, I.

Appendix to minutes of evidence taken before Her Majesty's commissioners of inquiry into the state of the law and practice in respect to the occupation of land in Ireland, part iv, [672], H.C. 1845, xxii, I.

Tables showing the number of criminal offenders committed for trial or bailed for appearance at the assize and sessions in each county in the Year 1845, and the result of the proceedings, H.C. 1846 (696), xxxv, 81.

Tables showing the number of criminal offenders committed for trial or bailed for appearance at the assize and sessions in each county in the year 1846, and the result of the proceedings, H.C. 1847 (822), xlvii, 189.

Tables showing the number of criminal offenders committed for trial or bailed for appearance at the assize and sessions in each county in the Year 1847, and the result of the proceedings, H.C. 1847–48 (953), lii, 361.

Tables showing the number of criminal offenders committed for trial or bailed for appearance at the assize and sessions in each county in the year 1848, and the result of the proceedings, H.C. 1849 (1067), xliv, 129.

Tables showing the number of criminal offenders committed for trial or bailed for appearance at the assize and sessions in each county in the year 1849, and the result of the proceedings, H.C. 1850 (1271), xlv, 529.

Tables showing the number of criminal offenders committed for trial or bailed for appearance at the assize and sessions in each county in the year 1850, and the result of the proceedings, H.C. 1851 (1386), xlvi, 97.

Report from the select committee on outrages (Ireland) together with the proceedings of the committee, minutes of evidence, appendix and index, H.C. 1852 (438), xiv, 1.

Homicide statistics, House of Commons research paper 1999/56.

Acts of Parliament

An act for encouraging and disciplining such corps of men as shall voluntarily enroll themselves under officers to be commissioned by His Majesty, for the defence of this kingdom during the present war (37 Geo. III, c. 2 [Ire.]).

An act for the union of Great Britain and Ireland (40 Geo. 3 c. 38 [Ire.]).

An act for the union of Great Britain and Ireland (39 & 40 Geo. III c. 67).

An act for the relief of His Majesty's Roman Catholic subjects (10 Geo. 4, c. 7).

An act to restrain for five years, in certain cases, party processions in Ireland (2 & 3 Will. 4, c. 118).

An act for the more effectual suppression of local disturbances and dangerous associations in Ireland (3 & 4 Will. 4, c. 4).

An act to continue for five years, and from thence until the end of the then next session of parliament, an act of the second and third years of the reign of His late Majesty, to restrain for five years, in certain cases, party processions in Ireland (1 & 2 Vict., c. 34).

An act to continue until the first day of June one thousand eight hundred and forty-five an act of the second and third years of His late Majesty, for restraining for five years in certain cases, party processions in Ireland (7 & 8 Vict., c. 63).

An act to restrain party processions in Ireland (13 Vict., c. 2).

Newspapers

Armagh Guardian
Banner of Ulster
Belfast Newsletter
Dublin Evening Post
Enniskillen Chronicle & Erne Packet
Fermanagh Mail
Galway Vindicator
Irish Times
Kilkenny Journal

Kilkenny Moderator
Leinster Express
Mayo Constitution
Newry Telegraph
Northern Whig
Strabane Morning Post
Sunday Tribune
Times

Contemporary works

Barrow, John, *A Tour round Ireland, through the Sea-Coast Counties, in the Autumn of 1835* (London: John Murray, 1836).

de Beaumont, Gustave, *Ireland: Social, Political and Religious* with an introduction by Tom Garvin and Andreas Hess [1839] (Cambridge, MA: Harvard University Press, 2006).

Blackstone, William, *Commentaries on the Laws of England: Book the Fourth* (15th edition, London, Strahan, 1809).

Inglis, Henry D., *A Journey throughout Ireland, during the Spring, Summer, and Autumn of 1834* (5th edition, London: Whittaker and Co., 1838).

Kendall, E.A., 'Letter to a Friend on the State of Ireland, the Roman Catholic Question, and the Merits of Constitutional Religious Distinctions', *Quarterly Review*, 38 (1828), pp. 535–98.

Lewis, George Cornewall, *On Local Disturbances in Ireland; and on the Irish Church Question* [1836], (new edition, Cork: Tower Books, 1977).

Mongan, James, *A Report of the Trials of John Kennedy, John Ryan, and William Voss, for the Murder of Edmund Butler, at Carrickshock, on the 14th December, 1831. Tried before the Hon. Baron Foster, at the Spring and Summer Assizes of Kilkenny, 1832* (Dublin: Richard Milliken and son, 1832).

Otway, Caesar, *A Tour of Connaught, Comprising Sketches of Clonmacnoise, Joyce Country and Achill* (Dublin: William Curry, Jun. & Company, 1839).

Trench, W.S., *Realities of Irish Life* (London: Longmans, Green, and Co., 1868).

Modern works

Akenson, D.H., *The Church of Ireland: Ecclesiastical Reform and Revolution, 1800–1885* (New Haven, CT and London: Yale University Press, 1971).

——, *Small Differences: Irish Catholics and Irish Protestants, 1815–1922: An International Perspective* (Dublin: Gill and Macmillan, 1991).

Alder, C.M., and Polk, Kenneth, 'Masculinity and child homicide', *British Journal of Criminology*, 36.3 (1996), pp. 396–411.

Archer, John E. 'Mysterious and Suspicious Deaths: Missing Homicides in North-West England (1850–1900)', *Crime, Histoire & Sociétés / Crime, History & Societies*, 12.1 (2008), pp. 45–63.

Bardon, Jonathan, *A History of Ulster* (Belfast: Blackstaff Press, 1992).

Bartlett, Thomas, 'Select documents 38: Defenders and Defenderism in 1795', *Irish Historical Studies*, 24.95 (May 1985), pp. 373–94.

——, *The Fall and Rise of the Irish Nation: The Catholic Question, 1690–1830* (Dublin: Gill and Macmillan, 1992).

Beames, M.R., *Peasants and Power: The Whiteboy Movements and their Control in Pre-Famine Ireland* (Brighton: Harvester Press, 1983).

——, 'Rural Conflict in Pre-Famine Ireland: Peasant Assassination in Tipperary, 1837–1847', in C.H.E. Philpin (ed.), *Nationalism and Popular Protest in Ireland* (Cambridge: Cambridge University Press, 1987).

Beattie, J.M., *Crime and the Courts in England, 1660–1800* (Oxford: Clarendon Press, 1986).

Blackstock, A.F., '"A Dangerous Species of Ally": Orangeism and the Irish Yeomanry', *Irish Historical Studies*, 30.119 (May 1997), pp. 393–407.

——, *An Ascendancy Army: The Irish Yeomanry, 1796–1834* (Dublin: Four Courts Press, 1998).

Brewer, John D., Lockhart, Bill, and Rodgers, Paula, *Crime in Ireland 1945–95: Here Be Dragons* (Oxford: Clarendon Press, 1997).

Broeker, Galen, *Rural Disorder and Police Reform in Ireland, 1812–36* (London: Routledge & Kegan Paul, 1970).

Burney, Ian, *Poison, Detection, and the Victorian Imagination* (Manchester: Manchester University Press, 2006).

Carroll, Stuart, 'Introduction' in Carroll (ed.), *Cultures of Violence: Interpersonal Violence in Historical Perspective* (Basingstoke: Palgrave Macmillan, 2007), pp. 1–46.

Carroll-Burke, Patrick, *Colonial Discipline: The Making of the Irish Convict System* (Dublin: Four Courts Press, 2000).

Clark, Samuel, *Social Origins of the Irish Land War* (Princeton, NJ: Princeton University Press, 1979).

——, 'The Importance of Agrarian Classes: Agrarian Class Structure and Collective Action in Nineteenth-Century Ireland', *British Journal of Sociology*, 29.1 (1978), pp. 22–40.

Clark, Samuel, and Donnelly, J.S., Jr, (eds), *Irish Peasants: Violence and Political Unrest* (Manchester: Manchester University Press, 1983).

Cockburn, J.S., 'Patterns of Violence in English Society: Homicide in Kent, 1560–1985', *Past & Present*, 130 (1991), pp. 70–106.

Conley, Carolyn A., *Melancholy Accidents: The Meaning of Violence in Post-Famine Ireland* (Lanham, MA: Lexington Books, 1999).

——, 'The Agreeable Recreation of Fighting', *Journal of Social History*, 33.1 (1999), pp. 57–72.

Connolly, S.J., 'Mass Politics and Sectarian Conflict' in W.E. Vaughan (ed.), *A New History of Ireland, V: Ireland Under the Union, I: 1801–70* (Oxford: Oxford University Press, 1989), pp. 74–107.

——, *Religion, Law and Power: The Making of Protestant Ireland 1660–1760* (Oxford: Clarendon Press, 1992).

——, 'Unnatural Death in Four Nations: Contrasts and Comparisons' in S.J. Connolly (ed.), *Kingdoms United? Ireland and Great Britain from 1500: Integration and Diversity* (Dublin: Four Courts Press, 1998), pp. 200–214.

——, *Priests and People in Pre-Famine Ireland, 1780–1845* (2nd ed., Dublin: Four Courts Press, 2001).

Crossman, Virginia, *Politics, Law and Order in Nineteenth-Century Ireland* (Dublin: Gill & Macmillan, 1996).

Cullen, L.M., 'The Political Structure of the Defenders' in David Dickson and Hugh Gough (eds), *Ireland and the French Revolution* (Dublin: Irish Academic Press, 1990), pp. 117–38.

Daly, Martin, and Wilson, Margo, *Homicide* (New York: A. de Gruyter, 1988).

——, 'An Assessment of Some Proposed Exceptions to the Phenomenon of Nepotistic Discrimination against Stepchildren', *Annales Zoologici Fennici*, 38 (2001), pp. 287–96.

D'Arcy, Fergus, 'The Decline and Fall of Donnybrook Fair: Moral Reform and Social Control in Nineteenth-Century Ireland', *Saothar: Journal of the Irish Labour History Society*, 13 (1988), pp. 7–21.

Daultrey, Stuart, Dickson, David, and Ó Gráda, Cormac, 'Hearth Tax, Household Size and Irish Population Change 1672–1821', *Proceedings of the Royal Irish Academy*, series c., 82.6 (1982), pp. 125–82.

Ditton, Jason, *Contrology: Beyond the New Criminology* (London: Macmillan, 1979).

Dooley, Enda, *Homicide in Ireland 1992–1996* (Dublin: Stationery Office, 2001).

Dooley, Terence, *The Murders at Wildgoose Lodge: Agrarian Crime and Punishment in Pre-Famine Ireland* (Dublin: Four Courts Press, 2007).

Donnelly, J.S., Jr, *The Land and People of Nineteenth-Century Cork* (London: Routledge, 1975).

——, 'The Rightboy Movement, 1785–8', *Studia Hibernica*, 17–18 (1977–8), pp. 120–202.

——, 'Pastorini and Captain Rock: Millenarianism and Sectarianism in the Rockite Movement of 1821–4' in Samuel Clark and J.S. Donnelly, Jr (eds), *Irish Peasants: Violence and Political Unrest* (Manchester: Manchester University Press, 1983), pp. 102–39.

——, 'Factions in Pre-Famine Ireland' in A.S. Eyler and R.F. Garratt (eds), *The Uses of the Past: Essays on Irish Culture* (Newark, DE: University of Delaware Press, 1988), pp. 113–30.

——, 'The Terry Alt Movement, 1829–31', *History Ireland*, 2.4 (winter, 1994), pp. 30–5.

——, 'Sectarianism in 1798 and in Catholic Nationalist Memory' in Laurence Geary (ed.), *Rebellion and Remembrance in Modern Ireland* (Dublin: Four Courts Press, 2001), pp. 15–37.

——, *The Great Irish Potato Famine* (paperback ed., Stroud: Sutton Publishing, 2002).

——, *Captain Rock: The Irish Agrarian Rebellion of 1821–1824* (Madison, WI: The University of Wisconsin Press, 2009).

Dunne, Tom, 'Popular Ballads, Revolutionary Rhetoric and Politicization' in David Dickson and Hugh Gough (eds), *Ireland and the French Revolution* (Dublin: Irish Academic Press, 1990), pp. 139–55.

——, *Rebellions: Memoir, Memory and 1798* (Dublin: Lilliput Press, 2004).

Edwards, Laura F., 'Women and Domestic Violence in Nineteenth-Century North Carolina' in Michael A. Bellesiles (ed.), *Lethal Imagination: Violence and Brutality in American History*, (New York: NYU Press, 1999), pp. 115–38.

Eibach, Joachim, 'The Containment of Violence in Central European Cities, 1500–1800' in Richard Mc Mahon (ed.), *Crime, Law and Popular Culture in Europe 1500–1900* (Cullompton: Willan Publishing, 2008), pp. 52–73.

Eisner, Manuel, 'Modernization, Self-Control and Lethal Violence: The Long-Term Dynamics of European Homicide Rates in Theoretical Perspective', *British Journal of Criminology*, 41.4 (2001), pp. 618–38.

——, 'Long-Term Trends in Violent Crime' in Michael Tonry (ed.), *Crime and Justice: A Review of Research, Vol. 30* (Chicago, MI: University of Chicago Press, 2003), pp. 83–142.

——, 'Human Evolution, History and Violence: An Introduction', *British Journal of Criminology*, 51.3 (2011), pp. 473–8.

Elias, Norbert, *The Civilizing Process: Sociogenetic and Psychogenetic Investigations* [1939], rev. edition, trans. E. Jephcott (Oxford: Blackwell Publishing, 2000).

Elliott, Marianne, *The Catholics of Ulster: A History* (London: Allen Lane, 2000).

——, 'Religious Polarization and Sectarianism in the Ulster Rebellion' in Thomas Bartlett, David Dickson, Dáire Keogh and Kevin Whelan (eds), *1798: A Bicentenary Perspective* (Dublin: Four Courts Press, 2003), pp. 279–97.

Emsley, Clive, *Crime and Society in England 1750–1900* (3rd ed., Harlow: Pearson Education Limited, 2005).

Ewing, C.P., *Fatal Families: The Dynamics of Intrafamilial Homicide* (Thousand Oaks, CA: Sage Publications, 1997).

Farrell, Brian, *Coroners: Practice and Procedure* (Dublin: Round Hall Sweet & Maxwell, 2000).

Farrell, Elaine, "Infanticide of the Ordinary Character': An Overview of the Crime in Ireland, 1850–1900', *Irish Economic and Social History*, 39 (2012), pp. 56–72.

Farrell, Sean, *Rituals and Riots: Sectarian Violence and Political Culture in Ulster, 1784–1886* (Lexington, KY: University Press of Kentucky, 2000).

Finnane, Mark, 'A Decline in Violence in Ireland? Crime, Policing and Social Relations, 1860–1914', *Crime, Histoire & Sociétés / Crime, History & Societies*, 1.1 (1997), pp. 51–70.

Fitzpatrick, David, 'Class, Family and Rural Unrest in Nineteenth-Century Ireland' in P.J. Drudy (ed.), *Ireland: Land, Politics and People* (Cambridge: Cambridge University Press, 1982), pp. 37–75.

——, 'Unrest in Rural Ireland', *Irish Economic and Social History*, 12 (1985), pp. 98–105.

Garnham, Neal, *The Courts, Crime and the Criminal Law in Ireland, 1692–1760* (Dublin: Irish Academic Press, 1996).

——, 'How Violent Was Eighteenth-Century Ireland?', *Irish Historical Studies*, 30.119 (May 1997), pp. 377–92.

Garvin, Tom, 'Defenders, Ribbonmen and Others: Underground Political Networks in Pre-Famine Ireland', *Past & Present*, 96 (1982), pp. 133–55.

Gatrell, V.A.C., 'The Decline of Theft and Violence in Victorian and Edwardian England' in V.A.C. Gatrell, Bruce Lenman and Geoffrey Parker (eds), *Crime and the Law: The Social History of Crime in Western Europe since 1500* (London: Europa Publications, 1980), pp. 238–337.

Gazmararian, Julie A., Petersen, Ruth, Spitz, Alison M., Goodwin, Mary M., Saltzman Linda E., and Marks, James S., 'Violence and Reproductive Health: Current Knowledge and Future Research Directions', *Maternal and Child Health Journal*, 4.2 (2000), pp. 79–84.

Gibbon, Peter, *The Origins of Ulster Unionism: The Formation of Popular Protestant Politics and Ideology in Nineteenth-Century Ireland* (Manchester: Manchester University Press, 1975).

Gibbons, S.R., 'Captain Rock in the Queen's Co.' in William Nolan and Pádraig Lane (eds), *Laois: History and Society: Interdisciplinary Essays on the History of an Irish County* (Dublin: Geography Publications, 1999), pp. 487–512.

——, *Captain Rock, Night Errant: The Threatening Letters of Pre-Famine Ireland, 1801–45* (Dublin: Four Courts Press, 2004).

Griffin, Brian, *Sources for the Study of Crime in Ireland, 1801–1921* (Dublin: Four Courts Press, 2005).

Gurr, Ted Robert, 'Historical Trends in Violent Crime: A Critical Review of the Evidence' in Michael Tonry and Norval Morris (eds), *Crime and Justice: An Annual Review of Research, Vol. 3* (Chicago, MI: University of Chicago Press, 1982), pp. 295–353.

Haddick-Flynn, Kevin, *Orangeism: The Making of a Tradition* (Dublin: Wolfhound Press, 1999).

Hanlon, Gregory, 'The Decline of Violence in the West: From Cultural to Post-Cultural History', *English Historical Review*, 128 (2013), pp. 367–400.

Hardwick, Julie, 'Early Modern Perspectives on the Long History of Domestic Violence: The Case of Seventeenth- and Eighteenth-Century France,' *The Journal of Modern History* 78.1 (2006), pp. 1–36.

Hay, Douglas, 'War, Dearth and Theft in the Eighteenth Century: The Record of the English Courts', *Past & Present*, 95 (1982), pp. 117–60.

Hempton, David and Hill, Myrtle, "Godliness and Good Citizenship': Evangelical Protestantism and Social Control in Ulster, 1790–1850', *Saothar: Journal of the Irish Labour History Society*, 13 (1988), pp. 68–76.

Hirst, Catherine, *Religion, Politics and Violence in Nineteenth-Century Belfast: The Pound and Sandy Row* (Dublin: Four Courts Press, 2002).

Hoppen, K.T., *Elections, Politics and Society in Ireland 1832–1885* (Oxford: Clarendon Press, 1984).

——, 'Grammars of Electoral Violence in Nineteenth-Century England and Ireland', *The English Historical Review*, 109.432 (1994), pp. 597–620.

Huggins, Michael, *Social Conflict in Pre-Famine Ireland: The Case of County Roscommon* (Dublin: Four Courts Press, 2007).

van IJzendoorn, Marinus H., Euser, Eveline M., Prinzie, Peter, Juffer, Femmie and Bakermans-Kranenburg, Marian J., 'Elevated Risk of Child Maltreatment in Families with Stepparents but not with Adoptive Parents', *Child Maltreatment*, 14.4 (2009), pp. 369–75.

Jackson, Alvin, *Ireland, 1798–1998: War, Peace and Beyond* (Oxford: Wiley-Blackwell, 2010).

Jenkins, Brian, *Era of Emancipation: British Government of Ireland 1812–1830* (Kingston and Montreal: McGill-Queen's University Press, 1988).

Johnson, E.A., and Monkkonen, E.H. (eds), *The Civilization of Crime: Violence in Town and Country since the Middle Ages* (Urbana, IL: University of Illinois Press, 1996).

Keane, Ronan, 'A Mass of Crumbling Ruins: The Destruction of the Four Courts in June 1922' in Caroline Costello (ed.), *The Four Courts: 200 years: Essays to Commemorate the Bicentenary of the Four Courts* (Dublin: Incorporated Council of Law Reporting for Ireland, 1996), pp. 159–68.

Kelly, James, *'That Damn'd Thing Called Honour': Duelling in Ireland, 1570–1860* (Cork: Cork University Press, 1995).

——, "A Most Inhuman and Barbarous Piece of Villainy': An Exploration of the Crime of Rape in Eighteenth-Century Ireland', *Eighteenth-Century Ireland/ Iris an dá chultúr*, 10 (1995), pp. 78–107.

Kelly, Jennifer, 'A Study of Ribbonism in Co. Leitrim in 1841' in Joost Augusteijn, Mary Ann Lyons and Deirdre McMahon (eds), *Irish History: A Research Yearbook No.2* (Dublin, 2003), pp. 32–42.

Kinealy, Christine, 'A Right to March? The Conflict at Dolly's Brae' in D.G. Boyce and Roger Swift (eds), *Problems and Perspectives in Irish History since 1800: Essays in Honour of Patrick Buckland* (Dublin: Four Courts Press, 2004), pp. 54–79.

King, Peter, 'The Impact of Urbanization on Murder Rates and on the Geography of Homicide in England and Wales, 1780–1850', *Historical Journal*, 53.3 (2010), pp. 671–98.

Kingon, Suzanne T., 'Ulster Opposition to Catholic Emancipation, 1828–9', *Irish Historical Studies*, 34.134 (November 2004), pp. 137–55.

Lee, J.J., 'The Ribbonmen' in T.D. Williams (ed.), *Secret Societies in Ireland* (Dublin: Gill & Macmillan, 1973), pp. 26–35.

——, 'Patterns of Rural Unrest in Nineteenth-Century Ireland: A Preliminary Survey' in

L.M. Cullen and François Furet (eds), *Ireland and France, 17th–20th Centuries: Towards a Comparative Study of Rural History* (Paris: Éditions de l'École des Hautes Études en Sciences Sociales, 1980), pp. 223–37.

Lenihan, Pádraig, *1690: Battle of the Boyne* (Stroud: Tempus Publishing, 2003).

MacDonagh, Oliver, *Ireland: The Union and its Aftermath* (London: Allen and Unwin, 1977).

——, *States of Mind: A Study of Anglo-Irish Conflict 1780–1980* (London: Harper Collins, 1983).

——, 'Ideas and Institutions, 1830–45' in W.E. Vaughan (ed.), *A New History of Ireland, V: Ireland under the Union, I. 1801–70* (Oxford: Oxford University Press, 1989), pp. 193–217.

Mc Mahon, Richard, 'The Courts of Petty Sessions and Society in Pre-Famine Galway' in Raymond Gillespie (ed.), *The Re-Making of Modern Ireland: Essays in Honour of J.C. Beckett* (Dublin: Four Courts Press, 2003), pp. 101–37.

——, '"For Fear of the Vengeance": The Prosecution of Homicide in Pre-Famine and Famine Ireland' in *idem* (ed.), *Crime, Law and Popular Culture in Europe 1500–1900* (Cullompton: Willan Publishing, 2008), pp. 138–89.

——, *Violence, the Courts and Legal Cultures in Ireland, 1801–1850* (forthcoming).

McGrath, T.G., 'Interdenominational Relations in Pre-Famine Tipperary' in William Nolan, (ed.), *Tipperary, History and Society: Interdisciplinary Essays on the History of an Irish County* (Dublin, Geography Publications, 1985), pp. 256–87.

McLoughlin, Dympna, 'Infanticide in Nineteenth-Century Ireland' in Angela Bourke, Siobhán Kilfeather, Maria Luddy, and Margaret MacCurtain, Gerardine Meaney, Máirín Ní Dhonnchadha, Mary O'Dowd and Clair Wills (eds), *Field Day Anthology of Irish Writing: Irish Women's Writing and Traditions Vol. 4* (New York: New York University Press, 2002), pp. 915–19.

McMahon, Kevin, and McKeown, Thomas, 'Agrarian Disturbances around Crossmaglen, 1835–1855, Part II' in *Seanchas Ard Mhaca*, 10.1 (1980–81), pp. 149–75.

McMahon, Michael, *The Murder of Thomas Douglas Bateson, Co. Monaghan, 1851* (Dublin: Four Courts Press, 2006).

McWilliams, Monica, and McKiernan Joan, *Bringing it out in the Open: Domestic Violence in Northern Ireland* (Belfast: HMSO, 1993).

Madden, Kyla, *Forkhill Protestants and Forkhill Catholics, 1787–1858* (Liverpool: Liverpool University Press, 2006).

Maddox, N.P., 'A Melancholy Record: The Story of the Nineteenth-Century Irish Party Procession Acts', *The Irish Jurist*, 39 new series (2004), pp. 243–74.

Malcolm, Elizabeth, *Ireland Sober, Ireland Free: Drink and Temperance in Nineteenth-Century Ireland* (Dublin: Gill and Macmillan, 1986).

Meagher, Timothy J., *The Columbia Guide to Irish American History* (New York: Columbia University Press, 2005).

Miller, D.W., 'The Armagh Troubles, 1784–95' in Samuel Clark and J.S. Donnelly, Jr (eds), *Irish Peasants: Violence and Political Unrest* (Manchester: Manchester University Press, 1983), pp. 155–91.

——, 'The Origins of the Orange Order in Co. Armagh' in A.J. Hughes and William Nolan (eds), *Armagh: History and Society: Interdisciplinary Essays on the History of an Irish County* (Dublin: Geography Publications, 2001), pp. 583–605.

Miller, K.A., *Emigrants and Exiles: Ireland and the Irish Exodus to North America* (Oxford: Oxford University Press, 1985).

——, 'The Lost World of Andrew Johnston: Sectarianism, Social Conflict and Cultural Change in Southern Ireland during the Pre-Famine Era' in J.S. Donnelly, Jr, and K.A.

Miller (eds), *Irish Popular Culture, 1650–1850* (Dublin: Irish Academic Press, 1999), pp. 222–41.

Mokyr, Joel, *Why Ireland Starved: A Quantitative and Analytical History of Ireland 1800–50* (London: Allen & Unwin, 1983).

Monkkonen, E.H., 'New Standards for Historical Homicide Research', *Crime, Histoire & Sociétés/ Crime, History & Societies*, 5.2 (2001), pp. 5–26.

——, *Murder in New York City* (Berkeley and Los Angeles, CA: University of California Press, 2001).

Morris, R.M., 'Lies, Damned Lies and Criminal Statistics: Reinterpreting the Criminal Statistics in England and Wales', *Crime, Histoire et Sociétés/ Crime, History and Societies*, 5.1 (2001), pp. 111–27.

Nordlund, Johanna, and Termin, Hans, 'Do Characteristics of Parental Child Homicide in Sweden Fit Evolutionary Predictions?', *Ethology*, 113 (2007), pp. 1029–37.

Ó Ciosáin, Niall, *Print and Popular Culture in Ireland, 1750–1850* (2nd ed., Dublin: Lilliput Press, 2010).

O'Donnell, Ian, 'Unlawful Killing Past and Present', *The Irish Jurist*, 37 new series (2002), pp. 56–90.

——, 'Violence and Social Change in the Republic of Ireland', *International Journal of the Sociology of Law*, 33 (2005), p. 101–17.

——, 'Lethal Violence in Ireland, 1841–2003: Famine, Celibacy and Parental Pacification', *British Journal of Criminology*, 45 (2005), pp. 671–95.

---. 'Killing in Ireland at the Turn of the Centuries: Contexts, Consequences and Civilizing Processes', *Irish Economic and Social History*, 37 (2010), pp. 53–74.

O'Donnell, Patrick, *The Irish Faction Fighters of the Nineteenth Century* (Dublin: Anvil Books, 1975).

Ó Gráda, Cormac, *Ireland: A New Economic History, 1780–1939* (Oxford: Clarendon Press, 1994).

O'Hanrahan, Michael, 'The Tithe War in Co. Kilkenny, 1830–1834' in William Nolan and Kevin Whelan (eds), *Kilkenny: History And Society: Interdisciplinary Essays on the History of an Irish County* (Dublin: Geography Publications, 1990), pp. 481–505.

Ó Macháin, Pádraig, *Six Years in Galmoy: Rural Unrest in County Kilkenny, 1819–1824* (Dublin: Poodle Press, 2004).

Ó Muirí, Réamonn, 'The Orangemen, Repealers and the Shooting of John Boyle in Armagh, 12 July 1845' in *Seanchas Ard Mhaca*, 11.2 (1985), pp. 435–529.

O'Neill, T.P., 'Famine Evictions' in Carla King (ed.), *Famine, Land and Culture in Ireland* (Dublin: University College Dublin Press, 2000).

Ó Tuathaigh, M.A.G., *Ireland before the Famine, 1798–1848* (2nd ed., Dublin: Gill & Macmillan, 1990).

——, *Thomas Drummond and the Government of Ireland, 1835–41* (Dublin: National University of Ireland, 1978).

Owens, Gary, 'The Carrickshock Incident, 1831: Social Memory and an Irish Cause Célèbre', *Cultural and Social History*, 1 (2004), pp. 36–64.

Palmer, S.H., *Police and Protest in England and Ireland, 1780–1850* (Cambridge: Cambridge University Press, 1988).

Pinker, Steven, *The Better Angels of our Nature: The Decline of Violence in History and its Causes* (London: Allen Lane, 2011).

Povey, David (ed.), *Crime in England and Wales 2002/2003: Supplementary Volume 1: Homicide and Gun Crime* (London: Home Office, 2004).

Powell, M.J., 'Popular Disturbances in Late Eighteenth-Century Ireland: The Origins of the Peep of Day Boys', *Irish Historical Studies*, 34.135 (May 2005), pp. 249–65.

Rogers, J.D., *Crime, Justice and Society in Colonial Sri Lanka* (London: Curzon Press, 1987).

Romani, Roberto, 'British Views on Irish National Character, 1800–1846. An Intellectual History', *History of European Ideas*, 23.5–6 (1997), pp. 193–219.

Roth, Randolph, 'Homicide in Early Modern England 1549–1800: The Need for a Quantitative Synthesis', *Crime, Histoire & Sociétés/ Crime, History & Societies*, 5.2 (2001), pp. 33–67.

——, *American Homicide* (Cambridge, MA: The Belknap of Harvard University Press, 2009).

——, 'Yes We Can: Working Together toward a History of Homicide that is Empirically, Mathematically, and Theoretically Sound', *Crime, Histoire & Sociétés/ Crime, History & Societies*, 15.2 (2011), pp. 131–45.

Rousseaux, Xavier, 'From Medieval Cities to National States, 1350–1850: The Historiography of Crime and Criminal Justice in Europe' in Clive Emsley and L.A. Knafla (eds), *Crime History and Histories of Crime: Studies in the Historiography of Crime and Criminal Justice in Modern History* (Westport, CT: Greenwood Press, 1996), pp. 3–32.

Ruff, J.R., *Violence in Early Modern Europe* (Cambridge: Cambridge University Press, 2001).

Ryan, David, '"Ribbonism" and Agrarian Violence in County Galway, 1819–20', *Journal of the Galway Archaeological and Historical Society*, 52 (2000), pp. 120–34.

Schwerhoff, Gerd, 'Social Control of Violence, Violence as Social Control: The Case of Early Modern Germany' in Herman Roodenburg and Pieter Spierenburg (eds), *Social Control in Europe, 1500–1800* (Columbus, OH: Ohio State University Press, 2004), pp. 220–46.

——, 'Criminalized Violence and the Process of Civilisation: A Reappraisal', *Crime, Histoire & Sociétés/ Crime, History & Societies*, 6.2 (2002), pp. 103–26.

Sellin, Thorsten, 'The Significance of the Records of Crime', *Law Quarterly Review*, 65 (1951), pp. 489–504.

Senior, Hereward, *Orangeism in Ireland and Britain, 1790–1836* (London: Routledge and Kegan Paul, 1966).

Sharpe, J.A., 'Domestic Homicide in Early Modern England', *The Historical Journal*, 24.1 (1981), pp. 29–48.

——, 'The History of Violence in England: Some Observations', *Past & Present*, 108 (1985), pp. 206–215.

Shoemaker, Robert, 'Male Honour and the Decline of Public Violence in Eighteenth-Century London', *Social History*, 26 (2001), pp. 190–208.

Sindall, Rob, *Street Violence in the Nineteenth Century: Media Panic or Real Danger?* (Leicester: Leicester University Press, 1990).

Spierenburg, Pieter, 'Faces of Violence: Homicide Trends and Cultural Meanings, Amsterdam, 1431–1816', *Journal of Social History*, 27 (1994), pp. 701–716.

——, 'Long-Term Trends in Homicide: Theoretical Reflections and Dutch Evidence, Fifteenth to Twentieth centuries' in E.A. Johnson and E.H. Monkkonen (eds), *The Civilization of Crime: Violence in Town and Country since the Middle Ages* (Urbana, IL: University of Illinois Press, 1996), pp. 63–105.

——, 'Violence and the Civilizing Process: Does it Work?', *Crime, Histoire & Sociétés/ Crime, History & Societies*, 5.2 (2001), pp. 87–105.

——, 'Theorizing in Jurassic Park: A Reply to Gerd Schwerhoff', *Crime, Histoire & Sociétés/ Crime, History & Societies*, 6.2 (2002), pp. 127–8.

——, *A History of Murder: Personal Violence in Europe from the Middle Ages to the Present* (Cambridge: Polity Press, 2008).

——, 'American Homicide. What Does the Evidence Mean for Theories of Violence and Society?', *Crime, Histoire & Sociétés/ Crime, History & Societies*, 15.2 (2011), pp. 123–6.

——, 'Questions that Remain: Pieter Spierenburg's Reply to Randolph Roth', *Crime, Histoire & Sociétés/ Crime, History & Societies*, 15.2 (2011), p. 147–50.

Steiner-Scott, Elizabeth, "'To Bounce a Boot off her now & then…': Domestic Violence in Post-Famine Ireland', in M.G. Valiulius and Mary O' Dowd (eds), *Women and Irish History* (Dublin: Wolfhound Press, 1997), pp. 125–43.

Stewart, A.T.Q., *The Narrow Ground: Aspects of Ulster, 1609–1969* (2nd ed., Belfast: Blackstaff Press, 1997).

Stone, Lawrence, 'Interpersonal Violence in English Society, 1300–1900', *Past & Present*, 101 (1983), pp. 22–33.

——, 'A Rejoinder', *Past & Present*, 108 (1985), pp. 216–24.

Taylor, Howard, 'Rationing Crime: The Political Economy of Criminal Statistics since the 1850s', *Economic History Review*, 51.3 (1998), pp. 569–90.

Temrin, Hans, Buchmayer, Susanne, and Enquist, Magnus, 'Step-Parents and Infanticide: The New Data Contradict Evolutionary Predictions', *Proceedings of the Royal Society: Biological Sciences*, 267 (2000), pp. 943–5.

Thuente, Mary, 'Violence in Pre-Famine Ireland: The Testimony of Irish Folklore and Fiction', *Irish University Review*, 15.2 (1985), pp. 129–47.

Townshend, Charles, *Political Violence in Ireland: Government and Resistance since 1848* (Oxford: Clarendon Press, 1983).

Vaughan, W.E., 'Ireland c.1870' in *idem* (ed.), *A New History of Ireland, V: Ireland under the Union, I. 1801–70* (Oxford: Oxford University Press), pp. 726–801.

——, *Landlords and Tenants in Mid-Victorian Ireland* (Oxford: Clarendon Press, 1994).

——, *Murder Trials in Ireland, 1836–1914* (Dublin: Four Courts Press, 2009).

Watson, Dorothy, and Parsons, Sara, *Domestic Abuse of Women and Men in Ireland: Report on the National Study of Domestic Abuse* (Dublin: Stationery Office, 2005).

Watson, Katherine, *Poisoned Lives: English Poisoners and their Victims* (London: Hambledon and London, 2004).

Whelan, Irene, *The Bible War in Ireland: The 'Second Reformation' and the Polarization of Protestant-Catholic Relations, 1800–40* (Madison, WI: University of Wisconsin Press, 2005).

Whelan, Kevin, *The Tree of Liberty: Radicalism, Catholicism and the Construction of Irish Identity, 1760–1830* (Cork: Cork University Press, 1996).

——, 'Introduction to Section III' in Tom Bartlett, David Dickson, Dáire Keogh, and Kevin Whelan (eds), *1798: A Bicentenary Perspective* (Dublin: Four Courts Press, 2003), pp. 189–94.

White, Philip, 'Homicide' in M.A. Walker (ed.), *Interpreting Crime Statistics* (Oxford: Clarendon Press, 1995), pp. 130–44.

Wilbanks, William, 'Homicide in Ireland', *International Journal of Comparative and Applied Criminal Justice*, 20.1 (1996), pp. 59–75.

Wilson, James, 'Orangeism in 1798' in Tom Bartlett, David Dickson, Dáire Keogh and Kevin Whelan (eds), *1798: A Bicentenary Perspective* (Dublin: Four Courts Press, 2003), pp. 345–62.

Wilson, Stephen, *Feuding, Conflict and Banditry in Nineteenth-Century Corsica* (Cambridge: Cambridge University Press, 1988).

Wilson, T.K., *Frontiers of Violence: Conflict and Identity in Ulster and Upper Silesia, 1918–1922* (Oxford: Oxford University Press, 2010).

Wood, Herbert, *A Guide to the Records Deposited in the Public Record Office of Ireland* (Dublin, HMSO, 1919).

Wood, John Carter, *Violence and Crime in Nineteenth-Century England: The Shadow of our Refinement* (London: Routledge, 2004).

——, 'The Limits of Culture? Society, Evolutionary Psychology and the History of Violence', *Cultural and Social History*, 4.1 (2007), pp. 95–114.

——, 'A Change of Perspective: Integrating Evolutionary Psychology into the Historiography of Violence', *British Journal of Criminology*, 51.3 (2011), pp. 479–98.

Wright, Frank, *Two Lands on One Soil: Ulster Politics before Home Rule* (Dublin: Gill and Macmillan, 1996).

Yager, Tom, 'Mass Eviction in the Mullet Peninsula during and after the Great Famine', *Irish Economic and Social History*, 23 (1996), pp. 24–44.

Young, T.J., 'Parricide Rates and Criminal Street Violence in the United States: Is there a Correlation?', *Adolescence*, 28.109 (1993), pp. 171–2.

Zehr, Howard, *Crime and the Development of Modern Society: Patterns of Criminality in Nineteenth-Century Germany and France* (Totowa, NJ: Rowman and Littlefield, 1976).

Zimmermann, G.D., *Songs of Irish Rebellion: Political Street Ballads and Rebel Songs, 1780–1900* (Dublin: Allen Figgis, 1967).

Reference works

Vaughan, W.E. and Fitzpatrick, A.J. (ed.), *Irish Historical Statistics: Population, 1821–1971* A New History of Ireland: Ancillary Publications II (Dublin: Royal Irish Academy, 1978).

The Waterloo Directory of Irish Newspapers and Periodicals, 1800–1900, Phase II (Waterloo, Ontario: Wilfred Laurier University Press, 1986).

Unpublished theses

Eiriksson, Andres, 'Crime and Popular Protest in Co. Clare 1815–52' (PhD thesis, Trinity College Dublin, 1992).

McCabe, D.J., 'Law, Conflict and Social Order: County Mayo, 1820–45' (PhD thesis, University College Dublin, 1991).

Moulden, John, 'The Printed Ballad in Ireland: A Guide to the Popular Printing of Songs in Ireland, 1760–1920' (PhD thesis, National University of Ireland, Galway, 2006).

Index